Choices in Approaching Conflict

Principles and Practice of Dispute Resolution

SECOND EDITION

Charles Ewert
Gordon Barnard
Jennifer Laffier
Michael L. Maynard

 emond ▪ Toronto, Canada ▪ 2019

Emond Montgomery Publications Limited
1 Eglinton Avenue E., Suite 600
Toronto ON M4P 3A1
http://www.emond.ca/highered

Printed in Canada.

We acknowledge the financial support of the Government of Canada.

Canada

Emond Montgomery Publications has no responsibility for the persistence or accuracy of URLs for external or third-party Internet websites referred to in this publication, and does not guarantee that any content on such websites is, or will remain, accurate or appropriate.

Vice president, publishing: Anthony Rezek
Publisher: Mike Thompson
Director, development and production: Kelly Dickson
Developmental editor: Sandy Matos
Production supervisor: Laura Bast
Production editor: Natalie Berchem
Copy editor: Geoff Graves
Permissions editor: Monika Schurmann
Typesetter: S4Carlisle
Text designer: Tara Agnerian
Proofreader: Holly Dickinson
Indexer: Karen Hunter
Cover image: qoppi/Shutterstock

Library and Archives Canada Cataloguing in Publication

Title: Choices in approaching conflict : principles and practice of dispute resolution / Charles Ewert, Gordon Barnard, Jennifer Laffier, Michael L. Maynard.
Names: Ewert, Charles, author. | Barnard, Gordon, 1951- author. | Laffier, Jennifer, 1973- author. | Maynard, Michael L., 1981- author.
Description: Second edition. | Includes index.
Identifiers: Canadiana 20189056770 | ISBN 9781772554953 (softcover)
Subjects: LCSH: Conflict management—Textbooks. | LCSH: Mediation—Textbooks. | LCSH: Dispute resolution (Law)—Textbooks. | LCGFT: Textbooks.
Classification: LCC HM1126 E94 2019 | DDC 303.6/9—dc23

Brief Contents

PART I Reconsidering Conflict

PART II Processes for Addressing Conflict

PART III Skill Sets and Knowledge Sets for Conducting Negotiations and Mediations

PART IV Professional Applications

Contents

PART I
RECONSIDERING CONFLICT

PART II
PROCESSES FOR ADDRESSING CONFLICT

PART III

SKILL SETS AND KNOWLEDGE SETS FOR CONDUCTING NEGOTIATIONS AND MEDIATIONS

PART IV

PROFESSIONAL APPLICATIONS

Preface

We are pleased to present this second edition of *Choices in Approaching Conflict*. The purpose of this textbook remains threefold. First, it is to challenge the widely accepted view that conflict is a negative force that should be avoided or suppressed at all costs. In place of this view, we promote the idea that conflict is a universal experience arising partly from our need, as people, to fashion new, shared meaning in fulfilling our aspirations. We look closely at conflict—its causes, its functioning, its phases, and its various types—because to intervene successfully in conflict situations, you must be able to identify the kind of conflict you are facing and understand its causes.

Second, this textbook seeks to point out that how we approach conflict is crucial to whether and how it is resolved. Our choice of approach is often a consequence of our social and cultural conditioning—to some extent, it is not a "choice" at all. Many of us automatically take an adversarial approach to conflict. When parties respond to conflict in this way—that is, aggressively and competitively—their positions become entrenched and their disputes escalate, causing stalemate, frustration, or even violence. A primary aim of this textbook is to make people aware that there is a deep difference between contending for results and cooperating in the crafting of results.

Third, this textbook has a practical purpose. To support our analyses of conflict and the processes surrounding it, we offer students questions for discussion as well as role-playing exercises that will equip them with the skills they need to intervene successfully in conflict situations. Our hope is that through practice of this kind, users of this text will learn to address conflict in a positive way and to move themselves and others to a mutual understanding of the underlying interests and needs of the parties to a given conflict. This knowledge will help them produce, for themselves or for others, win–win results for all concerned.

New to the Second Edition

The revised text has been expanded to include a new chapter on arbitration, its definition, and its implications and a new chapter on the multidisciplinary applications of the problem-solving skills outlined, including education, policing, social work, and psychology.

The second edition has also been reorganized into four sections encompassing common themes. These four sections contain a total of 14 chapters, aligning with the number of weeks in a standard college or university term.

- Part I fully defines conflict, its inception, causes, escalation, and analysis.
- Part II describes the major processes involved in meeting and dealing with conflict.

- Part III provides instruction on the skills and underlying knowledge necessary for promoting solutions to disputes.
- Part IV relates to applications of the dispute-resolving formulae set out in the book. It goes into actual areas of practice and the requirements necessary to employ these skills in a variety of personal and professional settings.

Acknowledgments

The authors wish to recognize the contributions of our families, who have supported us throughout our many long hours of researching and writing. We would also like to recognize our editing team: Mike Thompson, Sandy Matos, Geoff Graves, Holly Dickinson, Natalie Berchem, and especially Paul Emond for taking on our book for publication back in 2009. We also thank Carrie-Lynn Barkley, Algonquin Careers Academy; Shelagh Campbell, University of Regina; Amy Maycock, Fleming College; Suzanne McGirl, Northern College; and Deborah Pressman, George Brown College, for their review of the first edition. Their feedback and advice were invaluable—without it, this second edition would not be a reality.

About the Authors

Charles Ewert obtained his BA from Carleton University. He then studied law and earned his LLB from Queen's University in Kingston. Upon being called to the bar, he was invited to serve for a year as a clerk to the justices of the then High Court, the trial division of the Supreme Court of Ontario. He practised law in both St. Thomas and Newcastle, Ontario, before gaining a position as a professor in the legal administration program at Durham College in Oshawa. There, he taught courses in tort law, criminal law, contracts, and civil procedure, as well as general introductory courses to the law.

Having appeared in major court cases at trial and on appeal, he had a lasting concern about the costs, in monetary *and* human terms, of the adversarial processes underlying litigation. He entered the LLM program in mediation at York University and, upon graduation, was able to create and deliver courses in mediation at Durham College and University of Ontario Institute of Technology (UOIT), also in Oshawa. Those courses served as inspiration for his involvement in the writing of this text.

Gordon Barnard holds a Bachelor of Arts degree with a major in psychology from Concordia University in Montreal and is a retired professor of Human Resources Management. After working in the private sector at such organizations as Bell and Honda, he joined the faculty of the School of Business, IT and Management at Durham College in 1989.

For a number of years, Gordon was a member of the union–management Workload Monitoring Group at Durham, tasked with dealing with faculty members' issues regarding workload, as outlined in the college's and union's collective agreement, prior to the possible submission of a grievance. The focus of the group was to negotiate a solution that would prove acceptable to both college management and faculty.

Gordon co-developed and co-taught professional development courses in dispute resolution at Durham College that led to the creation of this text.

He retired in 2016.

Jennifer Laffier is a senior lecturer at UOIT. In 2014, she was appointed senior trainer with Mental Health First Aid Canada, a sub-division of the Mental Health Commission of Canada. She works with various organizations considering implementation of mental health first aid, including school boards, police services, and mental health agencies.

Michael L. Maynard is a mediator, arbitrator, and facilitator with ADR Chambers. He is also an investigator with the ADR Chambers Banking and Municipal Ombuds Offices and is the ADR Chambers Integrity Commissioner for municipalities.

As a neutral, Michael has mediated more than 2,000 disputes. His areas of expertise include administrative, civil, code of conduct/disciplinary, contract, insurance (including personal injury and Statutory Accident Benefits matters), landlord/tenant, public complaint, and workplace disputes. Michael has also facilitated a variety of meetings, workshops, summits, and conferences, including co-chairing a healthcare summit for an Ontario MPP, co-facilitating a three-day Northern Ontario economic development conference, and leading a number of public town-hall meetings.

Michael has a background in political and public policy matters and has consulted on organizational framework and ADR systems design. He has been an ADR instructor and course developer at Durham College and was a co-founder of Durham College and UOIT's campus mediation service.

PART I

Reconsidering Conflict

For centuries, scholars, philosophers, and wise men have sought to formulate the basis for a utopia on Earth. "Peace on Earth, goodwill toward men" has become a common mantra, hope, and prayer.

Nonetheless, our world remains a complicated and stressful place filled with conflict. We experience conflict at all levels—within our families, neighbourhoods, municipalities, and countries in the world at large. Moreover, in this complicated world, we often experience conflict within our own psyches.

Many of us have been taught from our youth on that conflict is a negative thing to be avoided, suppressed, and put down for the sake of the appearance of peace. How have our parents, siblings, bosses, co-workers, chosen spiritual leaders, friends, and enemies taught us to look at and respond to conflict and disputes in general? Is conflict, in your view, a negative thing that should be suppressed at all costs and ignored wherever possible? Or do you see it as a natural and unavoidable consequence of our living in a competitively ordered universe? Can we see it in a more positive light, offering an opportunity for mutual acknowledgment and the growth of common understanding between parties who need not remain adamant rivals?

Clearly, conflict is not going away, nor is it going to change the way it appears in the world, so we must change the way we see it.

The purpose of the first three chapters in this text is to encourage you to review, re-evaluate, and redefine your views of what conflict is and the ways you respond to and deal with it.

What Is Conflict?

1

LEARNING OUTCOMES

After completing this chapter, you will be able to:

- Define and understand the term *conflict*.

- Understand the underlying causes of conflict.

- Consider how cultural influences, such as values, beliefs, and principles, produce interests and aspirations that, in turn, cause conflicts.

- Challenge the prevailing view that conflict is something negative that ought to be suppressed.

- Promote a new perspective from which contending expectations, interests, and aspirations are seen in a positive light as catalysts for change.

- Apply the new understanding of conflict in class discussions and role-playing exercises.

Defining Conflict

The focus of this first chapter is conflict and the disputes that arise from it. What is conflict? Where does conflict come from? What choices do we have when it comes to responding to conflict?

Despite our best efforts, **conflict** seems to be an ever-present part of our human experience. Whether in the form of family breakdown, road rage, or terrorist activity, conflict is always occurring in our world. In our everyday lives, we constantly experience the tensions that give rise to it.

Utopian dreamers imagine a day when the world will be at peace and when conflict will be banished from our experience. But the reality is that conflict is a dynamic and necessary part of human life. Sometimes we need it to clear our collective thinking, overcome oppression, and promote change. Without it, life would probably be more boring and static than we would like. Yet with it, given the human capacity for destructive behaviour, our individual selves and our entire world can seem constantly in danger. That threat produces tension and stress.

So if we can't get rid of conflict, how do we come to understand and manage a dispute in more constructive ways?

First, we can accept the following as a basic truth: All people occupy the same Earth, but each of us inhabits a separate perceptual reality. How individuals, families, countries, and cultures make meaning in their lives varies radically. No matter what value, principle, or belief we select as sacred, we must accept that others will see things differently. Even a belief in the sacredness of life is not universal, as kamikaze pilots have shown. Kamikaze pilots came from the heritage of the Japanese samurai, who would readily offer up their lives because they believed that *to die samurai adds meaning to life* (Yamamato, 2002). To them, the concept of dying with honour had a higher value than living a life without it.

conflict
a state that exists when one party's aspirations are incompatible with those of another party

The Origins of Conflict

The fact that people have different values, beliefs, norms, and goals does not in itself make conflict inevitable. In *Social Conflict*, Rubin, Pruitt, and Kim (2004) point out that conflict occurs only when our underlying interests shape themselves into *aspirations* that are *incompatible* with others' aspirations. In other words, conflict arises from incompatibility of **aspirations**. De Bono (2004) points out that different belief systems do not lead to conflict until someone decides that his or her belief system is superior to someone else's and that the other system should not exist.

The same principle holds for cultural customs surrounding modes of dress, worship, eating, and social interaction: Conflicts occur only when one group becomes aggressively exclusive of another. A second point should be made here about the origins of conflict. Even when two parties have seemingly incompatible religious or cultural beliefs and therefore a great potential for conflict, no **dispute** actually exists between them until one sees the other's system as opposed to their own, is able to *name* this opposition as an injury, and is able to identify the other party as the offender and claim some sort of redress.

Without the acts of naming, blaming, and claiming, the conflict may exist but never become an actual dispute. These actions turn an uncomfortable but possibly short-lived conflict into a dispute requiring some form of intervention or resolution. In other words, the existence of underlying friction in a situation only leads to an actual dispute when one party seeks to make their aspirations predominate over another party's.

aspirations
the particular hopes and desires that arise from our underlying interests

dispute
what occurs when the parties in conflict (a) recognize they are opposed to each other, (b) view each other's opposition as an injury, and (c) lay claim to some form of redress

Ellis and Anderson (2005) suggest that most conflicts are characterized by the perceived presence of two or more of the following instigators of hostile feelings:

1. Different or opposing values or ideals (for example, democracy, security, and women's rights).
2. Divergent interests (tangible things—land, water, and money).
3. Different or opposing cognitions (for example, understanding of history, interpretation of statements, and perceptions of actions).
4. Identifying threats (for example, challenges to a person's sense of self as an individual; a group member who feels entitled to respect).

Admittedly, in our current world, most of the international conflicts that seem to exist involve an imbalance of, or limited access to, needed resources. Countries often fight over water, land, energy, and food, as well as other wealth-producing resources. But international, interracial, and sectarian disputes are often imbued with the other elements stated above. History has forged in different cultures different understandings of acceptable sexuality, the role of women, and the right to education and advancement, among many other things.

Claiming the right to ownership or possession of land can be the source of great conflict. Divergent claims can arise from different interpretations of what makes land sacred. Contrasting views of historical information can give rise to different understandings of what entitles parties to claim the land and its fruits. If we look at the Arab–Israeli conflict, there are numerous claims in regard to actual possession and sovereignty over areas of land, but there is also an incredibly rich history, differently interpreted, involving the core identities of the participants: Christians, Jews, and Muslims. This may be said to be true of Indigenous land claims in Canada, where the very meaning of land and its sacredness varies from culture to culture.

The determination of acceptable sexual practices also varies widely from country to country and culture to culture. Countries with harsh climates and high infant mortality rates often vested in men the right to marry more than one woman to maintain population and workforce. Some regions with limited food supplies, such as Tibet, often allowed polyandry—a practice in which a woman could marry more than one man—to maintain a lower or manageable birth rate. Some Indigenous societies in the Pacific were highly tolerant of homosexual relationships, whereas societies steeped in the Western religions have tended to be highly judgmental of such inclinations. In Canada, the ongoing movement toward accepting and supporting the LGBTQ+ community is shifting the population's understanding from judgment to acceptance of diversity. This shift in understanding has resulted in a true paradigm shift in the acceptability of individual choices. However, existing traditional attitudes die hard, and many judgments will remain based on historical and religious interpretations. Thus, as the underlying values and beliefs of societies shift and change, conflicts can resolve, but they can also expand, flare up, or commence anew.

We are living in times of change and acceptance in regard to the role of women in society. Saudi Arabia, for example, in 2018, lifted a decades-old ban on women driving. Closer to home, the #MeToo movement has, for example, rewritten and removed the power that used to exist around the director's *casting couch*. One rock star, after being accused of sexual misconduct in 2018, said that his sexual encounters were all consensual and his exploits were all just an acceptable part of *rock culture* ("Hedley Allegations," 2018). Rock culture, it seems, is also evolving. However, in some countries, there are still cultural norms that strongly dictate that women must wear culturally appropriate clothing and that their roles in public be strictly limited.

IN THE NEWS

IDLE NO MORE

In February 2018, Prime Minister Justin Trudeau announced that the federal government will create new legislation that is intended to make necessary changes to the way in which Canada deals with Indigenous peoples. This comes in the wake of a highly controversial acquittal in Saskatchewan of a white man who had shot and killed 22-year-old Colten Boushie, a member of the Red Pheasant First Nation. The intended legislative changes include how to deal with systemic racism in both broader Canadian society and the criminal justice system. They will also overhaul the process by which land claims and treaty rights are managed.

Some Indigenous people have responded to this announcement with hope, some with skepticism, and others with resistance. The latter group includes activists and others who support the Idle No More movement, a grassroots movement that has stated explicitly that it is opposed to, as it is framed by Coulthard in *Red Skin, White Masks* (2014), the "colonial politics of recognition." The term refers to the attempt by so-called *settler states* to gloss over past and present injustices to Indigenous peoples by recognizing certain rights within a liberal pluralistic democracy. Those in the Idle No More movement see this approach as a threat to Indigenous self-government while also keeping the door open to land grabs by the state, largely for the purposes of accessing mineral and oil and gas resources.

A fundamental values conflict can be seen here in terms of how "land" is viewed. Is it for the extractable resources that lie underneath it, or is it for the nourishment and well-being of those who live on it?

Source: Coulthard (2014).

Conflict and Meaning

Lederach (1995) proposes we do the following when we consider conflict:

1. See conflict as a natural, common experience in all relationships and cultures.
2. Understand conflict to be a socially constructed event; people are active participants in creating situations and interactions they experience as conflict.
3. Understand that conflict emerges through an interactive process based on the search for shared meaning.
4. Understand that this interactive process is accomplished through, and rooted in, people's perceptions, interpretations, expressions, and intentions, all of which are bound up with their commonsense knowledge.
5. Understand that meaning occurs when people locate themselves and social *things,* such as situations, events, and actions, in their accumulated knowledge. Meaning emerges when one thing is connected to another by an act of comparison. This perspective takes it for granted that a person's common sense and accumulated knowledge are the primary factors in how that person creates, understands, and responds to conflict.
6. Understand that culture is rooted in the shared knowledge and schemes that a group of people has developed for perceiving, interpreting, expressing, and responding to the social realities around them.

Lederach holds a social constructionist point of view: We create our own meanings. De Bono (1985) shares a similar view when he describes our minds as active self-organizing systems. Each of us actively takes in information about our worlds in our own way; new information is ordered in our minds according to what is already there.

Something shifts in our thinking about conflict when we stop seeing it as a negative thing and begin to see it as a common experience arising from the need for adaptation and new meaning. By adopting this perspective, we begin to see conflict not as a clash but as a creative opportunity.

Let us return to Lederach's list of considerations about conflict.

First, conflicts don't just happen arbitrarily; they can be seen as socially constructed events. Conflicts are not unnatural, fearful, or irrational happenings; they are often a necessary step in the evolution of **new, shared meaning**. Second, Lederach doesn't demonize conflict; he calls it a "natural, common experience" in "all relationships and cultures." This acceptance of the necessity and universality of conflict encourages us to acknowledge it in positive ways rather than to ignore, repress, or stifle it.

Finally, Lederach notes that culture is rooted in the shared knowledge and schemes that a group of people has developed for perceiving, interpreting, expressing, and responding to the social realities they face. As human beings, we always begin our lives as ego- and ethnocentric. The values, beliefs, and principles that come to us through family, religion, and culture are the ones we first adapt to and find comfort in. As we grow and branch out of our formative social circles, our academic and professional circles and the relationships we build within them help to shape our thinking. For example, those involved in legal professions are conditioned through training to view the world through a rights- and power-based lens. Social services and psychological support professionals are trained to view the world from a place of prioritizing human needs for personal growth and happiness. The extent to which

new, shared meaning
the shared understanding that can develop, through dialogue and an exchange of ideas, between parties in conflict

those values are taken on by any individual and how they are interpreted and acted upon will be influenced by the values established earlier in life. Our values mould our self-image and create a zone of comfort from which each of us can deal with the world of experience. What becomes real to each of us does so simply through the process of our living in a particular time and place. Social realities vary between families and between cultures.

IN THE NEWS

LGBT PURGE

Underlying social beliefs and values can either create conflict or create a platform of understanding that promotes acceptance of diversity.

In the 1980s, a woman was dismissed from the Canadian military for being a lesbian. Her case is one of many under a now defunct policy of systemic discrimination that has become known as the "LGBT Purge." This policy was recently the subject of a class action lawsuit against the Government of Canada and a historic apology from Canadian Prime Minister Justin Trudeau. The case was settled in Federal Court in 2018.

Individual Reality

Each of us has, of necessity, developed an individual world view—an individual reality. Our perception of our own interests, needs, fears, desires, and hopes will be shaped by our individual experience. It follows from this that another person's vision of the world is bound to be different from our own and may be difficult for us to grasp. Understanding this simple principle of subjectivity enables us to see that another's perceptions and interests, though inconsistent with our own, will make complete sense to him or her. Such understanding can make us more open-minded and help us look at issues in a broader context (De Bono, 2004). It can reduce our hostility toward opposing points of view so that we can appreciate another's perspective while maintaining our own.

By examining our own stereotypes, first impressions, and accumulated value judgments, we can get a clearer sense of how the other party's reality may be composed. Carl Rogers, in his seminal publication *Client Centered Therapy* (1951), set out four helpful rules of thumb for exploring another person's reality. To paraphrase him:

1. Every person exists in a continually changing world of experience of which he or she is the centre.
2. The individual reacts to his or her world as he or she experiences and perceives it; thus, his or her perceptual world is the reality for that individual.
3. The individual has one basic tendency, or drive, and that is to actualize, maintain, and enhance himself or herself.
4. Therefore, the best vantage point for understanding another person's behaviour is from within that person's internal **frame of reference**.

frame of reference
a person's subjective reality, shaped by his or her particular experience and culture, and the basis for his or her perception of the world

The important point here is that solutions to conflicts, if they are going to be real and meaningful for the disputing parties, must come from within the parties' own frames of reference. To create new, shared meaning that integrates conflicting realities, you must begin by understanding those realities.

Carl Rogers defined state of empathy, or being empathetic, as perceiving the internal frame of reference of another with accuracy and with the emotional components and meanings that pertain thereof as if one were the person (Rogers, 1980).

Changing Minds

When you seek to resolve a conflict, you are, by definition, promoting change and a transformation of the disputants' existing perceptions. Many people believe that our perceptions (that is, our way of seeing the world) cannot change because they are so strongly conditioned by culture and social environment. Marylyn Ferguson disagreed with this view in *The Aquarian Conspiracy* (2009) and pointed out that we can change our minds in four basic ways (as shown in Figure 1.1):

1. by exception,
2. by incremental change,
3. by pendulum swing, or
4. by paradigm shift.

Exception

Let us consider a woman who has lived through an abusive marriage. Her early experiences with her brothers and her father were also negative. She holds the perception, through her various experiences, that all men are untrustworthy, abusive toward women, and just plain bad.

If the woman were to meet one man, say a widower, who was kind to his children and gracious to her and other women, she might conclude that this one man was an exception to her general conclusion about men. Her basic perception of men would remain unaltered. The kind man would simply be an exception to the rule. This represents the most minimal type of change, **change by exception**.

change by exception
the mental change that occurs when a person with an absolute view of something acknowledges an exception to the rule

Figure 1.1   **The Ways in Which We Change Our Minds**

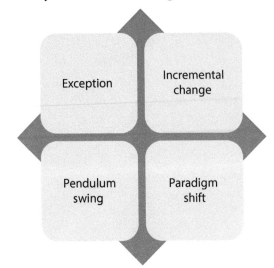

Incremental Change

If our woman started dating the widower and in time met many of his male friends, who were also gracious to her, her perception of men in general might remain basically the same and yet be incrementally changing—that is, changing a bit at a time. **Incremental change** is slow and tends to be unconscious.

Change by Pendulum Swing

Change by pendulum swing is the abandonment of one closed and certain system for another. Our woman falls head over heels in love with the widower and decides she was wrong before and now sees the truth—all men are kind and gracious. The problem with this type of change is that it completely abandons old experiences and fails to be discriminating about the new.

Paradigm Shift

In this scenario, the woman undergoes a **paradigm shift**. She could realize, very consciously, that she was a little bit right about men before and that with each new experience of men she has, her sense of them is becoming fuller and more accurate. She is not abandoning her earlier views on men; she is progressively adjusting them. Her fundamental pattern of perceiving men is shifting.

There are different ways for people to change their minds, perceptions, and positions. Not all of them are equally profound or durable. But through trust and the willingness to learn, we can effect change and acknowledge that all people are a little bit right (that is, right from within their own frame of reference) and that, through exploration and understanding, we can all be a little bit more right.

The value of trying to understand the interests and perceptions of others, particularly others with whom we are in conflict, is summed up in a prayer written by Chief Dan George (2017): "Speak to the animals that you may know them. For what we do not know, we fear, and what we fear we destroy."

---

incremental change
the gradual change of mind that occurs when a person starts finding numerous exceptions to a rule he or she once thought absolute

change by pendulum swing
the change of mind that occurs when a person abandons one closed and certain system for another

paradigm shift
the change of mind that occurs when a person integrates his or her old views with new perceptions and understands that experience will further refine these views

KEY TERMS

aspirations, 4	conflict, 4	incremental change, 10
change by exception, 9	dispute, 4	new, shared meaning, 7
change by pendulum swing, 10	frame of reference, 8	paradigm shift, 10

REFERENCES

Coulthard, G.S. (2014). *Red skin, white masks: Rejecting the colonial politics of recognition.* Minneapolis, MN: University of Minnesota Press.

De Bono, E. (1985). *Conflicts: A better way to resolve them.* Toronto: Penguin Books.

De Bono, E. (2004). *How to have a beautiful mind.* London, UK: Ebury Press.

Ellis, D., & Anderson, D. (2005). *Conflict resolution: An introductory text.* Toronto: Emond Montgomery.

Ferguson, M. (2009). *The Aquarian conspiracy.* Los Angeles: TarcherPerigee.

George, D. (2017). *The best of Chief Dan George.* Surrey, BC: Hancock House.

Hedley allegations put spotlight on music industry in wake of #MeToo. (2018, February 18). *CBC News.*

Retrieved from http://www.cbc.ca/news/entertainment/hedley-allegations-music-industry-1.4541231

Lederach, J.P. (1995). *Preparing for peace.* Syracuse, NY: Syracuse University Press.

Rogers, C.R. (1951). *Client centered therapy.* Boston: Houghton Mifflin.

Rogers, C.R. (1980). *A way of being.* Boston: Houghton Mifflin.

Rubin, J.Z., Pruitt, D.G., & Kim, S.H. (2004). *Social conflict, escalation, stalemate and settlement* (3rd ed.). New York: McGraw-Hill.

Yamamoto, T. (2002). *Hagakure: Book of the samurai.* Japan: Kodansha.

QUESTIONS AND EXERCISES

1. Choose and analyze a conflict you have experienced. First, analyze what was at stake. From your perspective, what was it that you believed in or needed? What did the other party believe in or need, from their perspective? Why or how were the needs *incompatible*? Was it easier to walk away from the differences, or did you strongly feel the need to prove yourself right and the other wrong?

2. Our sense of contradiction often leads us to conclude that there can only be one right answer or correct resolution to any disagreement. At the same time, on another level, we are aware that this simply isn't true; there can often be more than one right answer. To heighten your awareness of the differences in our perceptions, interpretations, and needs, try the following role-playing exercise.

   Three people are walking through an old forest on the outskirts of an urban area: an environmentalist, a real estate developer, and a lumberman. While viewing exactly the same forest, each sees it differently both in terms of its value and potential. Select three parties or groups to represent each of the individuals. Have them do the following:

   a. Clearly define what values each individual sees in the forest.

   b. Describe what personal interest each might have in developing the forest, harvesting it, or leaving it intact.

   c. Define what broader social interests each person sees themselves promoting.

   When people with differing interests or value systems approach the same situations or circumstances, they often tend to speak a different "language." Have each group or individual explain to the others their particular vision and aspirations for the use of the forest and why their vision is the most valid and justifiable.

3. George and Tang are from different cultural heritages. George was born in Canada and was raised in the Judeo-Christian ethic and belief system. From childhood, he was taught to believe in creationism. His family has always sponsored involvement in music because they believe music is the medium through

which people are connected to the angels. Tang, on the other hand, was born in China. He learned at an early age that one approaches the eternal by stillness, through meditation. The two men are now attending the same university and live in adjoining residence rooms. Each night after studying, George likes to play the "Hallelujah Chorus" loudly in his room. This usually happens at 10 o'clock, just as Tang, next door, is settling in for meditation. Tang's culture promotes a high degree of respect for others when it comes to allowing them to save face.

In discussion or through role-playing, determine the following:

a. Is there a conflict?

b. Does the conflict, if there is one, arise from the differences in cultural understandings or from the aspirations that each party has at a given time?

c. What will it take to raise this matter to an actual dispute, and is this likely to happen?

4. Set out in your own words why conflict may, in fact, be a necessary and positive phenomenon. Find examples in your own life of cases where positive shifts or understandings have grown out of what were apparently unresolvable conflicts.

5. Answer three of the following questions, all of which concern the environmental influences on your view of conflict and on your ability to define and respond to it. How did your parents compete with each other over ideas and interests when you were children? How did they react to competition and rivalry between you and your siblings? What views did they have on disputes in the community, the workplace, the country, and the world? How did your teachers deal with conflict in classrooms? How did the peers of your childhood and youth approach conflict, and what did they expect of your response to it both within and outside your peer group? How has the news media affected your perception of conflict? How do your boss, co-workers, and general work environment affect your understanding of what conflict is and how it should be responded to? How does your chosen religious affiliation, if you have any, add to or affect your view of conflict? Think for a moment of our politicians, of your current partner, of your friends and consider how these people influence, directly and indirectly, your perception of disputes in the world.

6. Imagine this scenario involving an elderly mother, whose health is becoming progressively poor, and her son, who is looking after her welfare. The mother lives alone in her own home, which she loves because it gives her independence. The son has growing concerns about his mother's house and her ability to look after herself. He wants her to move into a nursing home, where services will be provided. The mother insists that she can still do her own shopping, her own cooking, and her own cleaning. However, she has injured herself falling down stairs and has bouts of dementia.

In teams of two to four, reflect on the following questions:

a. Establish the legitimate interests, values, and needs of each party in the scenario.

b. Divide your team into two so that one team represents the son and the other represents the mother. Enter into a dialogue. Watch carefully for the tendency to slip into adversarial discussion, which, once entrenched, may escalate.

c. Think of how you might maintain a cooperative atmosphere and dialogue between the parties.

7. Research and consider the conflict in Canada in 2017–2018 over pipeline proposals (i.e., the Trans Mountain Pipeline, also known as Kinder Morgan) from Alberta to tidewater in British Columbia. Identify the various groups who are considered stakeholders in this conflict and list the points of conflict between each.

Choices in Responding to Conflict

2

Contents

LEARNING OUTCOMES

After completing this chapter, you will be able to:

- Understand that the standard responses to conflict are the following: ignoring, yielding, contending, or cooperative problem solving.

- Assess the strengths and weaknesses of the four standard responses to conflict.

- Consider the effects of argument-based problem solving as opposed to cooperation-based problem solving.

- Promote cooperative problem solving as a viable alternative to argument.

- Examine the elements of cooperative problem solving.

- Through class discussion, role-playing exercises, and individual activities, apply different problem-solving methods and approaches to conflict.

Reassessing Conflict

We have been taught to see conflict as the enemy of peace. We assume that if we can eliminate conflict, we can prevent human friction and the disorder it creates. Interpreting conflict itself as the adversary, we try to establish principles that will enable a legal- or power-based authority to declare a winner between disputing parties, end the conflict, and restore harmony. According to this view, an authoritative power eliminates conflict by imposing rules and making decisions; this process prevents the harmful effects of conflict and enables peace to return.

But what if conflict itself, and not the problem of how to remove it, poses the transformative challenge? How should we perceive conflict?

Kottler's *Beyond Blame* includes a chapter entitled "The Positive Functions of Conflict." Conflict, he asserts, may act as "a releaser of tension, a promoter of growth, a regulator of distance between people, a path to intimacy and to personal gain, and a preventer of stagnation" (1994, pp. 150–151). Kottler's positive view of conflict rests on the following idea: All conflict is based on human aspiration. In the terminology of interest assessment, an individual or group formulates an aspiration in order to end a fear, realize a hope, address a concern, or fulfill a specified need or desire. These are all positive aims. Conflict does not occur until the aspirations of one party are juxtaposed with another party's apparently contradictory or incompatible aspirations. Even then, as we saw in Chapter 1, a dispute will not arise until the aspirations and contradictions have been perceived, articulated, and expressed as some form of claim.

We can see, then, that suppressing a conflict through an imposed solution also suppresses the aspirations and needs that underlie it. Imposed solutions tend to be based on precedent, but every conflict is unique. Past resolutions to similar conflicts may be irrelevant to the underlying aspirations in the current case. A declaration of who is right and who is wrong may prevent escalation of the conflict, and this may benefit society as a whole. But this suppressive approach, by ignoring the disputants' needs and aspirations, may cause their individual problems to intensify.

CASE STUDY

MINOR VARIANCE, MAJOR MUNICIPAL CONFLICT

Vincenzo lives with his spouse, Fiorenza, and their three school-aged children in a dense urban neighbourhood of moderately sized, two-story, early 20th-century houses. Vincenzo's aging parents are frail and do not have the financial resources to afford quality care in a retirement residence. As Fiorenza is a stay-at-home mom, the family has agreed the best solution will be to move the parents in with them. However, their home must first be renovated. The proposed renovation includes the addition of two dormers to the sides of the second story, to create more bedroom space. This creates a massing effect, which changes the streetscape when viewed from the homes across the street. An addition will also be added to the back, and to make up for lost outdoor space, a rooftop patio will be built on top. Vincenzo and his family must apply for and be granted a minor variance in order to get a building permit. The neighbours across the road, Frank and Maureen, intend to oppose the Minor Variance Application on the grounds that the continuity of the neighbourhood streetscape will be harmed by the massing of the home, that street parking is already at maximum capacity and cannot support greater density, and that changes to Vincenzo's home will create a precedent that kickstarts a wave of change to a neighbourhood that has remained largely the same for several generations.

Figure 2.1   **The Four Responses to Conflict**

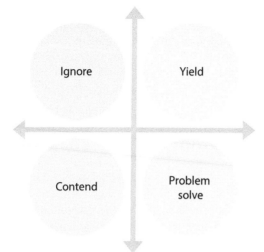

Source: Based on Robert, Pruitt, & Kim (2004).

The Four Responses to Conflict

As shown in Figure 2.1, above, conflicting aspirations seem to produce one of four responses in the parties involved: ignoring, yielding, contending, or cooperative problem solving (Rubin, Pruitt, & Kim, 2004). By **ignoring** or avoiding the conflict, the party shows they do not consider their underlying aspirations worth the effort of confronting the other party. The choice to ignore the conflict may at least remove it from conscious awareness. But it also may lead to its eventual escalation since the contrary aspirations still exist.

The second option for a party in conflict is **yielding** to the other party's claims. In this case, one party accepts the other's aspirations as more important than their own. Again, though, one party's giving up on their own aspirations may, in the case of an ongoing relationship between two parties, lead to retaliation down the way.

Third, the party may choose to contend—to contest the other's claims and seek to fulfill their own aspirations. In the case of **contending**, the party adopts techniques designed to defeat the other's aspirations. Here, the sole object is to win—to fulfill one's own aspirations while thwarting the other party's efforts to do the same. Parties who seek to contend may opt for either a power-based or a rights-based process. Power can take many forms and is shaped by such factors as culture, gender, the presence of wealth, and pure physical force. Power-based approaches tend to produce win–lose results. Rights-based processes are found in our legal system. Here, an adversarial system produces a winner or a loser according to well-defined principles and arguments, and the final determination is made by a third-party judge or arbitrator.

The fourth response possible for a party in dispute is to problem-solve. In the case of **cooperative problem solving**, each party will focus on both their own and the other party's underlying aspirations, with the aim of finding a solution that fulfills both. Here, the conflict is not resolved by imposed edict.

Clearly, if we see conflict as problematic and believe that society should be kept free of it, we will believe that an authoritative third party, equipped with reason

ignoring
pretending a conflict does not exist or suppressing conscious awareness of it instead of actively addressing it

yielding
resolving conflict by giving up one's own aspirations and accepting the other party's as more important

contending
adopting combative techniques designed to fulfill one's own aspirations while thwarting those of the other party

cooperative problem solving
focusing both on one's own and on the other party's aspirations, with a view to finding a solution that satisfies both

and socially approved principles, ought to have the power to nip it in the bud. If, on the other hand, we view conflict as a symptom of unmet aspirations, we will prefer a dispute-resolution process that unearths, examines, and incorporates those aspirations. The parties best equipped to resolve a dispute in this second way are the ones actually engaged in it. They best know their own aspirations. And if each party is willing to respectfully consider the other's needs and interests, together they can best determine how to fulfill both sets of aspirations. Together, they can *remove the cause of conflict from the inside out.*

Contending and Cooperative Problem Solving

Let us take a broad-spectrum approach to two of the responses to conflict we've been discussing: contending and cooperative problem solving. According to the literature, these are the two main approaches to conflict resolution: competition and cooperation (Deutsch & Coleman, 2000; Rubin et al., 2004). De Bono (1985) differentiates the thinking that underlies each approach as *argumentative thinking* as opposed to *explorative and design thinking*. They go by different names, but the perception of the two approaches is consistent. For the sake of simplicity, let's call one the **argumentative approach** and the other the **cooperative approach.**

If we isolate the basic ideas behind each approach, we will get a clear idea of how each is likely to work. How do they compare as alternatives? Our aim in asking this question is not to find out which approach is better but to establish certain facts about them—what the thinking is behind each, what their effects are, how they actually work, how well they work, and where they work best.

argumentative approach
an approach to conflict based on the traditional Western notion that we arrive at truth through a competitive clash of ideas

cooperative approach
a creative approach to conflict resolution that aims to create win–win solutions for the parties involved

The Choice to Contend

De Bono calls argument "the most venerated of western thinking traditions. Much of civilization is based upon it: for example, government and the courts. Whether we call it argument, debate, dialectic or clash it comes to the same thing" (1985, p. 18). Historically, the use of argument as an intellectual tool originated with the Socratic dialogues of Ancient Greece. It was later picked up and used by church thinkers in the Middle Ages to distinguish heretics from true believers. Our concern is how this approach to conflict works in theory and in practice. We would also like to show that it is the approach Western culture now expects.

How Argument Works

Argument is supposed to work on the basis of thesis–antithesis and a resulting synthesis. That is, someone proposes an idea, makes a case, adopts a political or moral stance, or takes up a point of view. This is the thesis. Then someone proposes an opposing idea, case, political or moral stance, or point of view. This is the antithesis. Promoting one's own idea while challenging or attacking the other person's produces a competitive clash. This leads to a synthesis that, ideally, combines the best of both positions, or at least a clearer view of what Lederach (1995) calls a "new, shared meaning," or truth.

So long as the argument is aimed at finding truth, it remains legitimate. However, once parties become enmeshed in debate, their main objective, usually, is to win the argument rather than to create new, shared meaning.

If winning the argument becomes the main goal—and winning is highly regarded in Western culture—the parties have no real motivation to consider each other's interests or needs. In reality, what the argumentative approach breeds is the notion that discrediting the other party's character, view, or position is as important as promoting our own. This approach encourages three aims simultaneously: promoting the merit of your own position, attacking the merit of the opponent's position, and defending yourself from your opponent's attack. These aims reflect the first principle of what legal scholars call the **rules of natural justice**—that is, the idea that the parties involved in a proceeding should be given the opportunity to present their case.

rules of natural justice a system of rules, based on English common law, that defines the elements of a fair hearing

Some of the most public debates in our society show us the argumentative approach at work. The opponents in the debates over abortion and capital punishment, for example, are deeply entrenched in their respective positions, each arguing inflexibly to undermine the other side and defeat them.

De Bono (1985, p. 19) summarizes what really happens with the argument method:

1. Each side gets more rigid.
2. Neither side attempts to develop an idea that is different from the two that are clashing.
3. Unlimited amounts of time, energy, and money are locked up in a sometimes long-standing impasse.
4. Each side's creativity and ingenuity are directed not at improving their own idea but at securing the defeat of the opposing idea.
5. The idea that triumphs in the end is the stronger but not necessarily the better one.

The other factor contributing to the rigidity of the argument process is the notion of **contradiction**. For some reason, our minds tend to work on an either/or basis. We want clear-cut answers. We assume that either this proposition or that proposition is true; they can't both be true at the same time. This person is either innocent or guilty. The defendant is liable, or she's not. This person is reliable and worthy of being heard, or he's not. This black-and-white thinking may produce clarity and predictability, but it also creates a trap; it assumes that there is only one right answer, one transcendent value, and one prevailing principle. It locks people into defending a single point of view rather than creatively exploring other points of view. And, inevitably, this either/or thinking makes the goal of argument to be winning, not finding new, shared meaning.

contradiction the principle by which our minds favour either/or thinking and assume that only one of two conflicting notions can be correct

The argumentative approach is, by definition, adversarial. We approach disputes as opponents—combatants in a battle over which side is right. Basic to this approach is the right to attack, diminish, and demean the opponent's point of view and, ultimately, the opponent. It clearly has the potential to destroy trust, limit communication, and compromise relationships. And yet it is, in Western culture, a widely accepted and conventional response to conflict.

Why Do We Argue?

In *The Argument Culture*, Tannen convincingly shows that members of Western culture are predisposed to approach conflict situations aggressively. She refers to this tendency as "a pre-patterned, unthinking use of fighting to accomplish goals that do not necessarily require it" (1998, p.8). Our language, she suggests, is full of militaristic metaphors that influence our competitive activities, such as debate or argument. Since language shapes thought, and thought shapes action, we automatically seek to defeat and obliterate our opponent's positions or ideas.

Western culture conditions us to respond to conflict by trying to win. Now consider the consequences of this. What does it mean that we, as a culture, are very skilled at arguing? We need to be more aware of how hastily we become contentious. Are there costs we are not considering?

The Costs of Argument

Argument and litigation can be useful for certain kinds of disputes. Disputes can arise over different things: ideas, values, property claims, relationship issues, and structural imbalances in societies and organizations. In situations involving power imbalances, courts do an admirable job of protecting individual rights. In situations where society requires clear answers and guidelines—as with capital punishment, for example—courts can be very useful. In most personal disputes, however, an adversarial stance is neither necessary nor appropriate. The price of winning these adversarial disputes is often higher than it appears, and this should encourage us to choose other modes of dealing with conflict.

Argument, debate, and litigation, because they emphasize winning, also promote *defeating*. Promoting your own argument tends to involve a personal attack on the other party or their position. This stance, it can be argued, is at the very root of rigid position taking. The costs of diminishing an opponent in this way are the loss of trust, the end of active listening, and the damaging of relationships. As Tannen said, "when conflicts are handled well, the participants form stronger, more open social bonds; when they handle it badly, they injure each other and diminish themselves" (1998, p. 44).

Tannen also points out the following: "The argument culture limits the information we get rather than broadening it" (1998, p. 20). What actually happens in argument and litigation is that we narrow and adapt issues to fit the perspective of the legal system. What is important to the parties—their personal, emotional, or psychological interests—may simply be irrelevant to the decision of the court or the arbitrator.

We might also consider the people who are left out of argument-based decision systems. Many people will simply opt to yield, abandon, or ignore their interest rather than enter the troublesome forum of debate. This acceptance of injustice is arguably a social ill that alternative, less abrasive forms of conflict resolution will help remedy.

polarization
the process by which parties in conflict become entrenched in disagreement, each assuming that their own view is the only correct one

The **polarization** promoted by the argument system is also commented on by Tannen:

> Our determination to pursue truth by setting up a fight between two sides leads us to believe that every issue has two sides—no more, no less. If both sides are given a forum to confront each other, all relevant information will emerge, and the best case will be made for each side. But opposition does not lead to the truth when an issue is not composed of two opposing sides but is a crystal of many sides. Often truth is in the complex middle not the oversimplified extremes. (1998, p. 10)

Compare this to de Bono's (1985) thoughts about what really happens in argument. A consequence of polarization, in his view, is that all creative energy goes into justifying a position rather than exploring the subtleties of truth or creating new ideas to reach an innovative solution. We might also consider what "winning" means in the context of polarization and its cost to the winners themselves. Barnett Pearce and Littlejohn relate this question to Machiavelli's unethical prince. They suggest that the prince who succeeds by acting dishonourably,

> "contrary to faith, friendships, humanity and religion" (Machiavelli, p. 283), may well have lost something more important than his princely entitlements. At least this prince has forfeited a variety of other relationships that Fisher and Brown (1988) call "good" relationships; he might also, as a young rabbi once remarked, have "gained the world and lost his own soul." (1997, p. 36)

Achieving success in debate or litigation often results in fractured relationships and lost opportunities. If this is the price of victory, maybe winning really isn't winning at all.

Tannen's criticism of the "argument culture" serves as a useful summary:

> The argument culture urges us to approach the world—and the people in it—in an adversarial frame of mind. It rests on the assumption that opposition is the best way to get anything done; the best way to discuss an idea is to set up a debate; the best way to cover news is to find spokespeople who express the most extreme, polarized views and present them as "both sides"; the best way to settle disputes is litigation that pits one party against the other; the best way to begin an essay is to attack someone; and the best way to show you're really thinking is to criticize. (1998, pp. 3–4)

The Choice to Cooperate

Let us now consider the cooperative method of dealing with disputes. Its assumptions about conflict are different from those of the argumentative approach.

How the Cooperative Method Works

When we adopt the cooperative approach, we no longer see conflict as a problem that needs to be stifled and ended. Instead, we see conflict as an inevitable part of relationships between separate individuals and between separate cultures. Each of us spends our lives developing a sense of reality and a way of behaving that are best suited to our particular surroundings so that we can survive, belong, and achieve. We are born into different contexts, and that is why we are all different. These differences between us lead to conflict.

Conflicts do not need to be seen as battles. They can be seen as opportunities for change and growth and for the creation of new, shared meaning. Such change and creative growth need to occur in an environment of trust, not a battlefield environment—a courtroom, for example—where the stage is set for the contentious interpretation of past facts and events.

When we adopt the cooperative method, we aim to accept and sound out the other party's reality in search of those needs, values, and aspirations that are of importance to them. We do this with no aggressive intention. It's the aggressive element in the argumentative approach that tends to harden people's positions. If we can stop seeing the other party's position, desire, or culture as being problematic, we can move on to a mutual exploration of those underlying needs, values, and aspirations that first brought us into dispute.

We can teach parties in dispute to listen for the merit in each other's positions rather than listening in order to attack those positions. We can teach these parties to go from **either/or thinking** to **both/and thinking**. Through exploring and honestly listening to each other, the parties may develop greater awareness of the common ground, actual or potential, between them. This awareness may enable them, in turn, to brainstorm solutions creatively and to choose a solution that maximizes both sets of interests. With the cooperative approach, the disputants' energies go not into attacking and defending points of view but into creatively exploring different points of view and potential solutions.

either/or thinking
assuming that only one of two conflicting notions can be correct

both/and thinking
assuming that there are many possible solutions to a problem, not just one

The Four Principles of Cooperative Negotiation

Fisher, Ury, and Patton (2011) sum up the thinking behind the cooperative approach in four basic principles of negotiation:

1. *Separate people from the problem.* If you personally attack another party for views they hold, for tactics they are using, or for aspirations they have, you will only put them into a defensive mode, which often breeds negative emotions and entrenches them further in their combative stance.

2. *Focus on interests, not on positions.* Freeing parties to understand and respectfully accept each other's interests is a much more fruitful measure than leaving them focused on their current positions.

3. *Invent options for mutual gain.* The principle here is the following: The thinking that got people into a dispute won't get them out of it. A new kind of thinking, sometimes called *brainstorming* or *lateral thinking*, is needed. To creatively, even playfully, invent options without prejudging their effectiveness is the aim. Options, once they are established, can be compared, analyzed, evaluated, and then adopted.

4. *Use objective criteria.* For the sake of equality and fairness, the criteria used in evaluating the parties' positions should be, according to an objective assessment, fair to both and not dominated by the will of one. This need for objective criteria applies to the process of discussion, as well as to the solutions eventually produced.

Practising the Cooperative Method

In the actual practice of dispute resolution, you will find people positioning themselves all over the argumentative–cooperative spectrum. Some people approach negotiation wanting only to prove themselves right and the other side wrong. Such people are bargaining in the traditional way, trying to be strong in their position and to concede as little as possible. Sometimes, right in the middle of a supposedly cooperative negotiation, one party will hit an emotional nerve, the other will hurl an insult, and the two parties will sink back into argument and standoff.

When you face opposition and conflict, you need to check your natural tendency to provoke, challenge, and confront; you need to consider, as Tannen suggests, that there are other ways of approaching a problem: "What about exploring, exposing, delving, analyzing, understanding, moving, connecting, integrating, illuminating …

or any of innumerable verbs that capture other aspects of what art can do" (1998, pp. 23–24)?

Problem-solving or cooperative approaches are based on what we have called *both/ and thinking*. Such thinking takes the following into account: Any party in dispute has their own unquestioned reality—that is, a firmly established *frame of reference* within which they organize their particular world. The aim of cooperative problem solving is to avoid attacks upon the integrity of the disputing parties or upon their particular frames of reference. Instead, it aims to clarify, explore, understand, and approve the underlying interests of both parties and to create solutions that benefit all.

Sometimes a party in dispute fears that, if they do not act aggressively, their position will be lost or overwhelmed. But a party that adopts the cooperative approach should not be seen as giving up their position. A key to cooperative problem solving is to adopt a "firm but conciliatory stance," a stance that "is efficient in generating creative solutions" (Rubin, Pruitt, & Kim, 1994, p. 191). You can be clear about your own interests and firmly resolve to pursue them and at the same time show your conciliatory intentions and be flexible about the final form of any agreement.

Offering to Cooperate

In terms of generating a clear intention to be flexible about the final form of the agreement and a willingness to treat the other's outcomes as important, parties entering into negotiations can do many things.

- They can show from the beginning that the other's welfare and benefit will be taken seriously and brought into consideration as part of the problem.
- They can demonstrate willingness to alter their proposals should new ways be discovered to bridge the interests of both parties.
- They can manifest their willingness and ability to problem solve through creatively developing new and useful alternatives and ideas.
- They can facilitate open lines of communication maintaining both the ability to contact and to be contacted in a spirit of cooperative openness.
- They can positively reinforce the other when they perceive the other is being cooperative.
- Finally, the parties can seriously take stock of their own interests and positions where they are clearly in conflict with and unacceptable to the other. If on re-examination a party's interests seem to be relatively unimportant, they might be dropped or minimized as an indication of cooperation. If, on the other hand, the interests are high priority, it may be possible to analyse them and determine what lesser interests underlie and make up those main interests being sought. In doing so, smaller component interests may be found that are not incompatible with the interests of the other and yet still go a long way to fulfilling the parties' own needs.

Cooperative problem solving, despite its many advantages, is not necessarily the conflict resolution strategy people choose first. Very often people will, because of their experience or their conditioning, go straight to a strategy of contending. But as people learn more about the costs of contending and about the merits of the cooperative process, they may begin to see conflict itself in a different light and see that it may be resolved cooperatively, without contention (see Figure 2.2).

Figure 2.2   Interpersonal Conflict-Handling Styles

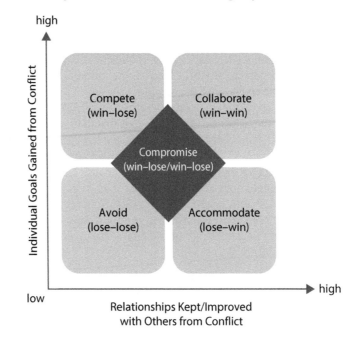

KEY TERMS

argumentative approach, 16

both/and thinking, 20

contending, 15

contradiction, 17

cooperative approach, 16

cooperative problem solving, 15

either/or thinking, 20

ignoring, 15

polarization, 18

rules of natural justice, 17

yielding, 15

REFERENCES

Barnett Pearce, W., & Littlejohn, S.W. (1997). *Moral conflict: When social worlds collide*. Thousand Oaks, CA: Sage.

De Bono, E. (1985). *Conflicts: A better way to resolve them*. Toronto: Penguin Books.

Deutsch, M., & Coleman, P. (2000). *The handbook of conflict resolution: Theory and practice*. San Francisco: Jossey-Bass.

Fisher, R., Ury, W., & Patton, B. (2011). *Getting to yes* (3rd ed.). New York: Penguin.

Kottler, J.A. (1994). *Beyond blame: A new way of resolving conflicts in relationships*. San Francisco: Jossey-Bass.

Lederach, J.P. (1995). *Preparing for peace*. Syracuse, NY: Syracuse University Press.

Rubin, J.Z., Pruitt, D.G., & Kim, S.H. (1994). *Social conflict, escalation, stalemate and settlement* (2nd ed.). New York: McGraw-Hill.

Rubin, J.Z., Pruitt, D.G., & Kim, S.H. (2004). *Social conflict, escalation, stalemate and settlement* (3rd ed.). New York: McGraw-Hill.

Tannen, D. (1998). *The argument culture*. New York: Random House.

QUESTIONS AND EXERCISES

1. Think of an occasion where you participated in a heated debate. Think about the issues involved in this debate. Did they seem to expand and become more detailed, or did they shrink and contract to the point where the dispute became narrowly personal? Also, describe what happened in terms of emotional states and quality of dialogue. Was there a point where effective listening stopped and it became more important to personally insult the other side than to succeed in the argument?

2. To sharpen your awareness of Western culture's commitment to argument, try the following exercises:

   a. Find a newspaper or magazine article or watch a television show in which a matter of public interest is being addressed. Analyze the content to determine how competing points of view have been polarized and whether they accurately represent all points of view and interests. Try to see how other interests could have been involved and how the focus and outcome of the discussion could have been changed.

   b. Watch a political debate. Try to determine whether either side is making any effort to see the merits of the opposing side's view. How much of the debate simply consists of one party attacking the other side's ideas or person? How effective a forum and process is this for creating new strategies? How could it be improved?

3. Return to the exercise in Chapter 1 where the three people—the environmentalist, the lumberman, and the developer—are walking through the forest. Now assume that the interest each has in acquiring the forest depends on the zoning of the property—the land use that the local municipality will allow for it. This is currently being decided. Select groups to represent each of the parties and to prepare presentations for the municipal council. If we assume that only one party will be successful in obtaining the zoning he needs, how does this affect the manner in which we proceed? Will we merely promote our own case, or will we attack the uses proposed by the others? Will we be prepared to withstand their assaults on our presentation? Is this the most appropriate method for determining the use of the land? Try to assess, as you do the exercise, the strengths and the dangers of the aggressive approach.

4. Return to the exercise in Chapter 1 involving George and Tang. Assume that Tang has now approached George and complained about the volume of George's music during his (Tang's) meditation time. George, embarrassed and taken aback by the charge, advises Tang that his music is important to him and that Tang, if he doesn't like it, should move or get earplugs. Tang reports the incident to the residence don, who has the authority to refer it to an appeal committee. What is likely to happen to the relationship between George

and Tang if a formal appeal is undertaken? Again, select groups to carry out the formal appeal in which George and Tang approach the problem as adversaries, each claiming the rightness of his own position and the wrongness of the other's. How much time and effort will each party spend if they focus only on the win–lose potential of the dispute?

5. Recall a time when you intervened in an argument between friends. Clarify and detail the strategies you used. What were the friends' strategies, and what were they seeking to achieve? What does this recollected episode tell you about argumentation and peacemaking?

6. Consider a time when you were personally involved in a conflict. Would you rather have had the power to create your own solution, with the other party's input, or would you rather have had a third party select and impose a decision on you and the other party? Why?

7. Return to the scenario of the three people and the forest. Set up an arrangement by which the three parties can all use the forest.

8. Return to the scenario with George and Tang. Have a mutual acquaintance of George and Tang attempt to intervene and to use cooperative problem solving to settle their conflict.

Conflict Analysis: Types and Sources of Conflict and the Potentials for Escalation and Intervention

3

LEARNING OUTCOMES

After completing this chapter, you will be able to:

- Recognize, define, and discuss the various types of conflict.

- Identify the underlying causes of these different types of conflict.

- Analyze actual conflicts to determine their source, type, and stage of development.

- Recognize what intervention strategy is appropriate for a conflict depending on its type and stage of development.

- Define and recognize zero-sum thinking and compare it with collaborative win–win thought paradigms in terms of processes and results.

- Understand how an adversarial approach to conflict leads to escalation.

- Recognize the various stages of escalation and the changes that occur at each stage.

- Clearly define the benefits of the cooperative method of addressing conflict.

- Through class discussion, role-playing exercises, and individual activities, apply the new understanding of conflict types, stages of escalation, and methods of intervention.

Zero-Sum Thinking

Zero-sum thinking is a mindset we are all familiar with. Its basic idea is that the world has limited, finite assets for which the world's inhabitants must contend on a win–lose basis. If two people are in conflict over assets, ideas, or values, the assumption, from the perspective of zero-sum thinking, is that only one of them can win or dominate. The other will lose. People influenced by this kind of thinking will automatically contend if they perceive themselves to be in conflict. This reflex severely limits how a dispute can be handled. It's a reaction that leads to entrenched positions and the use of rights-based or power-based tactics.

The competitive mode leads quickly to the situation described by de Bono:

> Each side gets more rigid. Neither side makes an attempt to develop an idea different from the two that are clashing. An indefinite amount of time, energy, and cost are locked up in a standoff, which may continue for a long time. The creativity and ingenuity of each side is not directed at improving their idea but in securing the defeat of the opposing idea and at the end the idea (or party) which triumphs is the stronger but not necessarily the better. (1985, pp. 19–20)

The aim of peacemakers, or mediators, is to help liberate disputing parties that have become locked into that competitive process. If we can understand the parties' reactions to conflict, then teach them to understand their own reactions, perhaps we can redirect them to more beneficial avenues of problem solving.

Types of Conflict

The first step in developing our awareness about conflict is to realize that there are different types of it, each requiring a different type of intervention.

There are different ways of classifying conflicts. We may differentiate them, for example, according to the level at which they are occurring. Conflict may occur at the *material* level, as when two parties are competing for scarce physical resources. Here, zero-sum thinking tends to promote win–lose tactics. The conflict between two parties may be *relational*. These conflicts are present where people miscommunicate, where power is unequally distributed, or where people engage in competitive social behaviours and strategies. Finally, conflict can occur at the *spiritual*, *perceptual*, or *symbolic levels* because of seeming incompatibilities between cultures or genders or between people with diverse personalities and world views.

In *The Mediation Process* (2014), Moore classifies the different types of conflict according to their *causes*. Focusing on causes makes Moore's approach quite different from the legal rights approach to conflict. From the legal rights perspective, it's more important to deal with the *effects* of divorce or of criminal or other anti-social behaviour than to examine the causes of the behaviour. This effects-oriented perspective ignores the fact that exploring the conflict's causes is fundamental to resolving it in a lasting way. Cooperative processes do understand this fact.

The Five Kinds of Conflict

Moore (2014) identifies five types of conflict:

1. **Relationship conflicts** are caused by misperception and stereotyping and often involve strong emotions (Moore, 2003). For example, two workers of different ethnic backgrounds who are constantly quarrelling are engaged in this kind of conflict. This kind of conflict tends to be fed by miscommunication and persistently offensive behaviour.

2. **Data conflicts** occur over information or misinformation, over what information is relevant, or over how it should be collected or interpreted. For example, people disputing the value of a property are engaged in this kind of conflict and may simply need more or better information or an expert third party to assist them.

3. **Interest conflicts** occur when parties believe they are in competition over substantive, procedural, or psychological interests. Siblings who don't believe they are getting their fair share of attention from parents would be engaged in this kind of conflict. Another example would be a woman who is angry at being denied fair treatment in a male-dominated workplace.

4. **Structural conflicts** are caused by destructive patterns of behaviour or interaction; unequal control, ownership, or distribution of resources; unequal power and authority; and geographical, physical, environmental, or time constraints that hinder cooperation. This can happen, for example, in institutions where employees with greater education are preferred to those with greater experience.

5. **Value conflicts** arise when people have different criteria for valuing ideas or behaviour or have goals based on mutually exclusive value systems. These conflicts occur where different, seemingly incompatible religions, ideologies, or ways of life come into contact.

Interventions for the Five Kinds of Conflict

Having outlined the different types of conflict, Moore goes on to suggest appropriate interventions for each. The suggested interventions are meant to address the root causes of the dispute rather than their effects.

For *data conflicts*, the intervention would seek agreement from the parties on what data is important, how to collect and interpret it, or how to use outside experts to break deadlocks. Two people battling over the value of a house, a painting, or an heirloom, while they may not agree on the actual value of the goods, may well agree on what criteria to use in valuing the goods—for example, on an expert they both trust to establish that value.

Interventions in *value conflicts* tend to be the most difficult. Moore suggests that, for this type of intervention, we avoid defining the situation as a value conflict and search for **superordinate goals**—in other words, goals that may appeal to both parties. Take, for example, the battle between pro-choice and pro-life advocates.

relationship conflicts
conflicts caused by stereotyping and misperception, often involving strong emotion

data conflicts
conflicts that occur over information (for example, disagreements over what information is relevant or how that information should be collected and interpreted)

interest conflicts
conflicts arising from competition over substantive, procedural, or psychological interests

structural conflicts
conflicts that arise from inequities or constraints in a social structure and that often take the form of destructive behaviour or interactions

value conflicts
conflicts that arise when people have different criteria for valuing ideas or behaviour or have goals based on mutually exclusive value systems

superordinate goals
goals that transcend the conflict situation and appeal to both parties

Here, any attempt by the two sides to discuss fundamental values is likely to break down quickly, even violently. In this case, the intervention should take the focus off abortion and move it to, for example, the superordinate question of how to educate young people about sexuality and its consequences. Both groups might contribute quite freely to such a discussion.

For *interest conflicts*, according to Moore, interventions should strive to clarify what the parties actually want, need, or fear, as opposed to what the grounds are for their entrenched positions. Other intervention methods for interest conflicts might be to:

- look for objective criteria,
- develop integrative solutions that address the needs of all parties,
- search for ways to expand options or resources, or
- develop trade-offs that will satisfy both parties.

Take, for example, the case of a married couple where the husband believes that, after the birth of their first child, the wife should leave her job and stay at home to raise the child. The wife clearly has an interest in raising her child, but she also has an interest in maintaining her career. An appropriate intervention strategy in this case would not simply invoke the traditional definitions of wife and mother; it would explore the possible ways in which the interests and needs of husband, wife, and child might all be satisfied.

Relationship conflicts often require interventions that use procedural guidelines, ground rules, caucuses, and restraints of that sort to keep the disputants' emotions in check. Other interventions into this type of conflict may need to work the opposite way; in other words, they may need to *promote* the expression of emotions. This kind of intervention would work by the following means:

- legitimizing feelings and providing a process to do so,
- clearing up misconceptions and building positive perceptions,
- improving the quality and quantity of communication,
- preventing offensive behaviour through structural change, or
- encouraging positive problem-solving attitudes.

For example, take a case in which two co-workers of different ethnic backgrounds continually clash over their stereotypical beliefs about the other. Influenced by these stereotypes, each sees the other as incompetent and uncooperative. An appropriate intervention strategy here would be to control the two parties' negative reactions while helping them to understand each other as individuals rather than as members of stereotyped groups.

PSYCHOLOGICAL FIRST IMPRESSIONS

Psychological research has shown that we make judgments about others' characters—their trustworthiness, aggressiveness, and competence, for example—when we are exposed to their faces for just one tenth of a second. Seeing these faces for longer periods of time serves simply to increase our confidence in our first impressions (Todorov, 2017).

Interventions in *structural conflicts* should be geared toward the following:

- clearly defining and changing roles;
- replacing destructive behaviour patterns;
- reallocating ownership or control of resources;
- establishing a fair and mutually acceptable decision-making process;
- changing the negotiation process from positional to interest-based bargaining;
- modifying the parties' means of influence by, for example, suggesting they use less coercion and more persuasion;
- changing the physical and environmental relationship of parties to ensure they have equal access to amenities;
- modifying external pressures on parties; or
- changing time constraints.

Take, for example, a company in which women are prevented from rising beyond certain mid-levels of management due to long-standing promotion practices that are geared toward men. The men in this company, as the current holders of organizational power, choose their own successors, who are almost always male. An appropriate intervention here might be to restructure the selection processes so as to create opportunities for talented women to advance.

Interventions that address the conflicts' root causes have the potential to produce all-inclusive and durable solutions. This is not the case with the one-size-fits-all approach that characterizes power-based or rights-based conflict-resolution procedures. Understanding that certain kinds of interventions are best suited to certain kinds of conflicts—as complicated as such a consideration may be—will help us fashion durable solutions to problems in an increasingly complex society.

The Growth of Conflict

Once a conflict exists, it is rarely static. Conflicts tend to grow in intensity, complexity, and size. In other words, they tend to escalate. Effective interventions counter this process of **escalation**.

For countering escalation, the crucial analytical tool is the ability to identify the conflict's tendencies and stages. This can help you return the parties to a simpler, less cluttered or emotionally charged perception of their problem. You will also find it useful to identify very precisely the dispute's underlying elements.

Rubin, Pruitt, and Kim (1994) outline the course of development that most conflicts follow. Once established, a conflict will tend to move through the following **phases of escalation** (see Figure 3.1).

1. Light to Heavy

Parties in conflict will tend to move from **light tactics of contention** to heavy ones. First, let us examine and recognize what we mean by contentious tactics. At the light end of the spectrum, a party in contention will attempt to get their way through the use of ingratiating behaviour toward the person who controls what the parties are competing for. Take a case, for example, where two siblings are competing to borrow their mom's car for Saturday night. Without saying why, one sibling cleans the house,

escalation
the growth of a conflict in intensity, complexity, and size

phases of escalation
the stages a conflict moves through as it intensifies—from light tactics of contention to heavy ones, from narrow issues to general ones, from moderate to destructive aims, from the involvement of few to the involvement of many, and from rational perspectives to demonizing ones

light tactics of contention
tactics that are designed to win the contest without injuring the other party (for example, persuasion, guilt trips, or simple requests)

does the dishes, and praises Mom over supper as the greatest mother ever. These actions seem generous, but the teenager's ultimate purpose is to outflank the sibling and get the car. Parties using these light tactics will seek to modify their behaviour to impress and court the favour of a judge, arbitrator, or mediator, to whom the behaviour may seem positive. But the other party in the conflict will recognize it as a tactic designed to win the competition and will likely proceed to step up their own competitive efforts, thus producing further escalation.

gamesmanship
a light tactic of contention that involves an attempt to destroy or upset the other party's rhythm in some way

Gamesmanship is another light form of contentious tactic. This involves an attempt to destroy or upset the other party's rhythm in some way. It might involve, for example, interrupting the other party at crucial moments in their talk, feigning lack of attention, abruptly changing the subject, or undermining the flow of logic in their presentation.

Guilt trips are also a light tactic of contention. They are designed to win the day rather than promote understanding.

heavy tactics of contention
tactics involving arguments and threats, often leading to the use of violent force

When lighter tactics fail, parties will often resort to **heavy tactics of contention**. Argument escalates to the level of threat. Commitments to a combative course of action become entrenched and unyielding, as in a hunger strike, a game of chicken, or Gandhi's 1930 march to the sea to obtain salt. The latter example demonstrates that a heavily contentious approach is sometimes consistent with a policy of non-violence.

Beyond these threatening tactics lie pure force and violence. Whether at the personal or international level of conflict, violence, once present, is more likely to escalate than not—and it is likely to escalate out of control.

Figure 3.1   Phases of Escalation

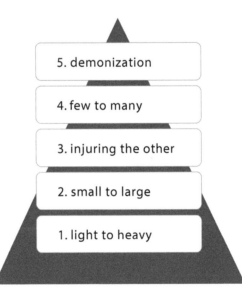

5. demonization

4. few to many

3. injuring the other

2. small to large

1. light to heavy

2. Small to Large

Contentious conflict may initially occur over small and limited issues. As the conflict proceeds, the issues tend to proliferate and to move from the specific to the general.

For instance, when Martha is upset with George for not doing the dishes, she may soon recall the uncut lawn, his poor financial habits, the women he slept with in college, and all the other offences of his life to date. To intervene effectively in this conflict, you might need to refocus attention solely on the matter currently at issue— that is, the dishes. Otherwise, George is likely to respond by highlighting Martha's own past shortcomings, and then they are into a pattern of blaming, attacking, and doing other things that lead to escalation.

After the parties have begun listing each other's specific faults, they will next shift to more general, all-inclusive statements. George will now become simply a "bad husband" and Martha a "bad wife." These labels, once established, make it harder to address the fundamental needs that gave rise to the dispute.

3. Injuring the Other

The next phase of escalation comes when a contending party becomes frustrated and stops merely trying to succeed in the matter at hand and starts trying to hurt the other. Hurting the other party becomes the main goal.

When one party aims to hurt the other, the other party retaliates, and further escalation follows. Matrimonial disputes over custody or property are especially liable to this development. The parties involved in these kinds of disputes have been known to squander their assets in a process that gains them little but ensures the other spouse will also get little. In an international context, suicide bombers offer many examples of parties willing to self-destruct in order to inflict pain on their adversaries and draw attention to their dispute.

4. Few to Many

In the next phase of escalation, the numbers of people involved in the dispute go from few to many. The primary disputants will reach out to others who are in sympathy with them, thus enlisting outside support. Soon, more and more people become involved, and the dispute grows ever more polarized. Again, the ability to identify and analyze the origins of the dispute will help you cut through the complexity caused by these additional participants.

5. Demonization

At some point in the evolution of a conflict, a psychological element enters the polarized situation and causes the parties to demonize each other. **Demonization** generally involves using stereotypes to belittle, accuse, or attack the other side. The Iranian mullahs' referring to America as *the great Satan* is an example of such demonization, as is George W. Bush's use of the phrase *Axis of Evil* in reference to governments he believed to be promoting terrorism. Demonizations tend to be simplistic, polarizing, limiting, and suffused with inflammatory meaning. They often involve inaccurate and reductive comments about race and gender, and they always falsify their targets.

demonization
a disputant's use of stereotypes and falsifications to belittle, accuse, or attack the other side

As a dispute moves through the stages described above, a pattern of mutual retaliation develops. This leads to a spiral of escalation that is increasingly difficult to stop or withdraw from.

IN THE NEWS

NORTH CAROLINA "BATHROOM BILL"

In March 2016, the state legislature of North Carolina passed a bill (the so-called "Bathroom Bill") requiring anyone needing restroom facilities in any public building to use the one that corresponded to their gender as identified on their birth certificate. As such, it served to block transgender people from using the restroom that corresponded to the gender identity they currently have. The bill was called the *Public Facilities Privacy & Security Act* but immediately ran into opposition from a variety of progressive organizations due to concerns that it violated the rights of LGBTQ+ people. The Republican-controlled legislature claimed that the bill was a "commonsense" move and served to protect, among other things, religious freedom. The National Basketball Association's 2017 All-Star Game had been scheduled to be played in Charlotte, North Carolina, but the league moved the game to New Orleans due to its opposition to the bill. In March 2017, the bill was repealed, due in large part to businesses leaving the state as well as the cancellation of sporting events and concerts.

Sources: Fausset (2017); Hanna, Park, and McLaughlin (2017); Robertson (2018).

Finding Underlying Interests

When parties are locked in conflict, they tend to develop positions from which they can defend and attack comfortably. The focus of each party is on cementing their position and making it as solid as possible while attacking and trying to weaken the other's position. To disrupt this tendency, you need to get the parties to refocus on the interests that underlie their respective positions. A party's **interests** are what they legitimately need to happen—their aspirations. You learn what they are by determining what people need, fear, hope for, or desire. Positions taken in disputes sometimes mask these underlying interests, but they may also reveal them. Conflicts, at their root, are really more about pursuing and trying to achieve legitimate interests than they are about thwarting the opposing party's needs.

interest
the legitimate need that underlies the position a person takes in a conflict

CASE STUDY

MINOR VARIANCE, MAJOR MUNICIPAL CONFLICT

Vincenzo has learned through the grapevine that Frank and Maureen intend to oppose his application for a minor variance at the Committee of Adjustment meeting in a few months' time. When Vincenzo confronted Frank about this, their discussion quickly devolved into a shouting match from one boulevard to the other. Vincenzo took exception to the height of the plants in Frank and Maureen's garden. Frank and Maureen expressed frustration over the children's sports equipment on the lawn and in the street. Vincenzo complained about the construction equipment and labourer vehicles that frequently blocked the road last summer while Frank and Maureen had their basement renovated and their rear yard fully landscaped. Frank complained about the never-ending games of road hockey that block the road year-round. Before storming off, Frank told Vincenzo he wasn't alone in opposing the minor variance application, and Vincenzo will be quite surprised by the neighbourhood opposition. Vincenzo pretended not to care, but secretly he worried that opposition from many of his neighbours would negatively impact his application and alienate his family from their neighbours.

The ability to look past two parties' opposing positions and reframe a conflict according to their underlying goals or interests can help de-escalate a conflict. Throughout this text, we will emphasize the following fundamental idea: Disputes are based on interests, not on positions (see Figure 3.2).

Figure 3.2   The Conflict Onion

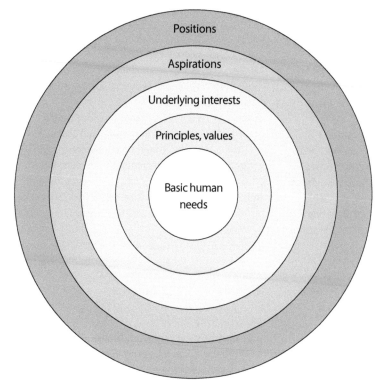

Source: Coltri (2010).

KEY TERMS

data conflicts, 27
demonization, 31
escalation, 29
gamesmanship, 30
heavy tactics of contention, 30

interest, 32
interest conflicts, 27
light tactics of contention, 29
phases of escalation, 29
relationship conflicts, 27

structural conflicts, 27
superordinate goals, 27
value conflicts, 27
zero-sum thinking, 26

REFERENCES

Coltri, L.S. (2010). *Alternative dispute resolution: A conflict diagnosis* (2nd ed.). Chicago: Pearson.

De Bono, E. (1985). *Conflicts: A better way to resolve them.* Toronto: Penguin Books.

Fausset, R. (2017, October 18). Deal on North Carolina bathroom law would expand transgender protections. *New York Times.* Retrieved from https://www.nytimes.com/2017/10/18/us/north-carolina-bathroom-bill.html

Hanna, J., Park, M., & McLaughlin, E.C. (2017, March 30). North Carolina repeals 'bathroom bill'. *CNN.* Retrieved from https://www.cnn.com/2017/03/30/politics/north-carolina-hb2-agreement/index.html

Moore, C.W. (2014). *The mediation process: Practical strategies for resolving conflict* (4th ed.). San Francisco: Wiley, Jossey-Bass.

Robertson, G.D. (2018, March 31). Tension over North Carolina's 'bathroom bill' lingers. *Boston Globe.* Retrieved from https://www.bostonglobe.com/news/nation/2018/03/31/tension-over-north-carolina-bathroom-bill-lingers/9FYiVJJeZ7sGKbbc7C5U1N/story.html

Rubin, J.Z., Pruitt, D.G., & Kim, S.H. (1994). *Social conflict, escalation, stalemate and settlement* (2nd ed.). New York: McGraw-Hill.

Todorov, A. (2017). *Face value: The irresistible influence of first impressions.* Princeton, NJ: Princeton University Press.

QUESTIONS AND EXERCISES

1. Consider again the three people in the forest, referred to in the questions from the first two chapters. Rewrite the situation so that the conflict underlying the parties' interaction becomes:
   a. a structural conflict,
   b. a data conflict,
   c. a relationship conflict,
   d. a values conflict, and
   e. an interest conflict.
   Which of these different conflicts would be most difficult to intervene in? Why?

2. Think of a relatively serious and enduring conflict between members of your family or between a couple of your friends. Trace the conflict's development, identifying the factors that caused it to escalate and the stages through which it grew. What tactics used by the parties contributed to the escalation? How far did they drift from the initial cause or causes of the dispute?

3. Consider your favourite drama in the movies, in the theatre, or on television. Generally, the plot of a drama is based upon some form of conflict between the leading characters and upon the tensions this creates between them before the conflict is resolved in the final scenes. Analyze an episode of your favourite show to determine the following: the cause of the conflicts, the underlying interests of the characters involved, the type of conflict involved, and the progressive stages of escalation.

4. Begin a personal diary that records your ongoing experience of conflicts—their causes and escalating elements. Pay attention to the people and circumstances around you and analyze the conflicts you observe. Practise defining the causes, elements, and interests involved.

5. Using the material recorded in your diary, consider some of the techniques you could use to intervene in and de-escalate the conflicts you have observed.

PART II

Processes for Addressing Conflict

Our effectiveness in dealing with conflict is mainly dependent on how we choose to respond to it!

How we respond to conflict will determine whether it escalates or is set on the path to resolution. People may choose to ignore conflict in the misguided belief that it will just go away. Or they may respond to it aggressively, using both rights-based and power-based methods meant to thwart another's interests and advance their own.

This portion of the text will examine the legitimate processes available for settling disputes. Although there are many variations for dispute-resolution processes, from engaging an ombudsman, to investigations, to mock trials, the four main approaches are:

Negotiation, Mediation, Arbitration, and Litigation

As you move from left to right, the above options become more formal both in terms of the procedures they follow and the criteria, principles, and advocacy they involve. Arbitration and litigation both authorize a third-party judge or arbitrator to impose a decision. With these two options, the disputants lose control over the process and over the final decision. Both processes are adversarial (win–lose) in nature; they pit the parties against each other and tend to destroy any positive relationship the parties may have.

Litigation involving the courts, while a legitimate process, is a complex and involved process better left to law school texts. Our focus here will be on the processes that leave the parties in control of their own fate. Negotiation and mediation offer disputants the opportunity to develop, with or without outside guidance, their own approach to the process, criteria, and solution to their conflict. Its resolution can be conducted in a collaborative as opposed to adversarial fashion.

In this part, we will look at the evolving definitions of negotiation and principled negotiation. We will also examine the goals, principles, and skill sets needed for confident, flexible, and successful negotiations and then move on to examine mediation, a form of assisted or *facilitated* negotiation. We will look at defining mediation clearly and again move on to the goals, principles, skill sets, and steps employed to maximize successful results in the mediation process. Finally, we will examine arbitration, which, while an adversarial process, can often remain at least partly in the control of the parties and create real possibilities for saving costs and time by avoiding rigidity of process.

What Is Negotiation?

4

LEARNING OUTCOMES

After completing this chapter, you will be able to:

- Define *negotiation*.

- Understand historical perspectives on negotiation.

- Understand the difference between distributive and integrative approaches to negotiation.

- Understand the effects of aggressive, as opposed to collaborative, negotiating techniques.

- Introduce new movements within the field initiated by Fisher, Ury, and Patton, especially their concept of principled negotiation.

- Practically apply the new understanding of negotiation in classroom discussions and exercises.

- Understand the preliminary steps involved in preparing to negotiate.

- Understand the practical aspects of preparing to negotiate.

- Recognize alternative theories of negotiation and understand what their effect will be on the proceedings.

- Become familiar with various procedural models for the conduct of negotiations and understand how they work.

- Participate in a negotiation process through role-playing exercises.

Responses to Conflict

How we respond to conflict can determine whether the conflict escalates or is resolved. As we have seen, responses to conflict vary. People may choose to ignore conflict. Or they may respond to it aggressively, using tactics, both rights based and power based, meant to thwart the other's interests and advance their own.

The tactics and the process a person chooses for dealing with a dispute will obviously affect the dispute's course and outcome. In this and the following chapters, we will examine the legitimate processes available for settling disputes. Despite the fact that our individualistic culture currently promotes competition and winning, we will focus primarily on cooperative or collaborative approaches.

Figure 4.1 illustrates the spectrum of options for dealing with conflict in Western culture.

As you move from left to right, the options become more formal in terms of the procedures the parties must follow and of the criteria, principles, and advocacy they involve. For example, arbitration and litigation both authorize a third-party judge or arbitrator to impose a decision; the disputants lose control over the process and over the final decision. Since both these processes are adversarial (win–lose) in nature, they pit the parties against each other and tend to damage any positive relationship the parties may have.

On the left side of the spectrum are negotiation and mediation. These processes leave the parties in control of their own fate. These processes offer disputants the opportunity to develop, with or without outside guidance, their own approach to process, criteria, and outcome. Negotiation and mediation can be conducted as collaborative as opposed to adversarial engagements.

Figure 4.1   Options in Conflict Resolution

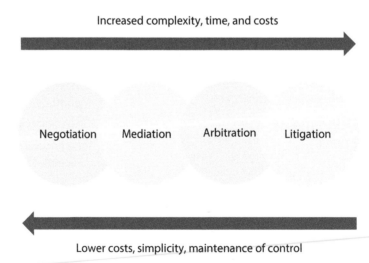

Increased complexity, time, and costs

Negotiation   Mediation   Arbitration   Litigation

Lower costs, simplicity, maintenance of control

The Need for Negotiation

Negotiation is part of all social, legal, and business activities. It is needed wherever separate parties seek agreement about beliefs, values, or actions. Countries inevitably have to negotiate when they are establishing international trade tariffs, international standards for human rights, peacekeeping policies, or defence arrangements. Activities in the business and legal spheres are also likely to involve negotiation: selling or purchasing goods, hiring employees, constructing a building, or settling a law suit.

Negotiation is a constant in our family lives too, needed for both big and small issues. Who gets the last piece of pie? Where will we go on holiday? How and by whom will housework be done? How will income be earned and allotted? How will the children be disciplined? What movie will we see this Friday?

Negotiation is something we've always engaged in with our siblings, parents, spouses, children, neighbours, and business associates. Our knowledge of how to negotiate has been acquired subconsciously, through instinct and observation, so we tend to be unaware of our own negotiating tendencies and techniques, though most people view themselves as competent negotiators. For similar reasons, we tend not to concern ourselves with the other party's interests, needs, and beliefs.

Defining Negotiation

Simply stated, **negotiation** is a process in which two or more parties communicate directly for the purpose of coming to agreement on some action that one or more of them will undertake. Chornenki and Hart (2015) suggest negotiation occurs when two or more parties in dispute communicate and engage in behaviour to see whether they can come up with something that is superior to what they have now or to what each of them could accomplish unilaterally. Negotiation is not just spontaneous conversation; it involves goal setting and measuring. It is also a process that involves only the interested parties; there is no intervening third party with the power to dictate procedure or to impose terms or direction on the process.

> **negotiation**
> a process in which two or more parties communicate directly in search of agreement on some action that one or more of them will undertake

When we enter into a negotiation, we generally expect the following to happen:

1. The parties will act in good faith.
2. The process will be efficient and not wasteful.
3. The process will produce a wise and advantageous agreement for all involved.
4. The process will improve the participants' relationship or at least not damage the relationship.

For many negotiators, however, relationship concerns and concern for the other party's interests are less important than winning at all costs. When negotiating yourself, you need to be able to deal with such win-at-all-costs people and with all types of negotiators. For that reason, we need to understand the different approaches to negotiation as well as their histories and underlying rationales.

IN THE NEWS

NAFTA NEGOTIATIONS

The public discourse around the NAFTA negotiations between Canada and the United States indicated a different philosophical approach to negotiation adopted by each side.

Publicly, the Canadian approach appeared to have been to establish cooperative bargaining based on creating and sharing greater value.

The American side as exemplified by Donald Trump had demonstrated a belief in competitive bargaining. Rather than value-creating, it was instead a value-claiming approach based upon the understanding that there are limited resources or a fixed pie in any given negotiation. This promotes a win–lose approach where whoever takes the bigger portion of that pie is the "winner" of the negotiation and the other party is seen as the loser.

The differences in approach have played out in full public view, with President Trump's decision to slap tariffs on imported aluminum and steel and his bragging about deliberately using false information in his negotiations with Prime Minister Trudeau. While these may be intimidating to the other party, they can also greatly affect credibility on the international scene, alienating existing allies and affecting future relationships.

Positional or Distributive Bargaining Theories

North American culture tends to support individual values over collective values. It honours independence, the individual's strength and success, and winners over losers. Finishing first and scoring high are the accepted measures of doing well. Winning and success are about money, fame, wealth, and outdoing your opponent. This win-at-all-costs attitude, combined with zero-sum thinking (the idea that we live in a finite universe with limited assets), has led to seeing negotiation as a competitive and adversarial exercise. Few people want their lawyer to go into a negotiation and be as reasonable as possible to the other party. Negotiating agents are expected to get as much as possible for their clients, not to be reasonable. Think about the vast sums that aggressive agents get for their clients in the sports and entertainment industries.

positional or distributive bargaining
bargaining aimed at getting as much as possible for the negotiating party, with no concern for the other side's needs

Parties who adopt this approach, which is known as **positional or distributive bargaining**, tend to see negotiation, like sport, as an adversarial, win–lose undertaking.

These parties tend to:

1. Design strategies that segregate, or separate, their interests or needs from the other party's, so that success is strictly a matter of satisfying one's own interests.
2. Focus on their own needs and ignore those of the other party.
3. Use techniques designed to overpower the other side, such as:
   a. distorting values (making excessively high demands),
   b. only partially disclosing facts,
   c. threatening and intimidating,
   d. making *take it or leave it* offers, and
   e. making no concessions.

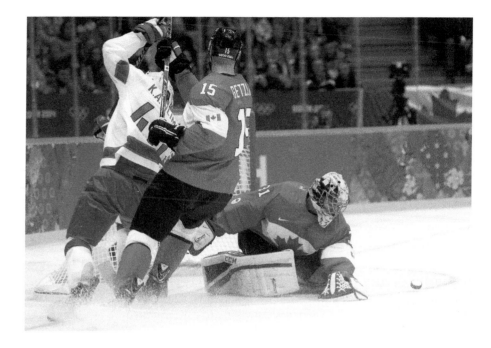

The usual game plan of the positional bargainer is to be as aggressive as possible. The goal is to intimidate your "opponent" so as to gain the larger, *distributive* share of the assets. In other words, positional bargainers aim to maximize their own gain and minimize the other party's. Your other objective, of course, if you are an agent negotiating on behalf of one party, is to justify and maximize your fee.

How Positional Bargaining Works

Negotiations conducted according to the positional bargaining approach tend to proceed as follows:

1. Parties establish their initial positions. This usually involves making an inflated or exaggerated claim. A party does this without actually expecting to get what they are asking for—that is, they *do* expect to move some way toward the other party's position. Their reasoning is as follows: "If I ask for twice what I expect to get, I can give up half my claim and still obtain what I am after."

2. Having established their respective positions, both parties put all their efforts into defending them. Here begin the take-it-or-leave-it offers and the attempts at overpowering argument. Neither party discloses much about their true needs or their advantages.

3. If both parties need a result, they will begin to **compromise**. To compromise is to give up parts of your claim and to move closer to the other party's position. Aggressive bargainers will give up as little as possible themselves while expecting the other party to give up much.

4. The parties will move slowly toward a point somewhere between their positions and, once they hit upon an acceptable compromise, come to an agreement. Otherwise, if neither party moves or changes their position, negotiations may break down.

compromise
give up parts of your claim and move closer to the other party's position

The Rationale for Positional Bargaining

Historically, this competitive form of negotiation has been very popular. Many expect it to be used in our society because our society is competitive in orientation. Positional bargaining offers a practical advantage too: The negotiator can easily jump in and participate without much preparation or much knowledge of the other party.

Think of how you approach a negotiation for a used article in a flea market or for the purchase of a used car. Even in legal claims for damages, the logic of positional or distributive bargaining often seems to prevail. But the fact that it is widely used in our society does not make it the best approach. In fact, the dangers of this approach outweigh the benefits.

The Disadvantages of Positional Bargaining

The problem with positional or distributive bargaining is that this approach is not really based on the needs or legitimate interests of the parties. The approach tends to limit the focus of negotiations to simplistic and inflexible criteria, such as monetary amounts. If the parties in dispute are unwilling to compromise, the process breaks down. If they are too aggressive in pursuing their own goals or in belittling the other party's goals, retaliation may result. Since positional bargaining is adversarial and competitive, it can damage social and business relationships. No one likes being intimidated or outmanoeuvered in any negotiation.

Desirable or not, positional bargaining is widely accepted in our society, and anyone preparing to negotiate needs to understand its principles and techniques.

Collaborative or Cooperative Negotiating Theories

The individualistic, win-at-all-costs, adversarial model of living and negotiating is everywhere in our society. But there have always been alternatives. We are all familiar with moral mandates to treat our neighbours as we would ourselves. Many of us understand that relationships—family, social, or business relationships—work better through cooperation and mutual respect. Sometimes we entertain thoughts like *nice guys finish last* or *you better look out for number one*, and sometimes we mock those who try to accommodate others' interests. And yet we know as well as that there are long-term costs—financial, emotional, and spiritual—to adversarial approaches and the retaliations they always involve.

The cooperative approach to life and to negotiating has produced the current trend toward mediation and **collaborative or cooperative problem solving**.

collaborative or cooperative problem solving
problem solving that integrates both parties' interests and seeks mutually beneficial solutions

How Collaborative Problem Solving Works

People engaged in collaborative or cooperative problem solving do the following:

1. Attempt to serve the interests of all parties, not just their own. Accordingly, they will seek to know and understand the other party's interests.
2. Integrate rather than segregate the interests of all parties, so that negotiation or problem solving is done with a win–win goal in mind.

3. Focus on:
   a. offering full disclosure of relevant information,
   b. establishing that each party is concerned with the interests of all other parties,
   c. creating new value (a larger pie) rather than unfairly dividing a fixed pie, and
   d. trying to deal collaboratively and cooperatively with all matters that arise.

Principled Negotiation

Fisher, Ury, and Patton (2011), in *Getting to Yes*, were largely responsible for reshaping our thinking about negotiation. In that brief but major work, they laid out the requirements and advantages of what they called **principled negotiation** (see Figure 4.2).

principled negotiation negotiation aimed at preventing parties from getting entrenched in positions; it works by separating people from the problem, focusing on interests rather than positions, and using objective criteria to assess creative solutions

Figure 4.2   Four Major Steps In Principled Negotiation

1. Separate people from the problem

2. Get parties to focus on interests, not positions

3. Invent options

4. Ensure the use of objective criteria

1. Separating People from the Problem

When people come to a negotiation, they often do so with a great deal of history between them, or at least with a tendency to negotiate as adversaries. Either way, positions can quickly become entrenched unless the parties, instead of simply trying to prove who was right or wrong in the past, are willing to clarify their own needs and their future interests.

Separating people from the problem can be brought about by several means:

- Promoting respectful verbal and non-verbal communication. Getting people to communicate with each other respectfully can help separate them from the cycle of blaming each other for past activities.
- Promoting active listening, so that the parties *feel* heard.
- Promoting the use of "I" statements. Statements beginning with "I feel," "I need," "I want," or "I fear" are much more effective than statements beginning with "You never" or "You always," uttered in a tone of anger or blame. The use

of "I" statements helps the parties stop blaming each other and enables them to tell which of their interests and aspirations might, if satisfied, lead to a resolution of the conflict.

2. Getting the Parties to Focus on Interests, Not Positions

position
the particular result a party wants to gain from a negotiation (as opposed to the *interests* that underlie this want)

A party's **position** is what they explicitly want from the negotiation; their *interest* is the underlying reason for their wanting it. You can discover what a party's interest is by exploring their hopes, expectations, and aspirations, as well as their fears and concerns. If both parties can define their underlying interests clearly and prioritize them, they are more likely to solve their common problem in a mutually satisfactory way.

Preparing to negotiate, then, involves not just establishing positions but trying carefully to identify the specific hopes and fears underlying them. You need to be clear not just about your own party's interests but about the other party's interests too. This will help you gauge which of your interests are priorities and which can be sacrificed even if desirable.

3. Inventing Options

Creative problem solving is much more productive than a clash of narrowly defined positions. In principled negotiation, you must have the creativity to generate options that, though not in themselves final or binding, may lead toward integrative solutions. The key is being open and flexible, not combative and fixed.

4. Ensuring the Use of Objective Criteria

To prevent the will of one party from dominating the negotiation, you must create solutions using criteria that are objective, identifiable, and measurable. This will anchor the negotiation and enable the negotiation to set fair and measurable outcomes and goals and test those outcomes for their reality, durability, and acceptability to all parties.

Following the above principles in a negotiation will help prevent positional stand-offs and increase the chance of a mutually satisfactory settlement. We will come back to these principles throughout the course of this textbook.

Keep in mind that every party is free to choose their own negotiating ideology and process. A party entering a negotiation must be prepared for any behaviour from the other side, whether adversarial or cooperative. The best way to prepare for and conduct negotiations is the subject of our next chapter. As we mentioned in Chapter 2, you can always signal to the other party, at the outset of a negotiation, your willingness to proceed cooperatively.

Preparing to Negotiate

Negotiation scenarios and contexts can be very different. But proper preparation for negotiation is always important and can ensure a number of things. It can increase confidence. It can ensure appropriate strategy. It can enable a party to identify and prioritize their current interests and potential interests. It can help establish interests in objective terms, so they can be discussed and evaluated. Good preparation will help a party clarify their negotiating range and set the outer limits of the concessions they will make. It can contribute to the fluid, flexible, yet principled conduct of a negotiation.

Preliminary Steps

The following are some important preliminary steps in preparing to negotiate.

1. Define and Prioritize All Your Interests

When preparing to negotiate, you must thoroughly consider all matters related to your party's interests: values and needs, timing considerations, and the resources available to meet your needs and to make good on your offers.

You may clarify your party's values and needs by determining which of their hopes and aspirations they aim to fulfill through the upcoming negotiations. You should consider their concerns and fears too, which can also reflect underlying needs.

Consider a husband and wife who are in the process of separating and trying to negotiate the custody of their seven-year-old son and four-year-old daughter. What are the hopes, goals, and concerns that in this case should be listed, summarized, and valued according to importance? The legal test is always to consider what is in the *best interests of the child*, but the choices in this regard are not always clear. For example, will the children have a primary residence, or will the parents have equal custody? What are the daily routines of all the parties? The children will need both parents to be supportive of them and not to fight in their presence. The parents' goal, on the other hand, may be to live as separately as possible. A negotiation of this sort requires that the parties consider all the questions, determine underlying interests, and clarify their goals.

In real estate transactions, turnaround time often becomes important, as do guarantees of timeliness and penalties for lateness of performance. These factors should be considered prior to any real estate negotiation as you try to establish the parties' interests. In sales or lease situations, monetary amounts tend to be important, but other considerations, such as convenience and the actual ability to pay, are important as well.

By clearly establishing the range and nature of its interests, a party can be much more flexible in terms of how those interests are met. This process can also help a party see what is indispensable to them—what they will not be bullied or bluffed out of.

2. Set Objective Measurable Criteria, Based on Reliable Information

Fisher et al. (2011), as we have seen, suggest that **objective measurable criteria** are needed for productive negotiation. These criteria can be established through research and through consulting with experts. In a case involving damages, for example, legal experts may be consulted about valuations and damages awarded in previous cases. For personal property like antiques or art works, evaluators can help establish a range of values. Real estate appraisers can prepare professional reports on the value of land or buildings. Actuaries can often help in assessing risk or future costs. Each industry or profession will have an abundance of experts who can value things objectively and authoritatively.

> **objective measurable criteria**
> standards of measurement or evaluation that would be acceptable to an unbiased third party

The poorly considered criteria that result from showing up at a negotiation unprepared often result in a stalemate or in a negotiation controlled by one party alone. In a negotiation over art, for example, the seller might take the following position: "This piece of art is an antique and collector's item. It is worth what I say it is worth, and you can take it or leave it." The party negotiating to buy the art will probably accept the seller's valuation unless they have criteria for determining its justifiable and measurable value.

Parties that show up to negotiate unprepared often try to bluff their way through. This often leads to defensiveness and rigid position taking. Parties that do this have no clear sense of what anything is worth and are therefore unable to explore alternative means of satisfying both parties' interests. For obvious reasons, such negotiations tend to produce poor results.

A cooperative, integrative style of negotiation does not necessarily require a party to compromise or to give up on their key interests. You must be clear and firm about what your key interests are and why they are important. And you must be able to demonstrate why your criteria for measuring value are reasonable and objective.

3. Establish a Bargaining Range

bargaining range
the range of solutions acceptable to a negotiating party, from most to least acceptable

For each element of your negotiation, set a **bargaining range** with high and low points of acceptability. Your goal, of course, is to satisfy your own interest in the most desirable way possible. In a hypothetical sales situation, for instance, it might be optimal to close a sale within two weeks but still acceptable to close it within a month. Closing it in a month or more, because it is your year-end, is unacceptable. In this case, your range of acceptance with respect to time is somewhere between two weeks (or less) and a month. In other words, you would be flexible enough, in consideration for the other party's interests, to extend your ideal frame by two weeks, but no further. You would walk away from the negotiation rather than extend it further. Knowing your bargaining range in advance is obviously advantageous, whether your negotiation involves monetary amounts, types of assurances or penalties, or services.

Figure 4.3   Key Points in Negotiation

1. Target Point

2. Resistance Point

3. BATNA or WATNA

4. Opening Bid

Have a Back Door

At this point in your preparations, you should also try to think of alternative solutions. How might you satisfy your needs and fulfill your interests other than by the upcoming negotiation? For example, are there other parties buying or selling what you are negotiating over, or offering at more reasonable prices the services you are seeking? Having a back door in the event of a standoff can relieve pressure on what may otherwise seem an all-or-nothing situation. You can also examine other avenues of dispute resolution that you could take to satisfy your needs. Would arbitration, mediation, or litigation be the most effective avenue should the current negotiation fail?

Once this preliminary work is completed, you can set or establish four key points for the upcoming negotiation (see Figure 4.3). These will guide your strategy.

Set Four Key Points

1. Target Point

Having preset your interests and goals, you need to establish your **target point** for each element in the negotiation. Your target point is the most desirable outcome for you. For example, in the hypothetical sales situation discussed above, one of your target points would be to have the other party agree to a sale within two weeks. Other target points might be having the other party agree to a price of $6,000, payable in cash upon delivery, with the delivery taking place two days after the purchase. Each of these elements is negotiable, but collectively, from your party's point of view, they would produce the most desirable sale and are therefore the target for these negotiations. Remember to set the target points in terms that are reasonable, measurable, and justifiable. Ask yourself honestly what facts support your setting this goal. Ask whether you should call on expert opinion to verify your sense of what the elements in the negotiation are worth.

> **target point**
> the most desirable outcome for a negotiating party

2. Resistance Point

Your **resistance point** is the lowest point of acceptability in your preset bargaining range. Knowing this point in advance helps prevent your being pushed into undesirable settlements. Your resistance point, in other words, is your *walkaway point*—the point beyond which you will not go. This point, too, should be measurable and clearly definable. When you have both a clearly defined resistance point and an alternative to the current negotiation—that is, a back door—you are more likely to feel certainty and confidence when negotiating.

> **resistance point**
> the lowest point of acceptability in a party's preset bargaining range

3. BATNA or WATNA

The acronym **BATNA** stands for *best alternative to a negotiated agreement*; **WATNA** stands for *worst alternative to a negotiated agreement*. Planning for a negotiation involves identifying your BATNA, occasionally referred to as your *Plan B, backup plan,* or *escape hatch*—that is, a course of action you can adopt should the upcoming negotiations break down or come to deadlock. Above, we discussed the concept of a resistance point—the lowest point of acceptability within your bargaining range. Your BATNA is established prior to entering into the negotiation as the best option available to you should you reach your resistance point and decide to walk away from bargaining. Having this option mapped out in advance releases the parties from the understanding that a negotiation is otherwise all or nothing. For example, we have been offered lumber from someone other than our present supplier at 50 cents a board foot. We are now negotiating with our present supplier to renew the contract we have with them; they are asking 60 cents a board foot. If they won't go below or

> **BATNA**
> the best alternative to a negotiated agreement; a course of action the negotiating party might adopt should the upcoming negotiations break down or come to deadlock

> **WATNA**
> the worst alternative to a negotiated agreement; the worst possibilities if the upcoming negotiations fail

at least come close to what the other supplier is offering, we are—all other interests being equal—better off breaking off our negotiations with them. Our target point is the 50 cents. If they don't meet it, we can opt for our BATNA; that is, we can walk away and enter a contract with the other supplier. The BATNA of a wife who is being abused by her husband during the negotiation of a separation agreement is to break off the current negotiations and take her husband to court; she will receive more protection and a fairer deal that way. In other words, an application to the courts is her BATNA.

To establish your WATNA, calculate what the worst possibilities are if the upcoming negotiations fail. To return to our lumber scenario, for example, let's say there is no alternative supplier offering a price of 50 cents a board foot; there is only our current supplier, offering 60 cents a board foot. If we walk away from the latter offer, we will have no supplier at all. That is our WATNA. The WATNA tends to show the negotiator just how important success in the present negotiation is.

Calculating your best and worst alternatives in advance will bolster both your confidence and your realism concerning the negotiation.

CASE STUDY

BATNA AND WATNA

A newlywed couple is purchasing a house. The one they have found has everything they want but is listed out of their price range. If negotiations fail to lower the price to within their range, there is an alternative house in the next neighbourhood that is acceptable in terms of price but less desirable due to its amenities and location. This second option represents their best alternative to a negotiated agreement or BATNA.

With the market moving quickly, their real estate agent warns the couple that they cannot afford to delay or they risk missing out on both opportunities. This represents their worst alternative to a negotiated agreement or WATNA.

These two factors should inform their negotiating strategy and influence their decision making.

4. Opening Bid

opening bid
the initial offer in a negotiation

The final key point to calculate before you begin to negotiate is your **opening bid**. This step can be crucial. A careless opening bid can set your bargaining range in a disadvantageous way.

If your opening is lower than it needs to be, and the other party accepts it, you will not be able to raise it. If you do not open yourself but allow the other party to do so, you may be brought in at a level that is much higher than you consider reasonable and have a difficult time lowering the range.

Since the opening bid can be crucial to success, you must consider all aspects of it carefully in the light of your needs, interests, and goals for the negotiation. Keep in mind that your opening bid holds out something measurable; you need to be able to justify it.

Remember, aggressive negotiators may double or cut in half opening bids as a way of controlling range. Thorough preparation is your best defence and guide. The important point here is that the opening bid can predetermine the range of the negotiation.

Assessing the Other Party and Your Own Assets

Having completed your self-analysis, you need to examine the other party. What is their reputation? What do your investigations or past experiences of them tell you about their character and preferred style of negotiating? What are their interests and corresponding objectives likely to be? What resources do they have—or lack—that could affect the directions of the negotiations? What are their likely BATNA and WATNA? In other words, you need to analyze the other party as you have analyzed yourself. Try to avoid surprises.

While examining the other party, take stock of the assets you have that might contribute to the negotiation. Coleman, Raider, and Gerson (Deutsch & Coleman, 2000, pp. 499–521) refer to these assets as "chips" and "chops." *Chips* are the positive benefits you can offer to the other party. *Chops* are deterrents or threats—a necessary element even in a cooperative negotiation. Imagine, for example, you are a parent negotiating with an eldest son about babysitting younger siblings and improving the quality of his babysitting performance. Chips for you to use as the parent could be an economic reward, an offer of privileges such as the use of the car, or expressions of respect and gratitude. Chops could be the withdrawing of privileges, a reduced economic reward, or using an alternative babysitter.

Chips and chops need not be directly involved in the current negotiations. They may be future options or may exist completely outside the current framework of negotiations. They can be aimed at removing the other party's pain or difficulty or at compensating them in some other way for undergoing these hardships.

Prior to any negotiation, take a thorough inventory of the chips and chops at your disposal.

Contacting the Other Party

Before meeting to actually negotiate, consider contacting the other party in order to confirm certain practical details and to telegraph your desire for collaborative negotiation.

Among the practical details you'll want to confirm beforehand are the location and the timing of the negotiations. Timing would include considerations about the duration of the overall process and the length of individual sessions. You should also consider which parties need to be in attendance so that there is authority to settle and the likelihood of a complete agreement. You can also suggest at this stage that an agenda be determined in advance and that some preliminary ground rules for the negotiation be set.

The **preliminary contact** and the discussion of these practical matters can set a positive tone for the negotiation to come.

preliminary contact
the parties' meeting or discussion prior to the start of negotiation

Foreseeing the Pattern of Negotiation

Parties are free to set the tone and the process for their own negotiation. Parties often jump in to negotiate without trying to foresee the overall pattern of a negotiation or the stages it is likely to go through. And yet it is possible to predict such patterns; to do so, you need to consider carefully the disposition of the parties as well as their likely attitudes and behaviours and the probable consequences of these.

Will the negotiation follow an adversarial format? In that case, the parties will try to maximize their own gains at the expense of the other. Or will the negotiation be patterned on a cooperative or collaborative model, with the goals of fairness and mutual gain?

We have already discussed how an intention to cooperate can be signalled beforehand. Ideally, both parties will favour an integrative solution. If, however, you conclude that the other party, on the basis of their past performance, their reputation, or their current conduct, is adopting an aggressive, distributive approach, you must be able to adapt.

Patterns of Negotiation

The Aggressive Mode

Williams (1983, pp. 70–72) suggests that adversarial legal negotiations are likely to involve four stages: opening, argumentation, crisis, and agreement (or breakdown) (see Figure 4.4).

1. Opening

The negotiators will meet and greet one another and begin to establish their relationship. Then they will establish and justify their respective positions. In the course of establishing the strength of their own case while undermining the other side's, they will establish their opening position.

Each party will claim that their opening position is absolutely sound and unalterable and that they have no intention of yielding on any part of it. If you have prepared sufficiently, you'll know whether the other's opening position is what Williams calls *maximalist*. A **maximalist position** sets a party's claim high, often well beyond what they can reasonably expect to obtain. A maximalist position is one sign that the negotiation will follow a more aggressive model. A sign that the proceedings may follow a more collaborative model is an opening offer that seems fair or even integrative. It is important to watch for the signals sent by the opening position.

The opening stage of an aggressive negotiation can go on for months or even years.

maximalist position
an aggressively high opening bid designed to preset the range of negotiation

Figure 4.4   Stages of Adversial Negotiation

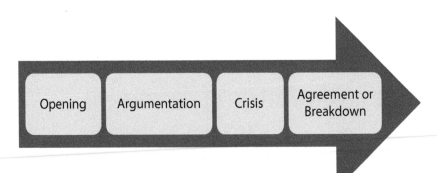

Opening | Argumentation | Crisis | Agreement or Breakdown

2. Argumentation

In this second stage, the stage of **argumentation**, the strategy is to present your case. This is in keeping with the rules of natural justice, which state that everyone has a right to a fair hearing. Here, tactics are typically intended to reveal the other party's *real position* while disguising your own and presenting your case in the best light possible. Presenting your own case in this way tends to involve emphasizing the weakness of the other's case. During this stage, parties tend to forget that the pursuit of truth is—ideally—the goal of argument; they resort to aggressive, unfair tactics.

During this argumentation phase, each party gains insight into the relative strengths and weaknesses of the other's case and may choose to modify their position through concessions. This is likely to follow the positional or distributive bargaining model we described earlier in this text. **Concessions** will move both parties closer to the middle ground between their positions. But it is important to realize that this movement is not driven by the actual needs of the parties; it is driven by a rights-based assessment of the strengths and weaknesses of each party's case. At a certain point, this concessionary process will produce either agreement or a final crisis in which both parties feel the pressure of impending deadlines.

> **argumentation**
> the second stage in an aggressive negotiation, where a party presents their own case in the best light possible while emphasizing the weakness of the other side's case

> **concession**
> the yielding of some part of one's position

3. Crisis

At the **crisis** stage, the parties understand that larger concessions or alternative proposals are required. They are likely to telegraph the kind of concession that might induce them to settle. Neither party wishes to concede any more themselves. Clients at this point worry about the advisability of settlement. Deadlines related to parties' agendas or court process are getting close.

At this point, the pre-established walkaway points and BATNAs come into effect as the parties reach the end of their ability to compromise. Either the imminence of deadlines will stimulate final offers or the parties will hit endgame—that is, the point at which parties will finally break off negotiation and give up hope of a settlement; they will proceed to court and allow a third party to determine the issue for them.

> **crisis**
> the stage in a competitive negotiation where further concessions are needed but neither party is willing to make them

4. Agreement or Breakdown

If final offers and last-minute pressure are compelling, the parties will come to an agreement, which will subsequently be reduced to **minutes of settlement**—that is, the document containing the final terms the parties have agreed upon. (The filing of this document with the court leads to a dismissal of the court action.) If no agreement can be reached at this stage, the negotiations will break down, and the best alternative will usually be costly and risky court proceedings.

The stages of an adversarial negotiation are quite predictable. Each party formulates their position based on rights and moves tentatively toward an acceptable centre by giving up elements of their original position. Giving up or compromising has nothing to do with clarifying and integrating actual needs. It is done for the sake of victory or defeat, and it often involves aggressive gambits and brinksmanship bargaining.

> **minutes of settlement**
> the written document containing the final terms the parties have agreed upon in settling their dispute

The Collaborative Mode

Deutsch and Coleman (2000) define the four steps of collaborative bargaining. They do so with reference to the five *communication behaviours* commonly found in the negotiating process. These communication behaviours are as follows:

1. Attacking

[This] includes any type of behaviour perceived by the other side as hostile or unfriendly: threatening, insulting, blaming, and criticizing without being constructive, stereotyping, patronizing, interrupting and discounting other's ideas. It includes nonverbal cues such as hostile tone of voice, facial expressions or gestures. (p. 511)

2. Evading

[This] occurs when one party or both parties avoid material aspects of the problem. Hostile evasions include ignoring a question, changing the subject, not responding, leaving the scene or failing to meet. Friendly or positive evasions include postponing difficult topics to deal with simple ones first, conferring with colleagues and taking time out to think or obtain relevant information. (p. 511)

Both these communication behaviours are aggressive techniques more likely to be found in adversarial negotiation. But they can be found in collaborative negotiations as well and need to be dealt with.

The other three communication behaviours commonly found in negotiation are the following:

3. Informing

[This] includes behaviour that directly or indirectly explains one side's perspective to the other in a non-attacking way. Information sharing can occur on many different levels: needs, feelings, values, positions, or justifications. (p. 511)

4. Opening

[This] invites the other party to share information. It includes asking questions about the other's positions, needs, feelings and values, listening carefully to what the other is saying, and testing one's understanding by summarizing neutrally what is being said. (p. 511)

5. Uniting

[This] emphasizes the relationship between disputants. This behaviour sets and maintains the tone necessary for cooperation during the negotiation process. The four types of uniting behaviour are:

1. building rapport;
2. highlighting common ground;
3. reframing the conflict issues; and
4. linking bargaining chips to expressed needs. (p. 511)

Stage One: Ritual Sharing

ritual sharing
the first stage of a collaborative negotiation and the point where parties develop rapport, discover common ground, and learn about each other's interests

The first stage of a collaborative negotiation is referred to as **ritual sharing**; in terms of communication behaviour, it involves *uniting*. This initial phase is always about defining the problem confronting the parties and trying to understand it from all perspectives. The matters each party wants to address will be prioritized according to their importance to the overall agreement. At this point, parties will often casually converse for the purposes of

- building rapport,
- establishing common ground, and

- listening for clues about the other party's value system or world view that might influence the negotiations.

Unlike the first stage of the adversarial model, the aim here is to unite the parties' perspectives as far as possible; it is not to have them establishing and defending their respective positions. The goal is to set a positive tone before moving on to establish the issues.

Stage Two: Establishing the Issues

The second stage of a collaborative negotiation involves *establishing the issues*. Each party informs the other of their opening position and its justification; each remains flexible about the other's opening position. After this, the parties move on to clearly define the interests (needs, hopes, aspirations, fears, concerns) underlying their respective positions. Each party informs the other about their own interests and probes the other about theirs. The communication behaviour that dominates this second stage is *informing*. Both parties clearly give and receive information about each other's underlying interests. This sometimes involves summarizing the two sets of needs on a single list. Then the parties move on to reframe and prioritize their issues.

Stage Three: Reframing

The third stage of the collaborative negotiation is referred to as *reframing*. One party or the other asks, "How can we satisfy the top-priority needs of both parties?" As with stage one, the communication behaviour that governs this stage is *uniting*. Reframing incorporates both parties' interests in a search for solutions. Each party formulates issues on the basis of their interests and lists them in order of importance. During this reframing stage, parties should reflect honestly on their own interest claims and decide which ones are truly important. They may determine that some are dispensable and can be dropped from the agenda.

Stage Four: Problem Solving

The fourth stage of the collaborative negotiation is the *problem-solving* step. Now, with their interests clarified, parties will brainstorm and list potential solutions. This is a creative, uniting behaviour that enables parties ultimately to select and refine the most desirable—and generous (chips)—ways of meeting their needs.

Once the best of the solutions have been selected and evaluated, the parties can combine their solutions to all issues and reduce them to agreement form.

In the next chapter of this text, we will look in much greater depth at the steps described above and at the skills involved in them. We will discuss the processes of determining interests and issues, dealing with emotion, reframing, creative problem solving, and selecting and testing solutions. Greater understanding of these matters will further clarify not just mediation, which is essentially facilitated negotiation, but the art of negotiation in general.

KEY TERMS

REFERENCES

Chornenki, G.A., & Hart, C.E. (2015). *Bypass court: A dispute resolution handbook* (5th ed.). Toronto: LexisNexis.

Deutsch, M., & Coleman, P. (2000). *The handbook of conflict resolution: Theory and practice.* San Francisco: Jossey-Bass.

Fisher, R., Ury, W., & Patton, B. (2011). *Getting to yes* (3rd ed.). New York: Penguin.

Williams, G.R. (1983). *Legal negotiation and settlement.* St. Paul, MN: West.

QUESTIONS AND EXERCISES

1. In groups, discuss whether the principle of good faith is entrenched deeply enough in the Canadian psyche that it should become binding in all negotiations carried out in Canada.
   a. When do you yourself expect good faith to be present in a negotiating situation?
   b. When, in your negotiating experience, can you rely on its presence as a matter of right?

2. Now consider the distributive, adversarial theories of negotiation. Are deception, revealing partial truths, concealing problems, and misleading the other party likely to be successful negotiating strategies? Where are you most likely to encounter these strategies? What are their short- and long-term effects? And what can you do to counter or diminish the effects of this kind of negotiation?

3. Consider which theory of negotiation—adversarial or cooperative—would be most likely and most effective in the following situations:
   a. You are buying a new car and turning in your used motor vehicle and are negotiating the value of your trade-in.
   b. You are negotiating with your spouse over where to go for next summer's holiday. Where to go and how to finance the trip are the main issues.
   c. You are negotiating a renewal of your investment contract with your financial advisor.
   d. You are a member of a union negotiating the next collective bargaining agreement with management.

   e. You are negotiating the sale of your house to people in the community you have known for some time.
   f. You are negotiating the sale of your house to strangers.

4. Consider the different theories of negotiation. Do you think the negotiation process is primarily about parties with diverse interests jointly establishing new value and direction? Or is it about individual parties getting as much as they can from other parties while giving up as little as possible themselves?

5. You are about to take on the role of negotiating agent for regional police service officers in their contractual dispute with police management over salary and work conditions. Outline and discuss the steps you need to take, the people you need to consult, and the information you need to gather. Deal with the four major points to be assessed and predetermined. Calculate your chips and chops and the negotiating strategies you will use. Try to find ways to make your demands measurable and justifiable. Go through the exercise again, this time focusing on the needs and likely strategies of the parties negotiating on behalf of police management.

6. Divide into two groups. One group should read situation A below. The other should read situation B.

Situation A: For Jay Silver

You are a collector of rare coins. You own several sets of coins, among them a partial set of gold and silver coins issued in the 19th century by Napoleon. This partial set, which includes five of the six coins needed for a complete set, is worth between $18,000 and $20,000. It is missing the "Head of Josephine" coin. If you had this coin, your set would be complete and would thereby increase in value to over $35,000.

Advertising in a coin magazine last month, Sam Samson offered to sell a complete set of the same gold and silver coins for $18,000, payable in cash. Your initial concern was that his coins could not be in very good shape. But you had a chance to inspect them and are satisfied that, while five of the coins are only in reasonable shape and are much less valuable than yours, the Head of Josephine coin is in nearly perfect shape; it would round out your set at maximum value. On its own, the Head of Josephine coin is probably worth $10,000 to $12,000 if offered to the right buyer.

The other coins could probably be sold off as singles for $2,000 to $3,000 each. But this would require time, effort, and advertising costs you would prefer not to spend. Still, Samson's advertisement says the sale is of the whole coin set.

Given the initial asking price in the newspaper advertisement, you seriously wonder if Sam is not very knowledgeable about coin collecting or possibly needs a quick sale and ready cash.

Also, you have $7,500 coming to you in a month's time—a commission on a sale of real estate. You could raise the money quickly on an existing line of credit, but you would rather wait and pay for the coins with the real estate commission and borrow the remainder at the time of purchase.

You have contacted Sam Samson and advised him that you wish to meet him and negotiate for the coins.

Required

Fully prepare for the negotiation by setting out and prioritizing your interests. Then establish your four main points of negotiation: target point, resistance point, BATNA, and opening bid.

Work out your strategy carefully, with a view to the negotiating techniques you want to employ.

Next, negotiate with Sam or his agent and attempt to come to an agreement. Throughout the exercise, be mindful of Sam's techniques as well as your own.

Situation B: For Sam Samson

You recently inherited from your uncle Jack a set of gold and silver coins issued by Napoleon in the 19th century. You are not a coin collector. Although you loved your uncle Jack, you wish to sell the coins.

You have recently had a run of bad luck and have lost a considerable sum of money on a business venture, so your credit and your ability to borrow money are very limited. In the meantime, you have the opportunity to pick up an option on a piece of property whose value will escalate substantially in the near future.

To be able to purchase the option on the property, you need $12,000 in cash within the next couple of days. Other funds will be available for this purchase upon exercising the option in a year. The owner and vendor of the property is a friend of yours. Your friend has already been offered $11,500 for the option by a third party and has told you that if he hasn't heard from you, cash in hand, by next weekend, he will give the option to your competitor.

Your only clear means of raising the funds is selling Uncle Jack's coin set.

You have had the coins appraised. You would like to get a second appraisal, but there isn't time. The appraiser valued the whole set at $17,000. One coin—the Head of Josephine coin—is in excellent shape and probably worth $8,000 to $10,000 on its own. The other five coins in the set, according to the appraiser, were of poorer quality and worth, on a quick sale, only about $1,000 each. On the basis of its being a whole set, the appraiser rated its value at $17,000. You didn't particularly like or trust the appraiser.

The appraiser also told you that if you really needed cash quickly, he would take the set off your hands at a discount, for $10,000.

You ran an advertisement in a coin collector's magazine last month offering the whole set for $18,000. So far, it has brought only one response, from Jay Silver, who would like to meet with you and negotiate to purchase the coins.

Required

Fully prepare to negotiate with Jay. Calculate and prioritize your interests. Set your four negotiating points: target point, resistance point, BATNA, and opening bid. First, work out your strategy and then enter into negotiations with Jay and come to an agreement if possible. Pay attention to Jay's negotiating style and techniques as well as to your own.

Mediation: Definition, Philosophy, and Boundaries

5

LEARNING OUTCOMES

After completing this chapter, you will be able to:

- Define the role of mediation and justify it as a means of dispute resolution.

- Review the backgrounds and bases for rights-based thinking and for cooperative problem solving.

- Discuss the purposes of mediation.

- Analyze and define the stages of mediation.

- Understand the purpose of each stage and the process each involves.

- Begin to learn the skills and strategies needed to mediate.

- Practically apply mediation skills in a role-playing exercise.

Introduction to Mediation

In previous chapters, we have emphasized the following point: If we view conflict as problematic and think society should be free of it, we will accept the idea that an authoritative third party, such as a court or tribunal, ought to have the power to end the conflict.

If, on the other hand, we see conflict as a symptom of unfulfilled aspirations, then we will think it best resolved through a process that unearths, examines, and incorporates those aspirations. The parties best equipped to resolve conflict in this second way are the ones actually engaged in it. They are in the best position to know and define their own aspirations. And if they are willing to consider the other party's aspirations, they are also in the best position to find mutually satisfactory solutions. Two parties working in this cooperative way can resolve their conflict from the inside out through negotiation. But even parties trying to resolve their conflict by cooperative negotiation can reach deadlock. They sometimes need a qualified expert to assist them. And so we come to the process of mediation.

A thorough treatment of mediation seems important for a number of reasons. First, it is a process distinct in nature from other forms of alternative dispute resolution, such as early neutral evaluation, mini-trials, and arbitration. Second, it has proven to be a very successful means of dispute resolution, one that deserves to be acknowledged. Third, those actually practising it may benefit from such a discussion. An understanding of the philosophy, procedures, and boundaries of mediation may reduce the anxiety of a new or confused practitioner.

Defining Mediation

Mediation is an increasingly popular process that has been adapted to many purposes and contexts. Trying to define mediation, given its diverse applications, is not easy. A working definition might look something like the following: **Mediation is the process by which a neutral or third party, upon being asked to do so, helps parties negotiate a dispute** (Chornenki & Hart, 2015). The mediator helps organize and control the process while leaving substantive outcomes and content decisions to the parties themselves.

mediation
the process by which a neutral or third party, upon being asked to do so, helps parties negotiate a dispute

Mediation is difficult to define with clarity because it tends to be needed on an ad hoc basis, in contexts that vary widely. Even the basic notion that a mediator is someone who has no role in determining the content of a dispute is questionable; the mediator can't always avoid getting involved in substantive issues. Take a case, for example, where the ignorance of one party is likely to produce a very unfair result if the mediator does not step in. Such an intervention amounts to a substantive contribution.

mandatory mediation
the formal requirement that parties who have brought an action in court must attempt to settle their dispute by participating in a minimum of three hours of mediation

Defining mediation is made more difficult by another fact: It is sometimes used in mandatory schemes that focus on settlement as success or that, in some cases, actually impose their own content code on the proceedings. **Mandatory mediation** schemes are now being established as part of the civil litigation process. In other words, when parties bring a lawsuit to the Ontario Superior Court of Justice, they are now required, by the Rules of Civil Procedure, to undergo, at a fixed stage of the process, three hours of mediation, with the aim of settling their action by mutual agreement. They are not formally obliged to settle their cases during this compulsory mediation, but they are required to put in the three hours. Success rates are high in this program, which has meant great savings in time and court costs. Mandatory mediation schemes are also being used for matters that are otherwise bound for arbitration tribunals, such as the Human Rights Commission or landlord and tenant boards. The term *mandatory mediation* is in some ways self-contradictory; mediation is by definition a voluntary process. In most of these programs, participation is mandatory, but the parties are free, once they have undergone mediation, to return to the trial process.

The mediator is obliged to remember, first and foremost, that the conflict being addressed and the aspirations that underlie it belong to the disputants alone. People trained in diagnosing, formulating, furthering, and controlling a rights-based agenda sometimes find this obligation hard to understand. But it is basic to an understanding of the mediator's role.

Sometimes questions such as "Who am I when I mediate?" and "Who are they when I mediate?" can help the prospective mediator clarify his or her role.

Mediators should see their role in terms of:

1. assisting in establishing a negotiating atmosphere that is open and trusting, conducive to problem solving and positive attitudes;
2. helping plan the steps to be undertaken throughout the process;
3. helping frame the issues to be dealt with and helping parties prioritize those issues;
4. helping parties explore their underlying desires, hopes, fears, and concerns;
5. promoting problem solving on the basis of the parties' own sharpening awareness of the facts and of their own interests;
6. enabling the parties to save face where possible;
7. helping the parties develop skills, such as active listening, that will permanently enhance their ability to problem-solve; and
8. asking the disputing parties the kinds of questions that will enable them to come to grips with their own interests and solutions.

The above list, though not exhaustive, suggests that the mediator is not someone who occupies a clear-cut position or job description. Rather, the mediator is the source of positive attitudes and functions that assist the disputing parties to problem-solve themselves. Mediation in practice is best understood in terms of its particular functions.

We can also define mediation in relation to three dichotomies:

1. Rights-based negotiation/Interest-based negotiation.
2. Distributive negotiation/Integrative negotiation.
3. Evaluative involvement/Non-evaluative involvement.

The last of these three dichotomies (the first two have been previously discussed) refers to two different approaches a mediator may take. In the case of *evaluative involvement*, the mediator evaluates a party's position and provides opinions about its merits, strengths, weaknesses, and potential success. In the case of *non-evaluative involvement*, the mediator plays a purely facilitative role in the negotiation—that is, he or she does not offer evaluative opinions.

The Backgrounds of Rights-Based Thinking

Western rights-based thinking, which is descended from the Mosaic code and from English common law, assumes that what keeps people from social chaos are rules, or laws. Obeying these laws produces acceptable human behaviour. Breaking them—so the thinking goes—produces chaos. It follows from this view of things that legal experts are needed to assess and judge departures from the law and thereby maintain social order. In such a society, the focus of dispute resolution is not the interests of the individual but the collective society and its norms. Those in power have the right to declare right from wrong and, in the case of a dispute, to choose winners and losers. They do so according to abstract principles accepted by the given society.

Aristotle is another source of our rights-based thinking about disputes. He believed the state is entitled not only to punish those who offend its norms but also to enforce distributive justice. Distributive or zero-sum thinking, remember, presupposes that while human desires are unlimited, human assets and wealth are limited and finite. Since property is finite, you cannot give to one person without taking from another; distribution is really just redistribution. The state has the authority to oversee and direct the distribution of money or property since conflicts over these things occur frequently and have the potential to upset societal order.

In a forum governed by rights-based, distributive thinking, conflict resolution will inevitably become adversarial in nature. The trick to winning the prize in an adversarial contest is to adapt your argument persuasively to your society's prevailing norms or principles (defined by precedents or statutes). Your aim is to show that your position in the conflict is more in keeping with your society's values than the other party's position. Judges or authorized third parties will measure the merits of the two positions according to those values or principles, then decide on a winner. For the sake of clarity and predictability, this kind of adversarial contest does not take into account the interests and desires of the contestants. Such considerations just muddy the water.

Why Contend?

As we have said before, the parties to a conflict are the ones most likely to understand its underlying causes and the conditions needed to resolve it. So why do disputants so often resort to the courts? Why do even negotiation and mediation so often have to take place in the shadow of the law? The answer lies in human conditioning and experience. People who find themselves in conflict seem to adopt automatically what we might call the **adversarial assumption**. This assumption is essentially fear based and related to zero-sum thinking.

adversarial assumption
a disputing party's assumption that they are locked in battle with the other side and can only win at the other's expense

Humans are driven to expand, enrich, and enhance their own situation and experience. Most people, assuming that material assets are limited, expect to enhance themselves at another's expense. So, when a conflict arises, the disputants think the following: *Someone is going to win and someone is going to lose, and the loser isn't going to be me.* The obvious choice, for someone who sees things this way, is to contend. Establishing a strong position and holding it seem the appropriate things to do. In this kind of environment, trust, disclosure, and consideration for the other party's needs have no place.

NEGATIVITY BIAS

Psychological and neurological research has identified our tendency toward a *negativity bias*. This refers to processes in the brain that overreact to negative thoughts, experiences, or possibilities as compared with positive ones. In conflict situations, this is likely to predispose parties to do whatever it takes to avoid losing.

What Is Wrong with Rights-Based Thinking?

We can challenge rights-based thinking on a number of grounds, most of them familiar to you by now:

1. Conflict itself is not an ill that needs to be banished from society; it is a symptom of two parties' underlying interests and needs. An attempt to satisfy those underlying needs, though they initially seem to disagree, may lead the parties to intimacy, growth, and renewed vitality.

2. While abstract legal principles are crucial to a society's sense of security, they are not the only means of resolving conflict. Satisfying the disputants' actual needs and interests is another way.

3. Attending to these needs and interests will not automatically produce chaos or violate a society's norms, so long as the rule of law is maintained.

4. The people best attuned to the deeper cause of a conflict are not necessarily the presiding judges; it is often the disputing parties themselves who best understand the frustration of their own aspirations. Real, lasting solutions are therefore more likely to come from the disputants.

5. Society as a whole will be enhanced rather than injured if individuals are empowered to resolve their own disputes.

A society's material assets may be limited, and people may seek naturally to get their share of the pie. But people are also motivated by other values—friendship, empathy, generosity—that have nothing to do with material reward. Remedying conflict need not be based only on zero-sum thinking and the redistribution of tangible assets.

Rethinking a Rights-Based Approach to Conflict

As we have seen in previous chapters, the Harvard Negotiation Project and its most famous members, Fisher, Ury, and Patton, have done much to challenge the old notions of conflict resolution with their understanding of principled, interest-based bargaining.

In *Getting to Yes* (2011), Fisher, Ury, and Patton's main thrust is the importance of getting the parties to move away from rights-based positions and not to view each other as adversaries. Rehumanizing the process—reminding parties of their shared status as human beings with real interests and aspirations—is essential to cooperative problem solving. Without some effort in this direction, one party is likely to demonize the other. This will simply escalate the conflict and force, eventually, some externally imposed solution. In a rehumanized negotiating atmosphere, parties can build an atmosphere of trust, explore each other's underlying interests (needs, desires, concerns, hopes, and fears), find compatibility, and create durable solutions. To the cynic, cooperative problem solving probably sounds misty-eyed and unrealistic. But if judged by its proven success rate—on the basis of fulfilled needs, durable results, continuing relationships, and reduced expenses—cooperative problem solving is clearly rooted in wisdom.

The Role of Mediation in Cooperative Problem Solving

How should we understand mediation and the mediator's role? Again, cooperative problem solving is based on the idea that the disputing parties themselves are best able to understand their problems and their ultimate interests. This means that the mediator is not there to impose his or her judgment on the process. The mediator's expertise will be used instead to counteract the adversarial impulse and to keep the parties focused on cooperative problem solving. This is done through skilled, probing questions that help the parties understand their own interests and see their conflict as a common problem, best resolved with mutually satisfactory solutions. The mediator can also help identify (name) those obstacles to the problem-solving process that the parties themselves aren't conscious of. By naming contentious strategies as they surface, the mediator can steer the disputing parties away from them.

Mediation, then, is a process that enables disputing parties to set aside the adversarial impulse. Mediation helps them explore the aspirations underlying their conflict, determine their true interests in a creative, conciliatory spirit, and fashion the solutions in their own way. The mediator is there to assist the negotiating parties, not to dominate them.

The Social Purpose of Mediation

Mediation is used more and more widely in our society, in many different situations, and there are different ideas about its social purpose. Speeding up negotiations, reducing legal costs, lightening the burden on an overworked court system—these are the clearest benefits of mediation. Some people take a more radical view of mediation's social potential, viewing it as a transforming force. The real purpose of mediation, they say, is to transform people by empowering them and encouraging them to recognize one another's interests. Through such a process, it may be possible to transform the world, one person at a time.

Perhaps the true social purpose of mediation is simply to offer a cooperative problem-solving process that is a practical, effective alternative to systems (for example, court proceedings) based on the adversarial impulse. To be effective, a system must work, and mediation does work. When you think about the number of transactions—court proceedings, arbitration, and even negotiations—that are based on the adversarial impulse, you can see how many potential roles there are for the mediator.

Even in supposedly cooperative negotiations, parties and their agents often try to maximize their own position. This causes them to slip into contentious behaviours and then into adversarial positions. The mediator's purpose is to oppose this tendency and hold out the benefits of cooperative problem solving—namely, empowerment of the parties themselves and recognition of each other's interests. This process can lead, in turn, to a successful solution that saves time and money and brings relief to an overburdened court system.

Cautions: Culture, Gender, and Power as Factors in Mediation

Culture, gender, and power have bearing on the question of what mediation's role should be. Mediation takes it for granted that both parties in a negotiation are willing and able, with assistance, to confront the issues and interests separating them and mould them into durable solutions. The key word here is *able*. According to conflict theory, as we have seen, there are four responses to conflict: avoiding (ignoring), submitting (yielding), contending, and cooperative problem solving (Rubin, Pruitt, & Kim, 2004). Sometimes a party will move from a problem-solving strategy to one of submission or avoidance. This movement may seem voluntary, but, in fact, it is driven by pre-existing imbalances that are bound up with culture, gender, or power. The question is how the mediator ought to deal with such an unbalanced situation. Should he or she refuse to mediate? Or should the mediator take an active role, during the negotiation, in trying to redress the imbalance?

Culture

One cultural factor a mediator must face is that *reality* is subjective—that is, different for every person. Every person adapts to the conditions and the culture surrounding them, and the result is that person's individual reality. Our culture is crucial in shaping us. The interaction of our individuality with the culture into which we are born results in a particular reality for each of us. But we soon learn that what is real to us is not necessarily real to other people, even members of our own culture. As Rogers (1951) has said, "What is real to you is real to you."

Another problem for mediators is that some cultures predispose us to contend. Western culture tends to view life as war. Images of war inform our ways of thinking and writing about the world. In light of this, it is not surprising that we tend to accept the adversarial assumption—the idea that we must compete with each other for scarce resources, must conquer and subdue in order to survive. Western culture does not condition people to choose cooperative problem solving. It is the mediator's role to steer people in that direction.

Gender

Gender can be a complicating factor in mediation. The potential for mistrust and misunderstanding between the sexes is great. Mediators often find themselves not just helping two people resolve a dispute but trying to bridge the gulf between the sexes. Negotiations in which privilege and role seem to be at stake can slide easily into zero-sum thinking; one gender sees the other's gain as their own loss rather than as cooperative achievement and rebalancing. Our society's sexual stereotypes don't help the process either. Historically, men have been seen as reasonable and logical and women as emotional, governed by feeling. Logic and reason are linked to law and seen as trustworthy, while emotions are seen as uncontrollable, unstable, and chaotic. Yet the literature of cooperative problem solving sees gender in somewhat different terms. It tends to view favourably the "feminine" world of soul and feeling, while "masculine" logic is seen to have destructive potential.

Power

The mediator will often find power imbalances between disputing parties in a negotiation. Sometimes these imbalances are due to cultural or gender conditioning; sometimes they arise from the psychologies of the people involved. How far the mediator should try to offset such factors is difficult to say.

Mediators must recognize that imbalances of power are common in negotiations—an inescapable reality. Once aware that imbalances between the parties exist, the mediator must decide whether mediation is the right process for addressing their dispute. In a case where one of the parties, owing to cultural or gender conditioning, is likely to adopt a submissive rather than a problem-solving response to the conflict at hand—thus giving up, effectively, their right to self-determination—the answer is probably *no*. Such people may be better off in a process where their rights will be protected in spite of themselves. In other words, the mediator may see that one party has submitted in a helpless spirit to the power imbalance, passively accepting their own disadvantage. In this case, the mediator should consider ending the process, to prevent an unfair result. Court processes may be preferable for such a case; they can focus on and guarantee the protection of individual rights.

The duty of a mediator faced with a power imbalance is to name it, not solve it. Naming the imbalance and having the parties explore it can have a powerful and beneficial effect. Probing questions can often alert the parties to what they are unconsciously doing or assuming about an imbalance. Once alerted, they can respond appropriately.

The Different Theories of Mediation

There are different schools of thought about mediation's purpose and how it ought to work. Which school of thought the mediator belongs to will obviously affect the strategies and techniques he or she chooses to use.

Facilitative mediators believe the aim of the process is to allow the actual disputants to maintain control of the outcome and to have the satisfaction of resolving the dispute themselves. This school of thought prizes the parties' autonomy most highly.

Others—*evaluative mediators*—believe the main aim of mediation is to reach efficient settlements. Quick settlements that save time and money are, according to this school of thought, what make mediation a useful alternative to court or other processes.

Others, as we have mentioned, have more ambitious ideas about mediation's purpose. They emphasize its power to educate and transform individuals, groups, communities, and perhaps even society as a whole. Mediation can empower an individual, for example, to problem-solve more effectively. It can help communities address imbalances of power and wealth, deal with questions of reparation, or develop consensus on future undertakings. Members of this school of thought believe that mediation, because it pushes disputants to deal thoroughly with the interests underlying their dispute, promotes a more stable kind of social change.

What follows is a brief account of different theories of mediation. Each theory offers a rationale, a form, and a direction for the mediation process.

The Facilitative Theory

One basic definition of mediation is facilitated negotiation, and the theory of mediation that follows this definition most closely is **facilitative mediation**. This is one of the two contrasting theories described by Riskin (2003). Facilitative mediators assume their role is to assist in the process of communication. In their view, a disputing party's autonomy and knowledge of their needs are the best guarantee of results. So, the mediator should not evaluate the legal or moral rights involved in the dispute. The mediator's role is to help the parties clearly see and understand what interests are actually in conflict. Mediators may help the parties develop and assess alternative solutions to the problem, but they leave the choice of solution to the parties themselves.

Facilitative mediators use their skills purely to help the parties problem-solve themselves. They don't try to impose their opinions about legal rights or about what the best solutions are. The rationale for this restraint is that mediators aren't really in a position to weigh in on a likely legal outcome. And they aren't as well positioned as the parties themselves to understand the needs and interests involved. Party autonomy and satisfaction are all-important to facilitative mediators. They will help parties develop and assess possible solutions. In the process, they may ask the parties to think about the consequences of failing to settle—the likely court costs, for example. But they will try not to influence the parties too much in the selection of outcomes. Their fundamental aim is to assist the parties through a broad, interest-based approach to the conflict. They trust that the parties are intelligent and fully capable themselves, with the mediator's help, of arriving at the best solutions.

facilitative mediation
an approach to mediation that aims to help disputing parties communicate and problem-solve themselves, on the grounds that they are better equipped than the mediator to resolve their conflict satisfactorily

The Evaluative Theory

The other theory of mediation described by Riskin is **evaluative mediation**. Evaluative mediators assume that the parties involved in a dispute need at least some advice and direction about an appropriate settlement of the conflict. This may sometimes require them to give a legal evaluation of a problem. Or it may call on the mediator's specialized knowledge of some industry or sector.

Evaluative mediators assume it is their role to give specialized advice. They can be quite influential in pushing parties toward a result they believe to be correct. Their influence reduces the independence of the parties. But this loss is seen as acceptable in light of the savings in time and court costs associated with this approach. Mediators of this type will evaluate the parties' legal cases. They will develop rights-based (or positionally based) solutions, or, in some cases, they will develop more broadly conceived interest-based solutions. But they will always fashion and direct the result. This is often done on the basis of a predicted court outcome or under the threat of high court costs.

Mediators who are lawyers or retired judges tend to be evaluative in their outlook and approach. Evaluative mediators tend to be used in the numerous court-annexed mandatory mediation schemes currently under way. Quick settlements are favoured in this context. Lawyers and judges with experience in court actions can be very persuasive in predicting the outcomes of cases and the likely costs. It's not clear whether the agreements brought about by evaluative mediation are as durable as the

evaluative mediation
an approach to mediation by which the mediator offers the parties advice and opinion about the appropriate settlement of the conflict

agreements reached through facilitative mediation, which emphasize party autonomy and independence.

The Transformative Theory

transformative theory of mediation
an approach to mediation that aims to transform the disputants by teaching them to recognize one another's interests and by helping them to become better communicators and problem solvers

Bush and Folger (2004) are the chief proponents of the **transformative theory of mediation**, briefly described above. This is the most radical view of mediation to date. Bush and Folger have written extensively about the potential of mediation to be a transforming force in our society. Its real purpose, they say, is to transform people by empowering them and encouraging them to recognize one another's interests.

The mediator, according to the transformative theory, is there to help the parties recognize their interests and to help them develop their skills in communication and problem solving. Thus empowered, they can make appropriate decisions for themselves. This approach emphasizes mediation's educational function and how mediation can transform individuals, groups, and society as a whole. It assumes, as does facilitative mediation, that party autonomy is central to the mediation process; it is not the mediator's role to transform the problem or conflict in a direct way. It is the mediator's role to transform people. Bush and Folger go so far as to suggest that settlement is not a key or even a necessary goal of mediation. The crucial thing is that people depart from the process better able to recognize and express their own interests and better able to recognize and acknowledge others' interests.

This view of mediation is uplifting, and it does capture something about the idealism of the mediation movement. But we need to recognize, too, that mediation is most often a response to a very real human conflict. Resolving conflict by reaching settlement is a crucial goal of the process. Still, Bush and Folger ought to be honoured for their idealistic conclusions. At the very least, mediators who spread the word about the benefits of a cooperative, interest-based problem-solving strategy will greatly benefit our society.

IN THE NEWS

BLACK LIVES MATTER

Lebron (2017) describes how Martin Luther King Jr and James Baldwin both focused on love as the best approach for African Americans to use while dealing with racism, segregation, and anti-Black violence. King's approach was based on self-sacrificing love, while Baldwin's was on brotherly love. The rationale for this was that everyone—Black and white people—needed to come together in a mutual understanding of their common humanity. While neither King nor Baldwin was acting as a mediator in the traditional sense, they can certainly be seen as mediators in a broader sense, specifically as transformative mediators who were attempting to educate people in order to transform society.

narrative mediation
a kind of mediation that aims to resolve conflict by uncovering and breaking down the disputants' stories so that they can be reconstructed into a larger narrative that integrates both parties' interests

The Narrative Theory

Another theory of mediation is the narrative model of Michelle LeBaron. **Narrative mediation** is based on a *relational understanding* of conflicts. According to LeBaron

(2002), conflicts are caused not by incompatible interests but by differences in identity and in the formation of identities.

LeBaron's view is that every person's self-image, belief system, and sense of meaning are based on the stories that have surrounded them since birth. These formative stories are endlessly diverse and equally valid. The narrative mediator deals with a conflict situation by trying to discover the formative stories belonging to each disputant. Having done that, the mediator helps each party break down their stories into their main elements and then reconstruct these elements into a larger narrative that integrates their own and the other party's interests. The mediator's main activity, in this scenario, is to gain the parties' trust and build rapport between them, so they can understand one another's stories. Through this process, parties are freed from the trap of their own socialization stories.

The problem with this approach to mediation is that it is, by definition, subjective; it lacks the objective standards that Fisher et al. (2011) see as crucial to negotiation. With its exclusive focus on relationships, it seems to cut out the objective criteria you find in an interest-based approach. Still, it is an approach that might help parties understand what underlies their conflict.

An Exit from the Theories

There are different schools of thought about the values and goals of mediation. Individual mediators will prefer one theory to another and conduct themselves accordingly, and every theory has something to recommend it. But perhaps we would do well to end this survey of theories of mediation on a practical note. Chornenki and Hart (2015) offer some useful reminders about the basic aims of mediation:

Mediators take many different approaches to their role, as various as their personalities, but some common elements can be observed in experienced mediators. They:

1. create an atmosphere conducive to discussion;
2. encourage the parties right away to agree on the goal of the session and on the rules they will abide by, which might include speaking in turn, without interruption, and without personal attacks;
3. elicit factual information about the conflict;
4. understand the dispute from each party's perspective and communicate that understanding so that each party feels *heard*;
5. manage the interplay between the parties—at some points engineering civility in their communications, and at others allowing them to vent;
6. help the parties identify the strengths and weaknesses of their case, often by playing devil's advocate;
7. work with the parties to go beyond their positions to discover their underlying interests, and to talk about them;
8. smooth communications between the parties in many ways—by listening to a *loaded* or angry statement made by one party and reframing it to convey the essential information to the other party without the potentially distorting emotional overlay, or by acting as the courier for information when the parties are physically located in separate caucus rooms, to name just two;
9. provoke the parties to be creative in generating options for settlement that go beyond what could be ordered by a judge trying the matter but which make sense and create value for these parties with these interests;

10. assist the parties to analyze and assess their alternatives to a negotiated resolution to the dispute;

11. control the pace of the negotiation to enable the parties to reach the moment of resolution on each point at the same time;

12. keep the parties working and focused on the future and on their goal of resolving their differences;

13. ensure that the parties' efforts are productive in moving them ever closer to that goal; and

14. display endless optimism that an agreement can be achieved and sustain commitment to the effort of its achievement. Good mediators do not give up easily. (p. 92)

Mediation in Five Steps

There are many models for mediation, and some of these models involve many steps. We have broken the process down into five fairly simple steps: preparing, introducing, framing the issues, determining interests, and, lastly, crafting solutions (see Figure 5.1).

Knowing these steps and having the skills to move through them effectively are the cornerstones of the mediator's art. Let's consider these steps in more detail.

Preparing

The Pre-Mediation Stage

The pre-mediation stage tends to vary with the circumstances and is therefore difficult to generalize about. Multi-level, public mediations involving many parties and agents will require more preliminary work than simpler situations will. But certain concerns are always part of the pre-mediation stage.

Practical Concerns

Generally speaking, the mediator at the pre-mediation stage is responsible for a number of practical concerns. Where will the mediation take place? Is the site accessible? Is there enough seating? Are there appropriate *breakout* rooms (that is, rooms for smaller group discussions) in case caucusing becomes necessary? Do you need to screen the parties with an eye to possible intimidation of one party by the other and the potential need to separate them? Will the mediation go long enough to require refreshments? These physical concerns may seem pedestrian. However, failure to fully consider them may result in delays, bad moods, and a process that lacks flow once the parties are at the table.

Figure 5.1 **Mediation in Five Steps**

1. Preparing 2. Introducing 3. Framing the issues 4. Determining interests 5. Crafting solutions

The mediator will need to sort out a number of other practical matters, either by telephone conference or by meeting directly with the parties or their counsel:

1. Do all parties wish to mediate? Does the mediator wish to take the mediation? For a successful mediation, you need general agreement beforehand that mediation is the right process for everyone. At this point, the reluctance of one party or the other to mediate needs to be addressed, as does any concern the mediator may have about power imbalance between the parties or about his or her own lack of expertise. Co-mediation—having more than one mediator—should be considered where cultural or linguistic lack of expertise on the mediator's part may hinder the proceedings. It should also be considered where the complexity of the issues or the number of parties warrants it.

   The mediator should discuss with the parties whether a **mediation brief** is needed. If so, the brief should be created and exchanged by the parties and forwarded to the mediator. The form and length of the brief are optional. Its purpose is twofold: to prepare the parties to make their opening statements during the introductory phase and to have each party tell their own story of the conflict without focusing narrowly on the issues. A brief that is a page or a page and a half in length is long enough; the mediator, being neutral, is not inclined at this point to hear a detailed account of the parties' complaints. A mediator shouldn't come to any conclusions based on the brief. It simply acquaints the mediator with the type of the conflict and its history. It may also give clues as to the best mediation process to use.

   Documentation other than the mediation brief should probably not be collected or reviewed at this point unless you are involved in a court or rights-based mediation. In that case, you may need pleadings or an agreed-upon technical report. *Pleadings* (for example, the statement of claim and the statement of defence) are the documents the parties exchange in accordance with the rules of the court; they elaborate on the facts of each party's case and the nature of each party's claim or defence. The presence of documentation shouldn't encourage the mediator to try to become judge upon the issues.

2. The mediator should forward the **agreement to mediate** to the parties. This agreement will be executed at the outset of mediation. Since the authority to mediate depends on all parties' consent, all parties should be aware of and accepting of the content of this agreement.

   To this point, courts have protected the confidentiality of the mediation. In the pre-mediation stage, it is wise to reinforce confidentiality. This is done by making sure the parties understand that the mediator cannot be asked in future proceedings to reveal what happens in mediation. The neutrality of the mediator and the *without prejudice* nature of statements made within the mediation process need to be protected. The term *without prejudice* means that anything said in mediation is said for the purpose of resolving the dispute; it cannot be used in the event of subsequent court proceedings.

   The parties' good-faith commitment to the mediation process and their commitment to full disclosure should also be written into the agreement. The agreement should also contain some reference to independent legal advice. Some such reference is crucial for avoiding subsequent liability.

mediation brief
a short document that the disputing parties create during the pre-mediation stage of a negotiation, setting out the history and context of the dispute

agreement to mediate
the contract, executed at the outset of mediation, that establishes the rules of the process, the parties' good-faith commitment to it, the mediator's neutrality, the confidentiality of the process, and the mediator's compensation

authority to settle
the power to resolve
all issues fully and
finally at the table

3. You need to establish who the disputing parties are. All parties with an interest in the dispute or its settlement need to be present at the table; you need to address this need with the parties themselves or with their counsel. A related question concerns who has the **authority to settle**. It's unlikely that the parties at the table will have unlimited authority to settle all issues themselves, and it is a good idea to have them think about this before arriving. Both parties, if unable to settle all issues themselves, ought to have some sense of the process by which they'll gain ultimate approval.

4. First impressions are important. For one thing, they can be difficult to dislodge. The mediator's preliminary work, though it is done outside the process of mediation itself, gives the parties a chance to assess the mediator's neutrality, competence, and credibility. The wise mediator understands this.

   The pre-mediation stage is also the best place for the mediator to begin developing rapport with the parties. This can be accomplished in a number of ways, including:
   a. exchanging social niceties;
   b. engaging in small talk and discussing general topics of interest, such as local sports teams or current events;
   c. demonstrating active listening and showing interest in and, where appropriate, empathy for the circumstances of the parties; and
   d. displaying boundless optimism and confidence in the process.

Chornenki and Hart (2015) describe one pre-mediation approach as follows:

> One outstanding mediator (whom we would choose as our mediator) routinely sees parties independently at first, if only briefly. She hears their stories and permits them to connect with her, a stranger in a one-on-one setting, without the pressure of the other party's presence. The goodwill she builds is money in the bank for later. (p. 89)

Introducing

At the Table

The introductory phase of mediation begins once the parties are at the table. It has several parts. First are the mediator's introductory remarks. These are meant to welcome the parties but also to inspire confidence in the process. Next comes the execution of the agreement to mediate. After that, the mediator and the parties establish ground rules for the conduct of the mediation. There will also be a brief account of the parties' narratives and a summary of those narratives, with the main points synthesized for the issue-framing stage to come.

Opening Remarks

The mediator's introduction should invite trust and establish a positive environment. It needn't be long, and it should simplify expectations about the process. The opening might go as follows:

Welcome, and congratulations on choosing mediation as the process to sort out and solve your differences. Statistics show that where willing parties undertake responsibility for the settlement of their own affairs in mediation, they succeed. You can expect through this process to come to a satisfactory conclusion on your own terms.

The mediator's introduction should briefly, in simple language, outline the steps in the process, and it should clearly define the role of the mediator.
For example:

I am not here to judge, advocate, or even advise you on your situation or decision. I am here purely to assist you in your discussions. This is as it should be and is usually enough to allow the process to work.

The mediator may refer to the agreement to mediate and should take the opportunity, at this point, to reinforce the openness of the discussion by reminding the parties how the rules of confidentiality apply to both the parties and the mediator. The question of authority to settle can be discussed too so that each party is at least clear about the importance of this final step and knows how the other party will handle it. Any questions about the agreement to mediate should be answered, and the document should be signed.

The mediator may wish to refer briefly to caucusing. **Caucusing** is the art of separating the parties and meeting with them privately, away from the table. This process should be described in simple terms. You would say, for example, that caucusing consists of private discussions or meetings that may be necessary from time to time. Given that caucusing may not be required in the mediation, the mediator may choose not to mention it until it becomes necessary.

caucusing
separating the parties and meeting with them privately, away from the table

Lastly, the mediator's opening needs to address the ground rules and the agenda for the mediation. The mediator is chiefly responsible for decisions about process and agenda. But it can be instructive for all concerned to involve the parties in these choices. **Ground rules** should be simple. One can normally expect them to be broken, but over the course of the mediation, they will be a useful tool for the mediator. The parties will agree to them at the outset, so when they are broken during the proceeding, the mediator can refer to them as a way of getting the parties back on course and restoring a positive mood.

Ground rules should always mention the following:

ground rules
the rules for the conduct of the mediation, covering such topics as the need for respectful behaviour and active listening, caucusing, and the circumstances in which the process might be terminated

1. *Active listening*. Each party should agree to concentrate on what the other is saying and—difficult though it may be—not to interrupt for correction or rebuttal until the other has finished speaking.
2. *Respect*. Parties will refrain from using profanity in their discussions and will not resort to personal attacks or accusations.
3. *Private meetings*. A party who wants a private meeting with the mediator need only request it.
4. *Termination*. Should anyone wish to terminate or leave the mediation, they agree not to do so without first meeting with the mediator privately.

The Parties' Narratives

With the mediator's introductory work completed, the onus shifts to the parties. It is time for the mediator to step back and for the parties to deliver, uninterrupted, their narratives. These stories will express each party's perception of what the conflict is about (as set out in the mediation brief, if one was prepared). The mediator needs to let the parties decide for themselves who will tell their story first, and why. This will remind them that it is their process.

It is also important at this stage to get the parties speaking to each other; they should not be purely focused on the mediator. Their stories are for each other's benefit, not the mediator's. As the mediator, you can encourage their interaction by pushing back from the table and clearly showing the parties you are in listening mode.

Once the parties have decided which of them is telling their story first, they may begin. Their stories should take a relaxed form and use language the parties are comfortable with. Speakers should be permitted to tell their stories without interruptions. If necessary, the mediator can seek clarification and offer the speakers encouragement but in doing so should be careful to maintain positive momentum. At the end of each narrative, the mediator should try to ensure its completeness by asking if there is anything to add. The completed narratives should be summarized. It is best if each party summarizes the other's narrative. If this won't work, the mediator should summarize the main points of each narrative in language the parties are comfortable with. The mediator should take care to do this accurately and completely. This distilled information will be used in the crucial next stage: framing the issues.

Framing the Issues

framing the issues
establishing and clearly defining the parties' specific concerns

The stage of **framing the issues** is all-important and is, in fact, where much of the theory behind mediation is brought to bear. The mediator's efforts at this stage should be twofold. One, he or she needs to resist the impulse to manipulate the content of the issues. It is up to the parties to confirm that the content of the issue statement is accurate. Their agreement about this is crucial. The mediator's second chief concern at this stage is to ensure the issues are framed in an integrative rather than a distributive format. It is important for the mediator to get the parties out of a rights-based, either/or way of seeing their problem and into a perspective that enables them to probe common ground and jointly incorporate underlying interests.

Framing each issue should follow three stages:

1. Introducing the issue comes first. This should employ "you" language—that is, language that emphasizes it is the parties' conflict, not the mediator's. The language should be *intentional* (that is, focused on intentions) and carefully chosen to get both parties looking at the problem together.

   Examples of intentional, "you"-directed language would be the following:
   a. The problem you have to address is … .
   b. The matter you want to solve is … .
   c. So, the matter you want to talk about is … .

2. The second step in issue framing is to link the intentional statement with the subject matter of the issue by using language that is *conjunctive*, not *disjunctive*. In other words, introductory words should be *what* or *how* as opposed to *either/or* or *whether or not*. The disjunctive type of introductory words (the either/or type) will produce a distributive, rights-based question that will move the parties back toward an adversarial stance. *What* or *how* will frame the issue in a unifying, prospective (that is, forward-looking) format that moves the parties toward an exploration of their underlying interests.

For example, imagine a mediation involving a manager and an employee. The employee complains that the manager is doing a poor job: He ignores the employee's good work and doesn't spend enough time instructing and supervising. As the mediator, you could frame this issue as follows: "So, you would like to address the question of whether or not Mr. Manager is giving you sufficient time and recognition?" But this would invite the taking of positions, offensive and defensive. Mr. Manager would insist he has given the employee lots of time and recognition. The employee would insist he has not. Posed in that way, the question creates a distributive problem, requiring a determination of who is right and who is wrong. Posed conjunctively, the question becomes: "So, what you want to discuss is how you may be able to receive more of Mr. Manager's time and more appropriate forms of recognition for your good service?" Framing the issue in this way opens up the dialogue in a positive, forward-looking fashion.

3. In the third phase of issue framing, the parties need to confirm the issue has been accurately framed. Questions like "Is that it?" or "Does that cover it?" or "Is that right?" will prompt the feedback you need.

If the feedback is positive, you may consider the issue framed. If negative, invite the dissatisfied party to explain themselves. Incorporate their feedback into the frame. Keep doing this until the frame is acceptable to both parties. The issue frame must meet both parties' approval if the mediation is to remain their own. All parties must completely agree on what they have come to solve before they begin exploring the needs and interests underlying their conflict. You may also have to order and prioritize the issues if there are a number of them. Once this is done, you are ready to move on to the next and perhaps most important stage.

Determining Interests

Positions and Interests

You must make every effort at this stage to establish perceived common ground. For this to occur, you must move the parties away from taking positions and blaming each other. You must move them toward a full and frank discussion of the **interests**—the needs, desires, hopes, concerns, and fears—that underlie the points at issue. It is through identifying the parties' underlying aspirations and actual interests that progress can be made. Where the positions of disputants may seem mutually exclusive, their underlying interests may be compatible, complementary, or even mutually desirable.

The term **position** has been defined in different ways. According to Fisher et al. (2011), *positions* are what a party wants in concrete terms, and *interests* are the underlying reasons for the party's wanting it. You might also define a position as *my proposed solution that works best for me* or as a disputant's *ideal solution from his or her point of view*. Position taking typically inspires defensive behaviour. Once a party takes a position, they will direct their energies toward defending and promoting that position in its fixed form. They will not direct their energy toward redefining their interests or exploring alternatives. The problem with negotiations involving fixed positions is that any movement toward settlement will require compromise. Compromise, while it may lead to settlement, is, by definition, a result that isn't optimal to either party.

interests
the legitimate need that underlies the position a person takes in a conflict

position
the particular result a party wants to gain from a negotiation (as opposed to the *interests* that underlie this want)

Mediation tends to be a successful process because it rests on the following straightforward assumption: Behind rigid, simplified positions lies a multitude of hidden interests. These interests may be emotional, procedural, temporal, psychological, or material in nature. Uncovering them is the mediator's task. If the mediator is successful, there will be abundant common ground on which to craft durable solutions.

For instance, a woman in dispute with her husband over an oppressive, abusive marriage may, because of culture or family history, believe she is obligated to take the abuse and remain married. In her culture, marriage is seen as inviolable and permanent, and the man is seen as the dominant partner. The mediator's work, in this case, would be to open this woman's awareness to the possibility that her own needs and health are at odds with her thinking and cultural upbringing. The mediator can help her challenge her existing beliefs by increasing her awareness of her own actual needs and interests, then help her investigate alternative ways of acknowledging and fulfilling her needs.

The Mediator's Role in Determining Interests

What tools does the mediator have for promoting this interest-based awareness in the parties? The main tools are questioning and reflecting. We will focus on these skills in Chapter 8, but we will briefly outline them here:

1. *The Art of Questioning*. There are various kinds of questions open to the mediator, including the following: probing questions, clarifying questions, and consequential questions.

    a. *Probing questions* from the mediator ask a party to look for deeper meaning behind an answer they have given or to expand on something they've said. (Returning to our employee–manager scenario, for example, the mediator might ask the disgruntled employee, "Could you tell me more about why the manager's time and instruction are important to you?")

    b. *Clarifying questions* encourage the party to come to a more precise, complete understanding of their own statement. (For example, "When you say you don't get enough instruction, what do you mean?")

    c. *Consequential questions* invite the party to use their prospective imagination to picture the consequences of change. (For example, "What in your estimation would happen if the manager could find ten minutes at the beginning of each day to consult with you?")

2. *The Art of Reflection*. Restating or paraphrasing the party's words can be a way of isolating important points for acknowledgment, emphasis, or clarification. The language the mediator uses for this should be the language of interests. (For example: "So you need … "; "So you hope to … "; "So you're concerned with or you fear … .")

    A good reflection will repeat only what has been heard from the party. The mediator will add nothing of his or her own to the content. At the same time, the mediator should not appear to be merely parroting what the party has said.

    As interests emerge in this stage of the mediation, the mediator should summarize them regularly. Out of this summarizing process come the statements from which solutions will grow. A good agreement is one in which well-defined interests are met by outcomes. The unfolding of interests should not be rushed. Go slowly and be thorough.

Two other tools at the mediator's disposal are caucusing and reframing. These are used primarily to counteract impasses or to oppose contentious and negative behaviour from the participants.

1. For the mediator, there seem to be two basic rules about *caucusing*. The first rule is that you should try to spend an equal amount of time with each party so as to avoid the appearance of favouritism or bias. The second rule is that you should not use caucusing unless there is a strong reason for doing so. Remember, the problem belongs to the parties; during the interest-setting phase especially, you need to keep them facing each other and engaged in open dialogue. Of course, there can be very good reasons to separate the parties—where, for instance, a party is clearly not fully disclosing information, where there is a significant power imbalance at the table, or where one party's misbehaviour at the table is the kind that can't be dealt with through normal techniques. In other cases, the mediator may choose caucusing as a way to clarify interests privately or to offer coaching in communication skills. Sometimes, caucusing simply enables the mediator to diffuse emotion through a cooling-off period.

   The caucusing process should include some preparation for reconvening. The mediator can try to get the parties motivated about returning to the table with the points gained in caucus.

2. *Reframing* is a reflective tool the mediator can use when a party's words or behaviour slips into a negative or contentious mode. Parties sometimes stop focusing on their interests and begin using accusatory language in their statements. These kinds of statements should be reframed. Remember, though, that it is simply the statement, not the party itself, you are reframing. A successful reframe will involve three steps. First, the mediator must listen for and guess at the need hidden behind the negative statement. Second, the mediator should try to express the need in a simple, positive, forward-looking statement. Third, the mediator should listen and watch for the parties' affirmation of the reframe. Let's return to our manager–employee scenario for an example of reframing:

> Manager's statement: "I'm not spending more time with Mr. Employee. He's an airhead, and he never hears anything I say anyway."

> Mediator's reframe (guessing the need behind the statement): "So, in order for you to be willing to spend time with Mr. Employee, you need to know he will be willing to listen and pay attention to what you say?"

> Manager's affirmative feedback: "Exactly!"

The way out of a reframe and back to normal discussion is for the mediator to begin asking probing or consequential questions that are based on the need that the reframe has clarified and reaffirmed. (For example, "How could your need best be accommodated?")

During the interest-formulation stage, the mediator's crucial task is to help the parties become aware of their own real interests, which may be hidden from the parties themselves. As a mediator, you need to do this even if it makes you feel stupid or feel that you're stating the obvious. Let's go back to our manager–employee scenario.

The employee's need for time, support, instruction, and feedback may accord with the manager's desire for better job performance, better relations with employees, and increased employee expertise. If so, the next step—formulating solutions to their problem—will flow smoothly. These microskills in mediation are absolutely essential and should be learned, reviewed, and practised as much as possible. They cannot be overemphasized. We will return to them in the next chapter.

Crafting Solutions

If the parties' interests have been clearly understood and defined, the step of creating appropriate solutions will be easy. Again, the solutions are the parties' domain, not that of the mediator. The parties will know the best responses to their own conflict. The mediator can help them at this stage by conducting open and non-judgmental brainstorming sessions and collecting their best ideas. The mediator should also use probing and consequential questions. These are a way to test the durability of the solutions proposed—to establish that they will satisfy the parties' interests in the future.

The mediator can also encourage the use of retrospective imagination as a double check, asking questions that begin as follows: "Given the situation in the past, what would have happened if ... ?" Or the mediator might encourage the parties to use their prospective imaginations—that is, to think about future difficulties they may not have considered. Questions that begin as follows will help with this: "In the future, what would happen if you were to ... ?"

Otherwise, the mediator's role during the solution-crafting stage is to engage only in the kind of questioning that helps the parties understand that the success of their solution consists in how well it meets their needs. You need to keep the parties focused on interest fulfillment, not compromise; this will increase the value and durability of any agreement made. Creative problem solving, which is an important part of crafting solutions, will be examined in greater detail in Chapter 10.

terms of agreement
the conditions on which agreement has been reached and the conflict resolved

Once the **terms of agreement** have been reached, you need to determine who should draft the agreement into legal form and when this should be done.

A mediator is not acting in the capacity of a legal agent and must make this absolutely clear to the parties. If the parties are not represented by legal counsel, the mediator may reduce the terms agreed upon to some form of letter or record of consensus. But you should emphasize that the parties need to seek independent legal advice and draftsmanship to convert the agreement to legal form. If the parties are represented by legal counsel, the mediator may report to this representative the agreements reached during the mediation process. But the mediator should emphasize that any legal consequences of those agreements will remain the counsel's responsibility. The mediator should also recommend accounting or tax follow-up where relevant. By asking the appropriate questions, the mediator can ensure the agreement is detailed enough to cover the following: mutual releases, withdrawal of any claims filed, and the timing and the manner of any payment between the parties that may be part of the agreement.

A good mediation process will produce a durable agreement that meets the legitimate needs of the parties. And perhaps, as Bush and Folger (2004) suggest, the process will have transformed the parties themselves into better problem solvers for the future.

KEY TERMS

adversarial assumption, 60

agreement to mediate, 69

authority to settle, 70

caucusing, 71

evaluative mediation, 65

facilitative mediation, 65

framing the issues, 72

ground rules, 71

interests, 73

mandatory mediation, 58

mediation, 58

mediation brief, 69

narrative mediation, 66

position, 73

terms of agreement, 76

transformative theory of mediation, 66

REFERENCES

Bush, B., & Folger, R. (2004). *The promise of mediation: The transformative approach to conflict*. San Francisco: Jossey-Bass.

Chornenki, G.A., & Hart, C.E. (2015). *Bypass court: A dispute resolution handbook* (5th ed.). Toronto: LexisNexis.

Fisher, R., Ury, W., & Patton, B. (2011). *Getting to yes* (3rd ed.). New York: Penguin.

LeBaron, M. (2002). *Bridging troubled waters*. San Francisco: Jossey-Bass.

Lebron, C.J. (2017). *The making of Black Lives Matter: A brief history of an idea*. New York: Oxford University Press.

Riskin, L.L. (2003). Decisionmaking in mediation: The new old grid and the new new grid system. *Notre Dame Law Review, 79*(1), 3–54.

Rogers, C.R. (1951). *Client centered therapy*. Boston: Houghton Mifflin.

Rubin, J.Z., Pruitt, D.G., & Kim, S.H. (2004). *Social conflict, escalation, stalemate and settlement* (3rd ed.). New York: McGraw-Hill.

QUESTIONS AND EXERCISES

1. Identify what—according to the different theories of mediation—are the most important elements of the mediation process. Decide which theory you find most appealing and explain why. Take what seem to you the best elements from each theory and create a composite theory of what mediation should be and how it should work. What do you end up with?

2. Imagine you are addressing a person who is deeply involved in personal conflict with a long-term business associate over a breach of contract. Tell this party, in your own words, what mediation is and how it might be preferable to a civil lawsuit for addressing their problem. Explain what mediation can and can't accomplish.

3. Consider a situation from your life where two co-workers, friends, or family members were in conflict. Imagine you are a mediator trying to help them resolve the situation. Work out a set of strategies for intervening in the conflict. How would you create a positive atmosphere? How would you facilitate communication? How would you help the parties set goals? How would you dissuade the parties from blaming each other and encourage them to focus on the future? In developing your strategy for

intervention, consult our list under the heading "An Exit from the Theories" of the 14 abilities all experienced mediators—regardless of their particular theoretical approach—possess.

4. Set out in your own words the steps involved in the mediation process. Describe the purpose or purposes of each step and briefly outline the skills each step requires of the mediator.

5. What are the purposes of the agreement to mediate? What provisions should it include, and how does presenting it early and having it signed first thing at the table create momentum and encourage the parties to buy into the process?

6. Sally is fifteen years of age and looks older than her actual years. She wishes to be independent of her rather conservative parents' control. Without their knowledge or consent, she has gone out and had a number of tattoos and body piercings done. She is dating a singer in a punk band and often sneaks out after her 10:00 p.m. curfew to meet him. Her homework is suffering—she considers school a waste of time. She rarely cleans her room or performs her other household chores. Her father, George, is informed by a co-worker in his factory that Sally

was out at a pub drinking until the wee hours on a Saturday night and that she was being openly and inappropriately familiar with the twenty-year-old singer in the band.

When George confronts Sally about the matter at home, she tells him it is none of his business. He lists the various complaints that he and her mother, Sue, have about Sally's recent behaviour. Sally becomes more defiant. Telling her father to go to hell, she starts to walk away. George grabs her housecoat, which comes partly away to reveal a large tattoo on her back.

George is furious.

Sue has been watching the altercation along with Sally's ten-year-old brother, Mike. Now she screams for George to let Sally go; she is terrified her husband will become violent with their daughter. George is prone to bursts of temper, particularly when he has been working hard.

George tells Sue in a raging voice to mind her own business and to take Mike out of the room.

Sue screams that she is tired of his temper. She takes Mike and Sally by the hand and tells her husband they are leaving until he learns to control himself. She leaves and takes the children to a women's shelter. It has been a week since the parties have talked. The housework isn't getting done. Sue and the children have little money. Sue wants to come home but needs assurance that she will be respected and her children safe. George wants his wife and children home. But he feels he has been undermined as the head of the household and demands apologies and humility from his wife and children.

In groups, mediate the problem. Assign the various roles in the scenario—George, Sally, Sue, the mediator—to different group members. The mediator should lead the parties through each step of mediation:

a. Negotiating ground rules.
b. Storytelling and assessing issues and interests.
c. Creative problem solving and brainstorming.
d. Selecting and refining solutions.

The person acting as mediator should try to use the skills of questioning, reflecting, summarizing, and reframing. Who should be the parties to the mediation? In what order should the issues be dealt with, given their importance and their relevance to each of the parties?

7. Return to the Questions and Exercises at the end of Chapter 3—the conflict-analysis exercise outlined in Question 3. Go to a television show or a movie where the characters have a conflict. Do a conflict analysis as if it were part of your pre-mediation with the parties to a dispute. How does the analysis help you to identify who needs to be involved in mediating the problem? What types of issues emerge, and what is their order of priority? Over which issues are the parties likely to take strong positions? Use this information to set up an agenda for mediation.

8. Practising by yourself or with another person, find the wording that enables you to do the following comfortably:

a. Explain, as part of pre-mediation, the mediation process to the parties involved.
b. Introduce ground rules at the outset of mediation.
c. Invite the parties to storytell.
d. Explain and introduce problem solving.

Arbitration

6

LEARNING OUTCOMES

After completing this chapter, you will be able to:

- Define arbitration and its role in dispute resolution.

- Understand the dynamic of tension between providing informality and more formal legal protections in the process of arbitration.

- Understand the process of arbitration and how it works.

- Identify the courts' deferential approach to arbitration awards.

- Determine the various areas where arbitration is a growing field, particularly in the area of mandatory arbitration.

- Determine where and why arbitration is a necessary complement to both mediation and full court procedures.

Arbitration: An Alternative to Negotiation and Mediation

Up until now we have taken the approach that in facing conflict, parties are best off using interest-based negotiation or mediation.

With negotiation, the ability to know what you seek and to listen carefully to the interests of the other party allows you to creatively incorporate both sets of interests in coming as close as possible to a mutually satisfactory conclusion. This is done while the parties retain control over their own affairs. They decide if, when, and on what terms they will settle. No one is there with the power to impose a solution upon them. In mediation, a third party enters into the process but without power to direct a conclusion. They are there to assist in the process but not to impose a solution.

While the autonomy and freedom of interest-based negotiation and mediation are much to be desired, particularly in building relationships, there are times when urgency, public need, or other factors necessitate coming to a timely and inexpensive conclusion that ends the conflict. Neither interest-based mediation nor negotiation can guarantee this result. This necessitates there being a different type of process, one where a third party or parties are empowered to give fair hearing to each of the disputants and then determine and impose the answer that brings an end to the conflict.

In *Introduction to Law in Canada*, Olivo (2009) defines arbitration as follows:

ADR

alternative dispute resolution—a broad term for forms of dispute resolution that are alternatives to court or other rights- and power-based systems (for example, mediation)

> Arbitration is the method of **ADR** that most resembles a court proceeding. A neutral third person, an arbitrator, is appointed and paid by the parties to make a decision on the dispute. Normally the parties agree that they will be bound by whatever decision is made, although the agreement setting up the arbitration process may provide that the decision may be appealed to a court. The parties also determine the manner in which the issues are presented to the arbitrator. They may decide to present their issues through a formal hearing process or they may agree to have the arbitrator base the decision on written submissions. (p. 115)

While the foregoing is a simple situation, it is easy to see how some conflicts involving the public interest cannot be allowed to continue without a proper conclusion. Certain public sector unions for services deemed to be essential, like police and fire services, will periodically go through negotiations in regard to their collective agreement. If negotiation and mediation fail, the next step in union affairs is often to call a strike. The dangers to the public of police officers or fire departments closing down and striking are pretty obvious. As a result, conflicts in their negotiations proceed directly to mandatory arbitration.

Understanding Arbitration

The *Arbitration Practice Handbook*, published by the ADR Institute of Canada (2006), states that "arbitration is a legal procedure for resolving disputes using one to three neutral, private persons called 'arbitrators.'" It points out that arbitrators may be appointed by the parties or may, in certain instances, be appointed for the parties or provided by some specific legal requirement. Usually, the handbook states, the decision of the arbitrator is final and binding unless otherwise agreed to by the parties.

CASE STUDY

CONFLICTING VACATION PLANS: A SIMPLE ARBITRATION EXAMPLE

Mary and Janet are nurses. They have travelled together on holidays for years. This year they wish to take a holiday in Asia but are disputing the country they wish to visit. Janet wants very much to go to Vietnam, while Mary wishes to go to Thailand. They have sat and talked about it. They have shared each other's dreams and hopes for the holiday but have each dug in on their choice of destination. The problem is that discounted flights and holidays are offered for a given length of time, and they are rapidly running out of time to make their decision. They contact a mutual friend whom they both trust. David, a fellow nurse, is known to be fair, impartial, and honest. Mary and Janet decide to ask him to make a decision for them and indicate they will be bound by it. He listens to both, allowing them a chance to put in their own positive reasons for their choice of destination and to challenge each other's. In the end, he decides that while both countries have beautiful beaches and islands and interesting cultures and history, the main consideration for both nurses is the total cost of the vacation, and Vietnam would be a much cheaper country to visit. Mary is not thrilled but accepts the decision and suggests they look at Thailand for next year's excursion. In this situation, the parties may have been locked indefinitely in their conflict, or at least past the point in time when the discount prices for the holidays would have lapsed. Here, David, pursuant to the friends' request, acted as an arbitrator: the third party empowered to make the decision on their behalf.

The binding nature of the decision is based "in the parties' agreement, a statute or a court decision." The handbook also allows for non-binding arbitration, where, in fact, the arbitrator's decision is directive only. This is a much rarer form of arbitration and is used principally to establish direction for the parties involved in labour disputes and is not recommended for arbitrations in commercial disputes. This latter approach is similar in some ways to an investigation process conducted by an ombudsman, which ends in recommendations based on findings of fact as opposed to a binding decision.

While arbitration, or other problem-solving forums similar to it, can be required by statute, arbitration is often a voluntary process undertaken by the contractual consent of the parties. The arbitrator appointed by the parties quite simply acts as a judge, but unlike in a civil lawsuit, the proceeding will be private and not held in an open court. Proceedings, therefore, do not form part of the public record.

Like a court proceeding, the parties are pitted against each other. The process becomes essentially a zero-sum process, where the parties see winning and losing as the only alternatives. It is an adversarial process, the desired result of which is to defeat the other party and win the judgment.

The purpose of arbitration is essentially to simplify and make more affordable a court-like process. It is there to simplify rules of entry, conduct, and evidence so as to enable parties to come to a quicker, more economical solution.

Coltri (2010) states that arbitration consists of eight basic steps:

1. Creating the arbitration contract.
2. Demanding, choosing, or opting for arbitration.
3. Selecting the arbitrator or arbitrator panel.

4. Selecting a set of procedural rules.
5. Preparing for arbitration.
6. Participating in the arbitration hearing.
7. Issuing the arbitration award.
8. Enforcing the award.

While much of the process in arbitration is similar to that in civil litigation, arbitrators will seek to strike a balance, enabling simpler procedures for the production and admission of evidence. They can, for instance, allow **hearsay evidence** at the hearing that would not be admissible in a court. An arbitrator can allow such statements but will determine what weight should be given to them depending upon the likelihood of their representing the truth.

Court proceedings have complete sets of rules governing civil procedure. They have to do with defining and issuing documents, the steps involved in starting a court process, pre-trial steps, the order of presentation at trial and appeal, and, of course, a multitude of rules about the types of evidence properly received by a court. Also, attendance in the court can be required by one party of the other through the issuance and service of documents like statements of claim, subpoenas, and so on.

Arbitration, on the other hand, is most often mutually sought out by the parties and is a voluntary process. The parties often have a say in who is to be appointed arbitrator, the methods for presentation of evidence before and at the hearing, and the limitation of issues to be heard.

The greater involvement of parties in the process means they often have a say in establishing who the arbitrator or arbitrators will be and identifying who the parties to the arbitration should be. This will be done at the stage of creating the arbitration contract. Items that could be taken into account will include the issues actually to be decided by the arbitrator—in other words, their jurisdiction; the format for scheduling a hearing or hearings; the confidentiality of things disclosed in the proceedings; and the types of evidence to be presented before and at the proceeding.

As mentioned above, the parties may simply offer to give written submissions to the arbitrator. Often arbitration can be kept simple by the parties agreeing upon the facts that are not in dispute. If they are contending only the specific interpretation of a contractual clause where no real facts are in dispute, they may simply agree upon all facts and submit the interpretation of the paragraph to the arbitrator for determination. The parties can also agree on matters of costs and whether an arbitrated decision will be subject to appeal to the courts. Generally speaking, the courts will honour the parties' decision to arbitrate and not interfere with the arbitrator's jurisdiction.

It should be noted here that in Canada there are both provincial and federal statutes that establish basic ground rules for arbitration. They specify that the arbitrator is to have no conflict of interest or predisposition in the matter to be determined. These arbitration codes also set up the requirements for courts to conduct judicial review of an arbitration or receive an appeal from an arbitration. The statutes have been posted online and can be accessed easily through the Internet for clarity of process across Canada.

The Process of Arbitration

The concept of natural justice established through the common law sets the parameters for fair hearing. Essentially, natural justice requires a party to know in detail what they are being charged with or accused of doing. They are to have an

---

hearsay evidence
composed of statements made by people who are not testifying before a court; these statements, heard by a party who is testifying before a court, will not be allowed in as evidence because the person testifying can attest to the fact the statement was made, but not to the truth of it; the opposing party will not be able to cross-examine the testifier to determine the veracity of the statements

opportunity to prepare and place their case before a judge or arbitrator as well as an opportunity to challenge the case against them. Arbitration can therefore be broken down into steps. First, there is the matter of what evidence is relevant and how it should be exchanged prior to the hearing so that the parties are fully informed about each other's case presentation and evidence. Then there is the matter of the actual hearing and what steps will be taken at that stage. Finally, there is the question of what follows the arbitration in terms of enforcing the award.

Pre-Hearing Stage

The pre-hearing stage is essentially to ensure that all parties are fully aware of what to expect at the hearing. It will therefore involve establishing agreed statements of fact, notice of proposed evidence and documents to be provided at the hearing, and often some indication of what each party seeks as an outcome of the arbitration. The stage really is to ensure that no one is surprised at the hearing and that all parties have an opportunity to properly prepare so the hearing can move as expeditiously as possible.

The Hearing Stage

There is no one set of rules to govern the hearing stage of an arbitration. It will depend largely upon the issues before the arbitrator and the level of agreement on the facts. As previously stated, if the parties are in complete agreement on the facts and simply wish an interpretation, there may be no need to hold a hearing at all. The arbitration can take place absent the parties upon the submission of written information to the arbitrator, and their decision and award will simply follow.

If there is a need to establish facts, then a lengthier process may be required. Usually, the process will begin with the party making the claim presenting their case. This may be facilitated at any time by directions from the arbitrator but generally means that documents will be placed into evidence and parties on behalf of the claimant will be presented for **examination-in-chief**. It is important to know that while lawyers are often very familiar with the adversarial process generally used in court or arbitration procedures, a party does not have to be represented by a lawyer. In fact, the arbitrator does not need to be a lawyer and is often chosen for his or her area of expertise. That is, one would want an engineer to decide engineering matters, an architect to determine architectural problems, and so on.

examination-in-chief
the questioning of a party's own witness under oath at trial

> **DID YOU KNOW?**
>
> Arbitration can also be conducted by teleconference or videoconference depending on the complexity of the issues, the length of time required for proceedings, and the parties' willingness to be flexible with the process.

Once the claimant has put their case before the arbitrator and the responding party has had an opportunity to cross-examine and challenge the evidence submitted, the claimant will rest their case.

The responding party will then have the opportunity to present their documents and evidence examining their witnesses in chief. The claimant will have an opportunity to cross-examine and challenge the evidence of the responding party.

When all of the evidence is before the arbitrator, the parties will usually be given an opportunity to give a final argument, at which point they will summarize the evidence, argue for their interpretation of what it means, and set out clearly what they see as an appropriate outcome and remedy.

The arbitrator will then either make a decision or reserve the decision to be delivered in a written judgment after the hearing.

Post Hearing

Although usually no post-hearing procedure need be undertaken with respect to the issues at arbitration, there are times when there is confusion involved in the actual judgment delivered by the arbitrator. In such cases, either the arbitrator or the parties may seek clarification of the arbitration award, and the arbitrator will be allowed an opportunity to establish a clear understanding of the impact of the award.

One type of proceeding that frequently arises following arbitration is around the matter of costs. In many cases, the parties will agree for the costs of the arbitration to be paid by the losing party to the victor. However, occasionally, no agreement is reached, and the arbitrator is re-engaged by the parties to make such a determination.

It should be noted as well that most arbitration awards can be enforced through the courts if parties do not comply.

IN THE NEWS

SUPREME COURT MAKES IT HARDER TO APPEAL ARBITRATION AWARDS

In a recent decision, the Supreme Court of Canada has made it even tougher to go to court to overturn decisions made by arbitrators. It has ruled that the courts, when reviewing an arbitrator's interpretation of statute, should use the reasonableness standard and tease out questions of law from issues of fact.

Source: Bourrie (2017).

Med-Arb: A Hybrid Process

Because the essence of problem solving outside a court is to ensure speedy and inexpensive resolution of parties' conflicts while leaving the matter in their control to the greatest degree possible, it should be noted that people often seek to combine the process of mediation with the process of arbitration. This is referred to as Med-Arb.

This process involves private parties hiring someone to act as a mediator who will initially, through interest-based methods, seek an interest-based solution. If after a time a solution does not seem possible, the process may be converted to an arbitration, with the mediator becoming an arbitrator. Initially, this process respects the autonomy of the parties to make their own decisions while allowing for the fact that a third party may be required to break deadlocks. If this process is used, it is essential that the mediator-arbitrator be objective and be capable of selecting and presenting clearly the facts upon which his or her judgment is finally rendered. Furthermore, he or she must remain demonstrably free of bias or conflict of interest.

A Glimpse at Some Types of Arbitration

As noted above, arbitration is often entered into by the parties by consent; however, there are some cases where arbitration is mandatory. Of the types of mandatory arbitration, some are statutory in nature, while others are contractual and can be found, for example, in consumer, employment, and labour contracts.

Different jurisdictions within Canada and elsewhere handle mandatory arbitration differently. For instance, under Ontario's *Insurance Act* (1990), disputes arising between insurers on matters of **loss transfer** "shall be resolved through arbitration under the *Arbitration Act*." Meanwhile, Ontario's consumer protection legislation specifically exempts consumer contracts from mandatory arbitration—leaving individual consumers to seek redress to contract disputes through the courts—while some other jurisdictions, like British Columbia, are less restrictive on the use of mandatory arbitration clauses in consumer contracts.

loss transfer
a mechanism by which, under certain circumstances, automobile insurers who pay no-fault benefits (the first-party insurer) may be reimbursed by another insurer (the second-party insurer) for all or part of a claim

International Trade Disputes

Investor-state dispute systems (ISDS) are common features of most current international trade treaties, such as NAFTA. They are meant to resolve disputes between corporations and governments, most of which are claims brought against governments by corporations in which the corporation in question believes its actual or potential profits have been negatively impacted by government legislation. The original rationale for such provisions in trade disputes was that a particular country's court system might be biased in favour of its own government, so "neutral" arbitration panels would rule on these disputes.

For example, Windstream Energy, a US corporation, sued Canada for $475 million, claiming potential losses due to the Government of Ontario's moratorium on offshore wind farms. The arbitration panel found in favour of the company and awarded Windstream $25 million in damages (Global Affairs Canada, 2013).

Similarly, Mesa Power Group, another US corporation, sued Canada because it felt it had unfairly lost a contract for onshore wind farms in Ontario. The company claimed $657 million in damages, but the arbitration panel dismissed the claim (Global Affairs Canada, 2017).

CAMVAP

The Canadian Motor Vehicle Arbitration Plan (CAMVAP) was derived from the Ontario Motor Vehicle Arbitration Plan in 1994. It is there to protect consumers who have bought cars that have defects that a dealer cannot or will not rectify. The plan is fully funded by the auto industry.

Arbitrators under the plan are all trained in CAMVAP issues and procedures. Many of the arbitrators under the program are retired lawyers.

If a party finds the dealership where they purchased their car is unwilling or unable to fix the car, that party may apply to invoke the plan. They will receive a list of three local arbitrators with the arbitrators' backgrounds and qualifications. The party is then free to choose one of the arbitrators to examine all documentation and hold a hearing between the parties. The hearings are usually informal and will often be held in the town of the party making the complaint. Arbitrators have the power to order repairs or the reimbursement of the purchase price of a vehicle. This is done with no cost to the party making the application because, as stated above, the plan is fully funded by the auto industry.

Olivo (2009), citing the results of the early years of the plan, states,

in 1997 … of the 469 cases processed, 329 were arbitrated (over half of which were in Ontario). About 200 were decided in favour of the consumer; in 148 cases repairs were made or the consumer was reimbursed for those already paid for (averaging over $1,000 per case), 49 involved the car being bought back (with or without a price reduction, averaging over $18,000 per vehicle) or, in three cases, replaced; and 15 consumers were reimbursed for miscellaneous out-of-pocket expenses. (p. 285)

Olivo goes on to explain that CAMVAP describes itself as "fast, fair, friendly, free, and final." The Canadian Motor Vehicle Arbitration Plan is one example where arbitration is used to provide consumers with a powerful remedy quickly and inexpensively.

IN THE NEWS

SALARY ARBITRATION: MARCUS STROMAN

Prior to the start of the 2018 Major League Baseball season, Marcus Stroman, a pitcher for the Toronto Blue Jays, went to arbitration after salary negotiations with the team had broken down. The league offers an arbitration process to players who have between three and six years of major league service. After six years, the player becomes a free agent. Prior to the arbitration hearing, both the team and the player (and his agent) submit final salary offers to the arbitration panel, which picks one of the two offers. It cannot decide upon a salary figure that is between the two offers. The panel's decision is based on comparable salary figures for other players who currently have contracts. Both the team and the player's agent state their respective cases before the panel. In Stroman's case, the panel decided in favour of the Blue Jays, which infuriated Stroman, in large part because, as he put it, "The negative things that were said against me, by my own team, will never leave my mind" (Griffin, 2018).

Arbitration in the Education Setting

There are times when conflicts arise in the public and higher education systems. There may be conflicts about workload, salary, or work expectations that need to be settled by way of a union grievance, or potentially litigation, but may also be settled through the process of arbitration. A collective agreement will often dictate the appropriate course for the resolution of such disputes. In higher education settings, professors may have concerns about intellectual property or patents. Elementary teachers may have concerns about workload-related issues such as time spent on extracurricular activities or lack of educational assistant support in the classroom.

Muniz (2017) argues that the fact that children are minors, and that schools act *in loco parentis* during school, warrants a different approach to arbitration in educator discipline cases. These cases should not be treated the same as employee–employer arbitrable disputes. Safeguards should be adopted to directly address the children's well-being now and in the foreseeable future when determining whether a teacher should be reinstated and continue to teach in a classroom.

NO FREE LUNCH?

In 1986, the Manitoba teachers' union indicated that teachers would stop all extra-curricular activities after it was determined in an arbitration process that teachers did not have to do this work if it was not paid work.

Source: *The Churchill Local Association No 37-3 of The Manitoba Teachers' Society and The School District of Churchill No 2264* (1988).

Overall, arbitration is an attempt at leaving as much power as possible with the parties to the conflict within a process that gives ultimate decision-making power to a third party to determine the outcome. It is there to constantly balance the rigidity, cost, and complexity of court proceedings with a simpler, more adaptable process. Parties may choose arbitration as a dispute resolution process because it can be voluntary, controlled, private, confidential, informal, and binding or non-binding to suit their needs.

CASE STUDY

FORT WAYNE EDUCATION ASSN V FORT WAYNE COMMUNITY SCHOOLS

The school terminated a long-serving substitute teacher who, while supervising a basketball practice, approached a female student, placed his hands inside his shorts, and told the student that he did not like the new underwear he was wearing. A few minutes later, he proceeded to tell her that he wanted to show her something "cool" but that she could not tell her parents, and then showed her his pierced nipple. He eventually apologized for making her feel uncomfortable. The arbitrator reinstated him, concluding that the penalty was too severe for the misconduct. The courts upheld the arbitrator's decision, indicating that the arbitrator simply interpreted the school code as best they could. Therefore, the substitute's reinstatement on the middle school's list of available substitute teachers and partial back pay was merited.

Source: *Fort Wayne Education Association v Fort Wayne Community Schools* (2001).

Finally, it should be mentioned that there are other processes that resemble arbitration that, strictly speaking, are not arbitration. Government tribunals are set up under statute for any number of reasons. Tribunals can be set up with single officers or up to three officers who will hold hearings. They can involve a broad range of subject matters involving various applications (for example, for immigration to Canada; for land division; for licensing the sale of liquor; and for allocations of quota for farm products, such as dairy or eggs). Occasionally, these bodies will refer to their adjudicative function as "arbitration," but, strictly speaking, their process is a statutory, quasi-judicial process, overseen by agents of the state and not a private process entered into by way of contract. There is a great many of these types of tribunals, both federally and provincially, across Canada. Appearance before these tribunals is governed by empowering legislation, and an advocate or consultant appearing before them should become familiar with their specific rules.

KEY TERMS

ADR, 80

examination-in-chief, 83

hearsay evidence, 82

loss transfer, 85

REFERENCES

ADR Institute of Canada. (2006). *The arbitration practice handbook.* Toronto: Author.

Bourrie, M. (2017, June 26). Supreme Court makes it harder to appeal arbitration awards. *CBA National.* Retrieved from http://nationalmagazine.ca/Articles/June-2017/Supreme-Court-makes-it-harder-to-appeal-arbitratio.aspx?lang=EN

The Churchill Local Association No 37-3 of the Manitoba Teachers' Society and the School District of Churchill No 2264. (July 1988, unreported. Arbitrator: Baizley). Retrieved from https://www.mbschoolboards .ca/documents/grievancesTeachers/Churchill%20Extra%20Curricular%20Award%201988.pdf

Coltri, L.S. (2010). *Alternative dispute resolution: A conflict diagnosis approach* (2nd ed.). Toronto: Pearson.

Fort Wayne Education Association v Fort Wayne Community Schools. Cause No 02A03-0006-CV-229 (Ind Ct App 2001). Retrieved from https://caselaw.findlaw.com/in-court-of-appeals/1472471.html

Global Affairs Canada. (2013). *Cases filed against the government of Canada: Windstream Energy LLC v Government of Canada.* Retrieved from http://www.international.gc.ca/trade-agreements-accords-commerciaux/topics-domaines/disp-diff/windstream.aspx?lang=eng

Global Affairs Canada. (2017). *Cases filed against the government of Canada: Mesa Power Group LLC v Government of Canada.* Retrieved from http://www.international.gc.ca/trade-agreements-accords-commerciaux/topics-domaines/disp-diff/mesa.aspx?lang=eng

Griffin, R. (2018, February 15). Stroman fumes after losing arbitration fight with Blue Jays. *Toronto Star.* Retrieved from https://www.thestar.com/sports/bluejays/2018/02/15/stroman-fumes-after-losing-arbitration-fight-with-blue-jays.html

Insurance Act, RSO 1990, c I.8, s 275(4). Retrieved from http://canlii.ca/t/534tb

Muniz, R. (2017). You are now entering the school zone, proceed with caution: Educators, arbitration, & children's rights. *Arbitration Law Review.* Retrieved from https://elibrary.law.psu.edu/cgi/viewcontent.cgi?referer=https://www.google.ca/&httpsredir=1&article=1196&context=arbitrationlawreview

Olivo, L. (2009). *Introduction to law in Canada.* Concord, ON: Captus Press.

QUESTIONS AND EXERCISES

1. Consider the following case and use this as a role–play opportunity. Working in a group of three, one person can be the arbitrator, another the student, and another the teacher.

   Colonial Intermediate Unit #20 v Colonial Intermediate Unit #20 Education Association

   A special education teacher was reinstated to his position after an arbitrator determined the teacher's conduct did not constitute immorality, cruelty, persistent negligence, or wilful neglect of duties in violation of the school code. The teacher had a history of humiliating students, calling them names such as "loser, sissy, liar, knucklehead, crybaby and chubby butt," twisting their arms, placing them in corners for up to three days, and placing an "I Abuse Animals" sign around their necks. (No 839 CD 2014 (Pa Cmwlth)).

2. Look up two arbitration companies and answer the following questions:
   a. Who are the arbitrators, and what education and qualifications do they hold?
   b. What are the mission statement, values, and goals of the company?
   c. What are the specialties of the company?

3. Look up three recent arbitration cases in areas of commerce, labour, and education and answer the following questions:
   a. How do they fit within the definition of arbitration?
   b. Were they mandatory or voluntary arbitrations?
   c. What were the presenting issues and sides?
   d. Who were the participants?
   e. What was the outcome of the arbitration?

4. A custodian is fired and has the right to arbitration. Management has the right to appoint the arbitrator, but the employee has the right to opt out. He is not familiar with arbitration. You are to explain to him what arbitration is and how this process works. How will you go about this?

5. Look up an arbitration case where the courts intervened. Why did they intervene? What was the outcome?

6. Discuss whether Med-Arb is the preferred choice or best option for the dispute in either Question 4 or the case you researched for Question 5.

PART III

Skill Sets and Knowledge Sets for Conducting Negotiations and Mediations

Having described the processes of negotiation, mediation, and arbitration, this part of the text will now examine some of the skill sets and knowledge sets necessary to be successful in the processes of negotiation and mediation.

Chapter 7 will look at the microskills used first to gather information and define the interests, needs, and aspirations of the parties, particularly where they are reluctant, unclear, unsure, or initially competitive. The chapter will then look at creative thinking skills helpful in overcoming differences and creating successful bridges between realities that allow for creative solutions.

Chapter 8 looks at how people create their frames of reference. It will begin to examine the evolution of self-image, cultural identity, and inevitability of cultural difference. Canada is home to many people who are from different cultures and whose first language is not English. Having English as an additional language means that, when it comes to negotiation, these people are challenged in ways that native English speakers are not. Speaking and interpreting a new language, both verbal and non-verbal, is difficult and often requires patience and guidance. Chapter 8 will also go on to examine how important it is for a mediator or negotiator to be able to be self-reflective, to see clearly, and to comprehend his or her own inner workings, choices, preferences, and blind spots.

From there, Chapter 9 will explore the issues of culture, gender, and power in more depth. Cultural differences bring challenges to the mediator. At some point in a negotiation, people from other cultures are likely to revert to thinking in their first language, particularly for difficult conceptual or abstract thinking. In mediation, this shift can create timing problems and comprehension challenges for the other parties at the table, including the mediator. People from other cultures will also have their own ideas about acceptable physical distances between people (proxemics) and about appropriate physical posture. And they will have their own ideas about acceptable forms and etiquette for communication. The mediator needs to take all of this into account.

Neglecting the sensitivities of people from other cultures may make them anxious and may lead to a breakdown in communication and stall the mediation process.

An effective mediator must also be aware of gender issues. Our understanding of what is male or female—with respect to thought, behaviour, perception, or activity—is to some extent culturally constructed. Our notions of gender come from our parents and from our local community, but also from the larger society we are part of. Sometimes there is disagreement between these sources. In other words, the ideas about gender we get from our parents and our ethnic culture may disagree with the prevalent ideas of our society. This can lead to conflict and can be problematic for the mediator. Sometimes a party's behaviour at the table—whether aggressive or overly deferential—is influenced by their thinking about gender.

Finally, this part of the text will look at the use of power by parties in mediation. As Part I of this book discussed, some parties facing conflict will try to ignore the dispute. Another party may yield or cooperate to help bring an end to conflict. The greater likelihood, however, given that we live in a world dominated by zero-sum thinking, is that parties will choose to contend. When this happens, each party automatically wants to achieve their goals by means of power.

Power is often seen as a negative factor in human relations and becomes a source of oppression if it is not balanced between the parties. But power can be brought into consciousness and viewed objectively. Its consequences can be examined, and alternative solutions in which it plays a modified role can be explored. Power can be balanced and managed and seen as a positive, creative, or even nurturing presence between parties in conflict.

Microskills, Storytelling, and Creativity in Conflict Resolution 7

LEARNING OUTCOMES

After completing this chapter, you will be able to:

- Define and explain microskills.

- Demonstrate the various microskills required for handling conflict situations.

- Apply the communication skills specifically needed for effective mediation and negotiation.

- Understand how stories are important to our understanding of ourselves and others and to how we define and approach conflict.

- Understand the cooperative method of conflict resolution as a heroic journey.

- Understand and explain the narrative style of mediation and how it can benefit the parties in dispute.

- Learn techniques for helping parties think creatively of options.

- Understand how different thinking styles can help in mediation and be able to apply these styles and brainstorming techniques.

What Are Microskills?

This chapter examines a variety of microskills that mediators must possess in order to move disputing parties toward resolution as well as looks at the use of storytelling within the narrative approach to mediation and, finally, to the process of generating creative solutions that will satisfy the parties' interests.

Dealing effectively with conflict does not come naturally to everyone. Some people negotiate and mediate quite well; others struggle. The successful people tend to possess **microskills**. Microskills are skills that are useful in very particular situations. There is a set of microskills useful for the conflict resolution process, and effective negotiators and mediators tend to possess them. The first aim of this chapter is to teach these skills.

microskills
skills that are useful in very particular situations

Active Listening

active listening
a way of listening that involves giving the other party our full attention, showing them in every way that we are trying to understand

The Chinese symbol for listening illustrates perfectly what **active listening** is. The symbol has several visible components: the ears, the eyes, and the heart. With our ears, we listen in a literal way. With our eyes, we pick up non-verbal communication. The heart is there to show that active listening requires being present in both spirit and body. Listeners must use their whole heart to fully understand the other party. We may listen to another person but not hear what the message is. Active listening involves giving the other party our full attention, showing them in every way—by our own body language, too—that we are trying to understand.

Ear — You — Eyes — Undivided attention — Heart — Respect

Use Effective Body Language

Effective body language is an important part of active listening. The acronym SOLER (Egan, 2007) represents the body language that is involved in active listening:

- **S**   Straight: Sit or stand up straight and focus on the person. This posture demonstrates that the listener is interested in what the other party is saying.
- **O**   Open: Body posture should be open; no crossed arms or legs, no obstacles or barriers between the listener and the other party. An open posture indicates readiness to listen and understand. It makes others feel more comfortable as they communicate.
- **L**   Leaning: Leaning in when the other party is speaking indicates that the listener is paying attention (although the significance of this body language can vary depending on the culture and gender of the person involved) and that they are interested in what is about to be revealed.

E Eye contact: Eye contact is important; it shows the listener is following what is being said. However, too much eye contact can make situations uncomfortable and hinder the conversation.

R Relaxed: A relaxed body posture tells the speaker that the listener is paying attention, is interested, and is not about to get up and leave. This will help them relax. If the listener shows anxiety, the speaker will pick up on this and reflect it back.

Give Full Attention

Active listeners give the other party their undivided attention; they shut out distractions. Recently, this ability to remain attuned to the present and not think of the past or future, and remove distractions, has been called *mindful listening*. Mindful listening goes beyond active listening to prompt the listener to monitor their own thoughts, feelings, or reactions that might affect what they hear (Shafir, 2000). Mindful listening helps a person become aware of distractions so he or she can refocus and listen consciously. In *The Zen of Listening*, Shafir (2000) says mindful listening helps you to:

1. Retain information.
2. Pause before you speak so you can consider the effect of your words.
3. Pay attention for longer.
4. Boost your self-esteem.

Imagine what it would feel like if you were telling a friend something very important to you while they were watching TV and checking texts. As you spoke, they began channel surfing. You would probably feel that your friend wasn't listening or that what you were saying was unimportant to them. That kind of distracted listening is common, especially now with cellphones and tablets. The active and mindful listener always puts aside any distractions until the speaker is finished. This communicates respect and interest.

Don't Interrupt

Active listeners should also avoid breaking in or making comments while the other person is speaking. It is important to let speakers express their feelings and thoughts without interruptions. Remember, actively listening is like a job. The listener is trying to understand the speaker, not to comment or judge. When the speaker is finished, it becomes the listener's turn to speak and the other person's turn to actively listen. Interrupting a speaker to express the listener's own views may stop the speaker from communicating honestly. In fact, some research demonstrates that frequent interruptions can cause memory retrieval problems and throw a person off his or her story (Coon & Mitterer, 2014). In a conflict situation, active listening ensures that both parties have an opportunity to speak freely, without interruption. This helps them reveal all relevant information.

Give Positive Feedback

Have you ever been telling a friend a story and she just stares at you blankly, not saying a word? Maybe it's never happened to you, but you can imagine what it would feel like. Would you assume she wasn't paying attention, that she was lost in thought, or maybe that you were boring her? By using encouraging words and positive non-verbal feedback, we can show that we are paying attention. You could nod your head or utter short words of agreement or encouragement, such as "Uh-huh," "I see," or "Go on." These are called *encouraging prompts* (Picard, 2016) and are often used by therapists and human service workers. Such responsiveness tells speakers, "Yes, I am listening," and it prompts them to continue speaking.

Be Alert to the Unspoken

Active listeners pay as much attention to what's not being said as to what is being said. For an illustration of this principle, read the following case:

> Mary bumped into Janice at the supermarket one day. They had not seen each other for three years, not since Janice moved away to go to university. Mary was very excited to see her and enthusiastically asked how she was doing. Janice looked nervous and lowered her eyes for a minute. She then replied, "I'm doing wonderfully. I moved to Calgary for school and graduated with honours. Things have been perfect in my career. Jackson and I are doing just great." She paused for a moment before repeating, with a hint of sarcasm, "Just great!" From Janice's tone and from what she left unsaid, Mary picked up that Janice and Jackson were not doing great and that something was probably wrong. She asked Janice if she would like to go for a tea so they could talk about things. Perhaps then, Mary thought, Janice would tell her how she was really feeling.

manifest content
what the words of a message actually communicate; the literal meaning

Mary picked up both the latent and the **manifest content** of Janice's message. The manifest content of a message is what is actually being said—what the words themselves communicate. The manifest content of Janice's message indicated where she went to school and how she fared academically, and it claimed that she and her husband were doing great. The **latent content** of a message is what is not being said explicitly but is there by suggestion. It is just as important as the explicit content. Latent content is usually expressed non-verbally. Janice's body language indicated she was nervous about discussing something; she looked down and paused. Her tone of voice was sarcastic when she repeated, "Just great." The latent content of Janice's message told Mary that something was not right between Janice and her husband. An active listener pays attention to both the manifest and the latent content of the speaker's message.

latent content
the part of a message, often conveyed non-verbally, that is not expressed explicitly but is there by suggestion

Active Listening as a Mediator

Within the process of mediation, a mediator demonstrates and models active listening for the disputing parties and encourages them to practise it themselves. Brief demonstrations or lessons in active listening may sometimes be required during pre-mediation. This ensures a smooth process. If the mediator senses that one party is not hearing the other's message or that there is a breakdown of communication, the problem should be addressed. A mediator could, for example, ask one party to repeat what the other has said to ensure understanding. This kind of request could be phrased as follows: "John, I would like to ask you at this time to repeat what Mary has just said, as you understand it, in your own words. I want Mary to be satisfied you understand her."

Communication Skills

Effective communication is crucial in resolving conflict situations. The heightened emotions in a conflict situation often impair the parties' rationality (Crisis Prevention Institute, 2017). This can prevent people from communicating effectively. A conflict can quickly escalate when parties are not communicating well. Conflict resolution requires all parties to communicate their interests, fears, needs, and values. There are several key techniques for promoting this process.

Paraphrasing

Paraphrasing involves repeating in your own words what someone else has said. When one party can paraphrase what the other has said, you know that the original speaker's message has been heard and understood. A paraphrase may start with phrases such as the following: "What I hear you saying is … " or "It sounds like … ."

paraphrasing
repeating in your own words what someone else has said

Example

Adam: "I worked hard at that job for 15 years. I gave them everything I had for all those years, and this is what I get—fired. I've had it!"

Jason: "It sounds like you're angry about the way they have treated you."

Adam: "Yes, exactly."

When we paraphrase the speaker's message, we are putting it into our own words. This helps us understand the message, but it also ensures that we have heard the speaker's message correctly. If our paraphrase misses something in the original message, the speaker will usually let us know. If Jason, in the example above, left something out of his paraphrase, Adam could correct him.

Example

Jason: "It sounds like you're angry about the way they have treated you."

Adam: "Yes, angry, but more tired. After all, it was 15 years, like I said."

The use of paraphrasing in this example has led to a full understanding of Adam's message.

Summarizing

Summarizing involves condensing the speaker's message while including all of the relevant points. It is a way for listeners to make sure they have heard all they were meant to hear. It is also a way of clarifying the message.

summarizing
condensing the speaker's message while including all of the relevant points

Example

Sharon: "I stayed with him for the first while thinking that it was my fault. I believed it really was after a while, but then when he started hitting the kids, I realized what danger we were in. I could no longer pretend that I deserved it. I knew the kids did not deserve this. So, I left. I packed up my things and left that night. I stayed with my mom and sister. They have always been supportive."

April: "You stayed, thinking it was your fault, until he turned on the kids. It was then that you left and went to your mother's. Your mother and sister are being very supportive for you."

Sharon: "Yes, that's correct."

When people are sharing information, there are often many facts to grasp. Summarizing is a way to make sure the parties and the mediator have heard all of the important facts.

Reflecting

reflecting
providing feedback that shows that the speaker's feelings and emotions have been recognized

Reflecting involves providing feedback that shows that the speaker's feelings and emotions have been recognized. It is important that both parties' emotions be acknowledged and understood in this way.

Example

Kim: "Why would they do this to us? We cannot afford it. I have lost everything now, including the house. I have nowhere to go. It's so frustrating!"

Nicole: "You're angry over what they are doing to you and your family."

Kim: "Very angry!"

When reflecting someone's feelings, we must not downplay or understate them. Our reflection should try to match the intensity of the feelings that have been expressed. If, for example, a party expresses their absolute devastation over something, we should not say, "You sound a little upset." This kind of understatement will cause frustration, anger, and annoyance. In a conflict, emotions are heightened. Sometimes it is hard for individuals to express how they feel; the right words get lost somewhere in the dispute. For the mediation to work, each party's fears and emotions need to be clearly understood.

Reframing

reframing
looking at a situation from a different perspective, often a more positive one, and restating it

Reframing involves looking at a situation from a different perspective, often a more positive one, and restating it. It allows a situation to be viewed in a fresh way, which can provide hope and objectivity.

Moore (2014) refers to three levels of reframing: detoxification, definitional, and metaphorical.

1. Detoxification reframing involves "changing the verbal presentation of a comment, idea, or proposal to remove judgmental, derogatory, and negative attributions, negative emotions, or extreme positions."
2. Definitional reframing involves "changing the conceptualization of a conflict or situation to make it easier to communicate more effectively in a less polarized way and conduct collaborative problem solving."
3. Metaphorical reframing involves trying "to find a new or altered metaphor for describing the situation or concept, thus changing the way in which it is viewed. Sometimes this means finding a metaphor that all parties can

use or translating one party's metaphor into a metaphor recognized by the other party" (pp. 344–345).

Reframing involves restating comments

1. to give them a more positive tone;
2. to eliminate blame and accusation;
3. to reflect underlying interests, fears, concerns, needs, values, or goals; and
4. to reveal common ground between the parties.

Example

Statement: "There's no way she's going to live with you with all those drugs and God knows what around!"

Mediator's Reframe: "You feel that this [the ex-partner's home] is an unsafe environment for your daughter and would rather she live with you."

Reframing is used to deal with a party's rigidly positional assertions, which may be negative or accusatory. It is a technique that seeks to uncover the underlying interests that these assertions have obscured. For example, the reframe of the sample statement above could take the following form:

Mediator's Reframe: "So, you're scared for your daughter's safety and you care about that. I think you need to be reassured about her safety; otherwise, you feel she is in a safer place with you."

This second reframe brings into focus the speaker's underlying need to be re-assured about the daughter's safety. This allows the communication to move forward instead of being stuck at a hostile impasse. The mediator's reframing of a party's statement should always be

1. mutually acceptable,
2. future focused,
3. non-judgmental, and
4. interest based.

Reframing is an effective tool; it promotes fuller understanding of the party that has spoken and of their situation. It is an especially useful tool for mediators who are trying to find common ground between clients. Once the clients can see what each other's needs are, they often become willing to cooperate.

"I" Messages

A useful technique for communicating during conflict is to use **"I" messages**. "I" messages have become an important component of conflict-management training for young children and youth in schools and at-risk youth in alternative settings (Gibbs, 2003). These require people to express themselves without criticizing the other party. Blame and accusation tend to mar communication during a conflict. We make statements such as "You make me so angry!" These are called **"you" messages**

"I" messages
messages that require people to express themselves from their own perspective in language that does not blame the other party

"you" messages
messages that use the pronoun "you" and thereby tend toward blame and accusation

because they single out the other party for blame. By using "you" messages, a person causes several things to happen:

1. They put the other party on the defensive.
2. They tend to express inaccurately what the other party did, and they don't take into account the other person's emotional situation.
3. They jeopardize their own emotional control by focusing negatively on the other's conduct instead of focusing positively on their own interests.

"You" messages cause escalation of the conflict and a breakdown of communication. Parties should be encouraged to use "I" messages. The general format of an "I" message is as follows:

"I feel … when you … because … ."

The "I" message version of "You make me so angry" would be something like the following: "I feel upset when you arrive home late because I worry about where you've been all night." The message clearly tells the other party what they have done to distress the speaker. At the same time, it decreases defensiveness and promotes empathy (Gibbs, 2003).

Clear Language

Clear language is important during conflicts. When individuals are upset, they often miscommunicate owing to loss of rationality, heightened emotions, or inattention. Language should be clear, concise, and to the point. A few tips for using clear language are the following:

1. Avoid jargon. The other party may not understand it.
2. Unclear, ungrammatical, or ironic statements (that is, statements that don't mean what they say) may cause confusion.

frozen words
absolute words, such as "always" and "never," that are usually inaccurate and tend to provoke defensiveness in the other party

3. Do not use absolute words such as *always* and *never*. Known as **frozen words**, they are usually inaccurate and they provoke defensiveness. A statement such as "You never help around the house!" is likely to produce a defensive response like the following: "Yes, I do; I just helped last week!" The frozen word *never* allows the responding party to deny the charge—even if last week was the only time they have ever helped.
4. Speak clearly and audibly.
5. Use factual descriptions instead of judgments or positional opinions. Facts create less defensiveness. For example, a supervisor examining a poorly organized report might say, "This work is sloppy." This would cause the person who produced the report to get upset. The supervisor could instead say, "If the pages of this report were reordered, it would make it easier to read."

Communicating as a Mediator

Having a repertoire of communication skills is essential for a mediator. Such skills are needed during all stages of the mediation process, from the first contact with the parties onward. Mediators should set an example for their clients of how to communicate effectively. The primary task of the mediator, apart from organizing the negotiation process, is to maintain a flow of effective communication between the parties. When the parties are not communicating effectively, the mediator should stop the process and encourage them to communicate better. A mediator can ask the clients to restate their feelings in a different way or to clarify something they have said. For example:

"Can you summarize the meaning of what Jim just told you?"

"Can you reword that statement describing why you are upset?"

"Can you clarify what that word means?"

A mediator needs to understand that not all individuals grow up in an environment where effective communication is enforced or encouraged. The parties may need a brief lesson in these skills. Although this may be viewed as time consuming, taking the time to brief participants on what effective communication would look like, sound like, and feel like at the beginning of a mediation process will actually save time and energy for all involved.

Observation Skills: Being Aware of Non-Verbal Communication

Being able to recognize non-verbal messages or signals is crucial in dealing with conflict. Kinesics is the study of non-verbal physical language: tone of voice, body language, or facial expressions (CPI, 2017). Remember, communication is 90 percent non-verbal (Fromkin, Rodman, & Hyams, 2019). Each party in a conflict sends non-verbal messages that indicate what they are feeling and thinking. They convey these messages by the way they stand, hold their hands, or contort their faces. The following are some examples of the mental states that people might reveal non-verbally:

- Aggressive: A person whose anger is escalating and who is becoming impatient or frustrated is likely to be aggressive. Physical indicators may include finger or foot tapping, staring, leaning forward, finger pointing, fist clenching, and moving into the other party's personal space.
- Responsive: A person who is interested in the topic and is paying attention is responsive. Physical indicators may include nodding, holding the end of a pencil in the mouth, stroking the chin, pursing the lips, and rubbing the neck or head. The responsive party may also incline their head toward the speaker, give lots of eye contact, maintain a high blink rate, lean toward the speaker, and smile.
- Non-responsive: The person who is not interested in the topic and wants to leave is non-responsive. Physical indicators of a person's non-responsiveness may include staring into space, slumping, doodling, foot tapping, chair swivelling, putting their jacket on, looking around the room or sorting through their materials, sitting back with their arms crossed, putting their head down, frowning, or packing up their things.

These three modes of response match the styles of approaching conflict described by Rubin, Pruitt, and Kim (2004) and referred to in Chapter 2. The responsive person would be interested in cooperative problem solving. The non-responsive person would prefer to ignore the conflict. The aggressive person would choose to contend.

By watching and monitoring non-verbal communications in a conflict situation, a mediator can see if the conflict is escalating. If it is, they can apply proper conflict-management de-escalation techniques at the appropriate times and bring things under control (CPI, 2017). Remember, though, not all physical behaviours convey emotions or thoughts; be careful not to overread or misinterpret body language. For example, a party who crosses their arms may simply be cold or be someone who finds it comfortable to brace their arms against their body; they may not be communicating standoffishness or non-responsiveness. A frown may indicate confusion, not unhappiness. Body language isn't always clear, and we need to consider alternative reasons for behaviours we observe.

Another consideration, when it comes to interpreting non-verbal language, is culture. Different cultures communicate non-verbally in their own particular ways. For example, the North American hand sign for "OK" (making a circle with the thumb and index finger, while leaving the remaining fingers open) is an insult in some European countries. It is a way of calling someone a *zero* or a *nothing*. Another example is the act of making eye contact. In some cultures, making direct eye contact is considered rude, whereas in others, it is considered polite (Gowman, 2011).

Observing as a Mediator

Mediators need to pay constant attention to the flow of communication, verbal and non-verbal, between the parties. Sometimes they need to address the parties' non-verbal language directly in order to reveal underlying tensions or hidden feelings and beliefs. These unspoken matters need to be revealed as soon as possible. Otherwise, they may erupt later in the mediation process and damage the work done to that point.

Questioning Skills

To question seems like a natural human ability. After all, we start questioning everything in our environment at the age of two (Coon & Mitterer, 2014). But knowing the right kinds of questions to ask in conflict situations is not a natural ability for most people. It is a very important skill for mediators. When negotiating a conflict, a mediator may need to elicit more information than is being offered, clear up confusion, or lead clients in a new direction. The good mediator needs to know what types of questions to ask at what times.

The following are some types of questions a mediator might find useful:

open-ended question
a question that allows the person responding to answer with a variety of answers and to have control of the conversation and room to express feelings and underlying interests

1. **Open-ended questions**: An open-ended question allows the person responding to answer with a variety of answers. It gives the respondent control of the conversation and room to express feelings and underlying interests. An open-ended question looks like the following:

   "How do you feel about brainstorming some ideas now?"

   Open-ended questions are appropriate during the storytelling phase of mediation. They give each party freedom to paint their own picture.

closed question
a limiting question that requires only a "yes" or "no" response

2. **Closed questions**: Closed questions are limiting; they usually require only a "yes" or "no" response. An example would be the following:

   "Do you like brainstorming?"

Closed questions would not be appropriate for the storytelling phase of mediation because they would not elicit enough information. Closed questions can be effective, though, with emotional individuals; they can help such people focus their attention and control their emotions. They are also helpful with children, who tend to lack developed language skills, and with parties who tend to dominate conversations.

3. **Clarifying questions**: Clarifying questions are used to bring out more information or to clarify a point someone has made. The mediator, or any of the parties at the table, may ask clarifying questions, which are very useful in mediation. They can help to clear up any confusion or misunderstandings that exist, so the process can flow smoothly. Following are some examples of clarifying questions:

> "I am not sure what you mean by 'rigid'; can you explain?"

> "Can you explain what you mean by 'ignorant'?"

> "People may feel different levels of anger. Can you explain how angry you felt?"

4. **Consequential questions**: Being able to ask consequential questions is a key skill in mediation. With these questions, you ask a party to use their prospective (that is, forward-looking) imagination to consider consequences—for example, to assess risks and likely outcomes of current decisions or actions. Consequential questions can be very useful during the stage of mediation where parties are exploring or evaluating creative solutions that will satisfy their interests. Some parties may not think ahead effectively because their emotions have impaired their foresight or simply because they haven't taken enough time to weigh the outcome of their actions. Participants should be encouraged to consider both short-term and long-term consequences (Picard, 2016).

Consider a case where a woman on social assistance is involved in a mediation concerning the custody of her children. Though she has no home or job, she proposes that, as the natural mother, she ought to have the kids living with her full-time. The mediator knows she needs to consider something—namely, how she will support the children and herself. So, the mediator asks a consequential question:

> "Let's say that all three of the children do come and live with you. Where will you live? What school will they go to, and how will you provide food and necessities?"

Parties in mediation sometimes make agreements too quickly, without fully considering the consequences. They may do this out of guilt, impatience, lack of knowledge about the mediation process, or a desire to avoid conflict. The mediator has a responsibility to ensure fair, long-lasting agreements and can use consequential questions to challenge and test any agreement made.

Take a case where an elderly woman is in a mediation session with her three grown children, who are fighting over her estate and family-owned business. The woman is of sound mind and body, fully capable of making decisions. She hates hearing her children fight, so in an attempt to

clarifying question
a question that is used to bring out more information or to clarify a point someone has made

consequential questions
questions that ask a party to consider the possible consequences of a prospective course of action—for example, to assess risks and likely outcomes of current decisions or actions

restore harmony, she announces that they can have the business and her house. The mediator senses this will cause future problems and is not in the best interests of the elderly client. So, he asks her a consequential question:

> "Can I ask you a question, Mrs. Jones? If this happens, where will you live and how will you support yourself in the future?"

justifying questions
questions that are used to resolve inconsistent or contradictory statements and to ensure clarity and understanding

5. **Justifying questions**: Justifying questions are used to resolve inconsistent or contradictory statements and to ensure clarity and understanding. Inconsistencies in a party's statements can have negative consequences in mediation. Following are some examples of justifying questions:

> "Your opinion on that matter is different from what you said in the last session. Have you changed your mind?"

> "Earlier you mentioned that she was not present, but just now you said she was. Can you clarify which one it was?"

Justifying questions should be used with caution because they can come across as accusatory or belittling. If used inappropriately, they may cause defensiveness and may actually shut down communication.

probing questions
questions used for exploring a subject when the respondent seems wary of full disclosure

6. **Probing questions**: Probing questions are for exploring. When one party gives a vague response or when the mediator wants to get to underlying issues, he or she may use probing questions. When clients are reluctant to discuss certain things, probing questions may be necessary. Probing questions might look like the following:

> "And how did you feel about that?"

> "Can you explain that in more detail?"

Mediators should be cautious when using probing questions. If used too often or with the wrong verbal tone (for example, patronizing or condescending), they may cause defensiveness or suspicion in the client.

Storytelling in Mediation

The truth about stories is that that's all we are.

—Thomas King (2003)

narrative mediation
a kind of mediation that aims to resolve conflict by uncovering and breaking down the disputants' stories so that they can be reconstructed into a larger narrative that integrates both parties' interests

Keeping in mind the skills discussed above, this section looks at the use of stories and storytelling in relation to discovering, defining, and deciphering conflict and its underlying interests. By using various questioning techniques, we can elicit the stories that are representative of conflict. By using our skills to deconstruct the conflict stories we tell, we are able to define and decipher underlying meaning and ultimately suspend the disbelief that a meaningful resolution can be reached. We therefore look at storytelling both as an important part of any mediation process and as the basis of a particular style of mediation—namely, **narrative mediation**. This kind of mediation brings parties to a better understanding of their conflict by viewing it objectively in narrative terms (Winslade & Monk, 2000).

Our Stories

Stories and Gender Roles

Faced with conflict, we often turn to the stories we have heard over the course of our lives. These stories teach us about our traditional roles in all forms of human inter-action, including conflict, and they influence our sense of self and how to behave (Rule & Bishop, 2006). Sometimes our defining stories are embedded in verbal cues. For example, referring to a little girl as *princess* and to a little boy as *sport* or *champ* can profoundly affect how that girl and that boy see themselves and their role in relation to conflict. Whether people choose fight or flight in response to conflict is strongly influenced by their self-defining stories—of victory and loss, heroes and villains, bravery and fear.

Gender stereotypes are clearly a factor in this. Boys and girls are shaped from birth by the different expectations they feel from parents, teachers, and peers. Boys often feel the need to be strong and brave, girls to be graceful and clever. These expectations are less rigid than they used to be and continue to be challenged as acceptance of diverse gender roles and gender fluidity grows in Western society. Still, the old stereotypes are alive and well in children's movies, television programs, and books. Failure to conform to these traditional gender roles can still lead to social isolation, antagonism, and inner turmoil.

Conflict as Story

You might even say that conflict itself comes with certain narrative expectations and with certain stereotypes attached to it. Some view it as an absolute evil that needs to be conquered or at least avoided. To others, conflict is a dramatic source of both crisis and opportunity. Conflict can be viewed as a resource to be exploited, such as we find in the 24-hour news cycle typified by the oft-repeated phrase *if it bleeds, it leads*. Conflict can also be viewed as a learning opportunity for growth and change. As we become familiar with alternative models of dispute resolution, including interest-based negotiation and mediation, we can begin to look at conflict not as evil but as something potentially positive. We can begin to see that conflict, though born of mismatched aspirations, is in fact a vital opportunity to discover compatible interests.

Stories and Self-Definition

Every individual comes furnished with his or her own set of stories. Some of these stories are highly personal, unique to that person alone. Others are family stories, shared among kin. Other stories belong to a slightly larger group or class—shared, for example, by students in a course about conflict resolution. Other stories belong to particular subcultures and ethnicities; to people of certain ages, religions, and socio-economic classes; or to inhabitants of nations or continents. Other stories, based on archetypes and drawn from what psychologists call the *collective uncon-scious*, belong to people the world over.

National myths or foundation myths are stories that are created and repeated over generations within cultures in order to clarify what the culture is and who belongs to it. As such, they provide a narrative that is central to the identity of the members of the culture. It is not necessary for these myths to be historically accurate. Rather, it is necessary that the stories be both simple and durable.

For example, Canada has the myth of two founding nations, the British and the French. The United States has the myth of the founding fathers, the Declaration of Independence, and the Constitution.

Both Canada and the US have subscribed to the concept of *terra nullius*—nobody's land—to describe the Americas prior to European colonization. In other words, the Indigenous peoples who were actually there were considered inconsequential. This idea is deeply embedded within the national myths of both Canada and the US and continues to be a source of many conflicts.

Some stories may be true, based on real historical events; others may be factually false—myths. But whether true or false or somewhere in between, these stories and myths are very important to the people who possess them; they add truth and meaning to their lives. As we come to recognize how uniquely important our stories are for each of us, we are reminded again of what Carl Rogers (1959) said about the uniqueness of each person's reality: "What is real to you is real to you." In other words, reality is different for every person.

Our privately held stories and myths, whether true or false, contain the beliefs we hold most dear. Many of them have come to us from our ancestors, have shaped our national and family histories, and continue to inform our cultural identities. But the diverse origins of these stories, many of which we share with other people, indicate that we are capable of belonging to more than one culture and of holding more than one set of beliefs at once. The psychological term **cognitive dissonance** describes a condition in which a person holds two contradictory ideas simultaneously and is driven to reduce *dissonance* by changing his or her attitudes, beliefs, and behaviours (Coon & Mitterer, 2014). You might say that the diverse narratives each of us contains keep us in a constant state of cognitive dissonance.

We draw on our stories for self-definition and for guidance in our behaviour. They shape and define our world view and offer a pattern for our social interactions.

cognitive dissonance a condition in which a person holds two contradictory ideas simultaneously and is driven to reduce "dissonance" by changing his or her attitudes, beliefs, and behaviours

Stories and Conflict

In the context of these self-defining stories, conflict occurs when one party's culture, based on their stories or narratives, differs from another party's. This cultural disagreement can escalate from the level of interests (one party saying, for example, "This land is our land; you do not belong here") to the level of beliefs or values ("My god is more righteous than your god; my people's ways are superior to your people's ways") to a level that is religious in nature ("It is therefore sacrilege for you to be in our sacred land; if you do not leave, we will destroy you to protect the sanctity of our god and our way of life"). LeBaron (2002) works with similar distinctions in her account of conflict. She identifies three kinds of conflict:

1. material and analytical;
2. relational; and
3. perceptual and symbolic.

Conflict is material and analytical when it arises out of competing material interests and zero-sum thinking. It is relational when it arises out of miscommunication, misconception, and misunderstanding. It is perceptual and symbolic when it arises out of differences in culture, gender, world view, and personality and when it leads to rival rituals and competing core beliefs. Conflicts of the latter kind (that is, perceptual and symbolic) are often connected to stories—stories that reflect people's deep-seated beliefs about who and what they are. Consider, for example, the ongoing conflict between evolutionists and creationists. The biblical "story" of God's creation of the world stands in opposition to the "story" of evolution.

Stories in Conflict Resolution

The Hero's Journey

In *The Hero with a Thousand Faces*, Joseph Campbell (1972), a pre-eminent cultural anthropologist, deals with something called the monomyth. He argues that any story about a hero, whatever the story's cultural or historical origins, follows the pattern of the **Hero's Journey**. This pattern, familiar to us from a thousand action-adventure films, works in the following way. The protagonist, who may or may not be an extraordinary person, is living in a very ordinary way. Confronted with a problem, the hero perceives a call to action and adventure and moves into new and dangerous territory where formidable foes exist. At this point, heroes confront their worst fears and in doing so achieve an extraordinary state. In the course of these trials, our hero meets new friends, gains knowledge and new powers (for example, special weapons), and, after a last, bitter struggle, emerges victorious. Then he or she returns home to a seemingly ordinary life, albeit with the experience of a lifetime and an epic story to tell.

Hero's Journey
the narrative pattern according to which an ordinary person undergoes lessons and hardships and, by facing his or her fears, becomes extraordinary—a hero

Figure 7.1 is a visual representation of the traditional Hero's Journey. You will note that in order to overcome the journey's obstacles, heroes must enter the depths of their own selves, face their deepest fears, and discover their unrealized powers. Only then can they achieve victory and return to familiarity.

Figure 7.1   The Hero's Journey

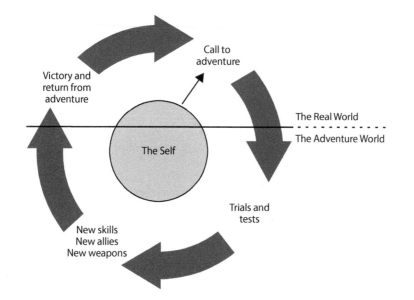

The Heroic Journey of Conflict Resolution

The Hero's Journey is an important narrative in the context of dispute resolution. Diamond (1996) takes the heroic journey of self-discovery and growth as the model for those engaged in the conflict resolution process. Drawing on the transformative theory of conflict resolution, Diamond argues that the conflict resolution process provides disputants with an opportunity for personal growth and learning.

Following are the stages of the conflict resolution process as seen in terms of a transformative heroic journey:

1. **The Source:** As Diamond says, we all desire peace. When heroes find their peace threatened, they feel chaos in the core of their being. Likewise, when we find ourselves in conflict, we are deeply shaken, and this gives us the desire to resolve the conflict. We begin to steel ourselves for battle, so to speak.

2. **The Quest:** When we choose to resolve conflict, we hear a call to adventure, like the call the hero hears. In this case, the adventure consists in entering and committing to the conflict resolution process. Many, despite making this commitment, are tempted to revert to battle mode, and it is the mediator's job to return them to a collaborative approach. The contracting stage of the mediation process, when the parties sign the agreement to mediate, helps secure the parties' commitment to this stage of the heroic journey.

3. **The Test:** Heroes experience pain and suffering in the course of facing tests and foes. The parties involved in resolving conflict suffer, too, as they face the blame, the pain, and the fears associated with conflict. To move past this stage, the hero requires new powers, such as special weapons. For the disputant who is trying to resolve conflict by the collaborative method, these weapons are enhanced communication and problem-solving abilities.

4. **The Shift:** Like the hero who must, despite some initial reluctance, ultimately accept his or her role, the party engaged in dispute resolution must take responsibility for their part in the conflict, and they must ultimately ask for or accept forgiveness. The disputants may feel mourning or remorse at this stage, but this will ultimately lead to final absolution.

5. **The Renewal:** In the last part of the journey, heroes reach a deeper understanding of their enemies' motives. This understanding enables the hero to achieve personal victory and growth, and it allows life to return to normal. Likewise, each party involved in conflict resolution must come to a deeper understanding of the other party. This mutual understanding enables both sides to generate options for resolution and peace, and this ultimately allows them to return to a normal existence, empowered by their new skills and abilities in conflict resolution.

Figure 7.2 is a visual representation of the conflict transformation model seen in heroic terms. You will note how closely it follows the model of the Hero's Journey. In both models, the horizontal line running nearly through the centre of the *Self* or *Source* can stand for the dividing line between the conscious (upper) and unconscious (lower) world. We as humans, whether our adventure involves a heroic journey or a conflict resolution, must venture into that lower world to face our fears and discover our interests.

Figure 7.2   The Heroic Journey of Conflict Transformation

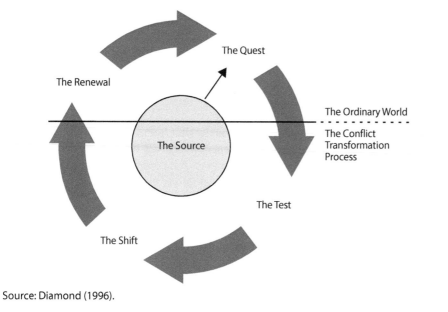

Source: Diamond (1996).

Narrative Mediation: Resolving Conflict Through Storytelling

Storytelling is an essential part of any mediation process. The goals of mediation lie in the future, but the disputing parties need to reflect on the past in order to reach these goals. Such reflection can occur through the telling and deconstruction of stories and the creation of new, shared narratives. As we have stressed in this chapter, people call on stories to explain all aspects of their lives and to understand their feelings. Stories shape our core beliefs—the world view that determines how we experience and respond to life. These stories contain images, symbols, and archetypes that we use to explain the thoughts, ideas, and truths that are most important to us. Our stories and the beliefs they embody shape us profoundly and can even determine our future. Mahatma Gandhi, the Indian political and spiritual leader, traced the connection between our beliefs and our future behaviour when he said the following:

Your beliefs become your thoughts.
Your thoughts become your words.
Your words become your actions.
Your actions become your habits.
Your habits become your values.
Your values become your destiny.

The narrative style of mediation (Winslade & Monk, 2000) is based on the idea that people understand their lives in terms of stories. Storytelling plays a role in all kinds of mediation. But in narrative mediation, storytelling is the primary focus. The literal truth of the stories is secondary. As Winslade and Monk (2000) have said, "Mediators who use a narrative orientation are interested in the constitutive properties of conflict stories ... Whether a story is factual or not matters little to the potential impact it has in someone's life" (p. 2). In narrative mediation, the emphasis "is on how the story operates to create reality rather than on whether it reports accurately on that reality" (p. 2).

A central idea in narrative mediation is that people resort to **totalizing descriptions** in telling the stories of their conflicts (Winslade & Monk, 2000). Totalizing descriptions reduce the complexities of a conflict situation to sweeping generalizations about the conflict and the disputants. Narrative mediation tries to undo these generalizations and create a new version of the conflict story. In other words, narrative mediation tries to develop a **preferred story** through "destabiliz[ing] the totalizing descriptions of conflict so as to undermine the rigid and negative motivations that the conflicted parties ascribe to each other" (Winslade & Monk, 2000, p. 3).

The Stages of Narrative Mediation

There are a number of steps involved in the narrative mediation process (Winslade & Monk, 2000, p. 3):

1. Building trust in the mediator and in the mediation process.
2. Developing externalizing conversations.
3. Mapping the effects of the problem on the person.
4. Deconstructing the dominant storylines.
5. Developing shared meanings about the conflict and its solutions.

Step 1: Building Trust

In narrative mediation, as in other types of mediation, the mediator's first task is to develop trust and rapport with the parties. From the beginning, the parties must understand that "the mediator has grasped the depth of their distress." The mediator must convey this empathy "without appearing to collude with each party's problem-saturated descriptions of the other" (Winslade & Monk, 2000, p. 4). The narrative mediator's key tools, during this first stage, are active listening, empathy, and an assumption that "everyone is doing their best to deal with the conflict with the resources they have at hand" (Winslade & Monk, 2000, p. 5).

Step 2: Externalizing Conversations

Having earned the parties' trust, the mediator will direct them to engage in **externalizing conversations**. This requires them to examine and understand the conflict story "as if it were an external object or person exerting an influence on the parties" (Winslade & Monk, 2000, p. 5). The principle is similar to Fisher, Ury, and Patton's (2011) principle of "separating people from the problem." Here, the parties separate themselves from the storyline at points where they identify with the conflict. The narrative mediator helps in this process by reframing the conflict and by changing

---

totalizing descriptions
descriptions that reduce the complexities of a dispute to sweeping generalizations about the conflict and the disputants

preferred story
a new narrative, composed by the parties in a narrative mediation as they resolve their dispute, that is based on their new understandings of themselves, of each other, and of the conflict itself

externalizing conversations
the stage in a narrative mediation at which the disputing parties are encouraged to talk about the "conflict story" as if it were external to them, influencing them both

blaming language into language that reflects the parties' specific interests (fears, concerns, goals, aspirations) and specific feelings (grief, anger, and disappointment).

Step 3: Mapping the Effects

In "mapping the effects" (Winslade & Monk, 2000, p. 6) of the conflict, a mediator helps the parties dig deeper into its history, with the aim of revealing how it evolved, how the parties were affected by it, and how their understanding of it developed.

This historical approach brings in a time dimension that enriches the parties' perspective on the conflict. They are able to see more clearly the conflict's rhythms and patterns—how it is changing and possibly escalating. Hearing about the conflict's origins and development gives the mediator a chance, as well, to start discovering the formative stories (also known as *socialization stories*) belonging to each disputant. These are the self-defining narratives, unique to each party, that precede and stand outside the conflict but may be contributing to it (Winslade & Monk, 2000, p. 6).

By having an honest dialogue about the conflict's effects, the parties can begin to see each other differently, not as monsters but as fellow victims of something unfortunate—namely, the conflict itself. Resolving the conflict becomes their common goal. This prospect becomes the basis for a new, preferred story in which the parties move out of conflict and into peace.

Step 4: Deconstructing the Dominant Storylines

The fourth step in the narrative mediation process is "deconstructing the dominant storylines" (Winslade & Monk, 2000, p. 3). This involves examining the stories that have shaped and defined each disputant. Having the parties examine each other in this way—in the light of such influences as culture, gender, age, and relationship expectations—enables them to understand each other better and to understand better how each sees and understands the conflict. The mediator may wish to isolate and focus on certain statements made during this process—statements that reflect something significant about each party's cultural context.

For example, one of the parties in a marital dispute may be a wife who reveals at this stage that she feels her life pressured by two storylines, or discourses. In one storyline, her role is to take care of her family, as her mother did. In the other storyline, she pursues the career for which she was prepared by her education and work experience. The first storyline comes from her traditional upbringing; the second, from her educational and social experience, which have taught her that she ought to use her work skills and that marriage should be an equal partnership. The woman's description of these storylines becomes an important building block for change; the pressures themselves are externalized—viewed as causes of conflict that come from outside the woman herself. As Winslade and Monk (2000) suggest, "This kind of discursive analysis maps out territory from which ways out of the conflict can be found" (p. 15).

When the parties begin to develop their understanding of the myths, stories, and discourses that have shaped both themselves and the other party, they typically begin to open up to new, alternative solutions to their problems.

Step 5: Developing Shared Meanings

At this point in a traditional mediation, the parties would engage in generating options and negotiating a settlement. In narrative mediation, the parties, after deconstructing their own and the other side's storylines, are encouraged to form a new story or discourse together based on their fresh understandings of themselves and each other and on the needs and interests they have identified. With this done, the parties can begin to give up their negative generalizations about each other—to "disengage from their totalizing descriptions of the other as hurtful and destructive"—and begin to compose a "preferred story" (Winslade & Monk, 2000, p. 16). The narrative mediator will encourage the parties to focus on the positive changes they have made throughout the process and to compose the new story on the basis of their now-stabilized relationship. This preferred story, which will define their future relations, corresponds to the settlement portion of a traditional mediation. The mediator will test the preferred story by asking hypothetical, prospective (that is, forward-looking) questions—in other words, questions that invite the parties to think about how their solutions will play out in the future. Such prospective thinking is essential to a durable agreement. In this way, "the parties who were formerly in conflict [will] reflect on the strategies, techniques, and problem-solving abilities they are putting in place" (Winslade & Monk, 2000, p. 21).

Narrative Mediation: Summary

Narrative mediation's starting point is that we make meaning "through the filter of language and the subjective interpretation of 'facts'" (Hansen, 2003). The interpretation of facts is always subjective, narratively shaped by a particular individual. Narrative mediation invites these individuals to engage in a storytelling process. This process involves their examining and deconstructing their different stories about the current conflict as well as their own self-defining stories—that is, the stories that inform their perception of the world and their own place within it. Finally, parties are encouraged to create for themselves a new, preferred story that is based on their new understandings of themselves, of each other, and of the conflict itself. The narrative mediation model may "particularly appeal to mediators … who prefer to work with the accounts of parties in conflict rather than attempting to get at 'the truth,' recognizing that any truth brings with it implicit bias" (Hansen, 2003). Narrative mediation also works well in mediating cultural or relational conflicts—those cases where cultural differences or a bad relationship between the parties makes it difficult for them to negotiate over issues or interests. Narrative mediation is exceptionally complex; it requires specialized study and training. But it can be a very effective and valuable tool in alternative dispute resolution.

Generating Solutions: Creativity in Mediation

Once the parties' interests have been clearly discovered, defined, and deciphered through storytelling, the process of searching for, demonstrating, and ultimately deciding upon integrative solutions can begin. You may recall the third principle in Fisher et al.'s (2011) model, discussed in Chapter 2: "Invent options for mutual gain." Interest-based negotiation, with its emphasis on collaborative problem solving, makes such options possible. They would be unthinkable in a more adversarial context.

At the outset of this creative stage, parties often make the mistake of trying to determine immediately what the best solution is. Their thinking is as follows: "Now that we have done the hard part (identifying our interests), we can get to the easy part—coming up with the best solution." Coming up with the best solution, however, is not as simple as it sounds. For one thing, it requires a shift in thinking styles. An awareness of the various types of thinking styles and mastery of them becomes essential in shifting from the storytelling and interest-identification stage to the creative, solution-finding stage.

Up to this point, the mediator has been helping the parties identify their interests. The mental operation needed for this kind of identification is **convergent thinking**. Convergent thinking analyzes a situation in order to identify what is actually going on; it uses logical, rational thought processes. The mediator, using the various questioning and reframing techniques, has the parties engage in convergent thinking to produce a clear statement of their needs, goals, and desires. This process removes the confusion that usually surrounds a conflict situation. It enables the parties to see accurately, often for the first time, what it is they need. Once the parties have arrived at this point, the next step is to invent options that will satisfy their needs and interests. Such invention requires a diametrically opposed type of thinking—**divergent thinking**.

convergent thinking
a type of thinking that uses logical, rational processes and focuses on a specific goal, solution, or way of doing things

divergent thinking
a type of thinking that starts from a single point or issue and expands outward, encompassing a wide range of solutions

Divergent thinking, or lateral thinking, as de Bono (2000) calls it, starts from a single point or issue and expands outwards. Given a problem or issue, a person engaged in divergent thinking considers a wide variety of solutions as opposed to searching for the single correct one. This is exactly what is needed at this stage of the mediation process in order to *expand the pie*. Parties using this thought process are able to craft solutions that would never be considered in dispute-resolution forums (for example, courts and tribunals) that resolve problems by way of rights or power.

The expression **expanding the pie** refers to the process of creating new benefits for both parties in a negotiation. Traditional approaches to conflict look at the pie as being of a fixed size and type—the pie is an apple pie, no other kind, and there are six slices, no more, each slice a certain size. Divergent thinking allows us to enlarge the pie, change the number and the size of the slices, and add other kinds of pie.

expanding the pie
creating new benefits for both parties in a negotiation

Creativity now becomes an important part of the process. Divergent thinking is creative insofar as it encourages you to look at any interest that is on the table from a number of perspectives. Each perspective reveals different ways of satisfying the interest.

The stage of mediation concerned with generating options, according to Fisher et al. (2011), has two basic steps: inventing options and deciding on options. They offer certain practical guidelines for helping parties brainstorm solutions that can potentially satisfy their interests.

1. Seat the participant's side by side, both facing the problem.
2. Clarify the ground rules, including the no-criticism rule.
3. Brainstorm.
4. Record the ideas in full view of both parties.

Brainstorming

There are many approaches to **brainstorming**, but some basic rules usually apply:

1. Speak freely. Parties should feel free to suggest solutions that may not be feasible. This is not yet the time to be concerned about practicality. Generally

brainstorming
generating a wide variety of ideas without worrying about which are feasible

speaking, parties should have the freedom, during brainstorming, to say whatever comes into their heads; this is much more likely to produce creative solutions than if the parties are looking for the one "right" answer. Looking for the one right answer will merely lead the parties to where they were at the outset of mediation, that is, to solutions that are tied to their fixed positions.

2. Do not criticize the other side. At this point in the process, the focus should be on generating ideas, not on deciding which ideas are acceptable or feasible. If parties are allowed to criticize each other's ideas, the brainstorming process will stop.

3. Produce as many ideas as possible. One of the key ideas behind brainstorming is that the quality of the ideas increases with the quantity. In other words, the more ideas that are generated, the greater the possibility that one or more of them will be workable in the real world. For example, a municipality may have a significant traffic congestion problem and members of city council may have a variety of fixed positions regarding how to fix the problem. Moore (2014, p. 390) points out that parties "often adhere to positions because they see no other way to develop new options."

   But consider how many possible solutions there might be for a municipality or region to deal with traffic congestion—road tolls, increased parking fees, more public transit, less public transit, free public transit, increased gas tax for private vehicles, more high-occupancy vehicle (HOV) lanes, fewer HOV lanes, carpooling, more roads and highways, adding lanes to existing roads and highways, more one-way streets, fewer one-way streets, more taxis, and so on.

4. Build on each other's ideas. When parties get into the flow of brainstorming together, they can begin working in a truly cooperative way, generating ideas they would never have produced alone. Brainstorming helps the parties combine ideas about how to satisfy both their interests; that is one of its great strengths. By this point in the process, the parties will have come to see their interests as substantially connected and will have thought hard about how to satisfy their own interests as well as the other party's.

The "Six Thinking Hats" in Mediation

Edward de Bono asserts that our habitual thinking processes limit our problem-solving abilities. Mediators may find his *Six Thinking Hats* (2000) method a help in promoting creativity. De Bono's theory is that most of us rely on one or two styles of thinking rather than on the entire range of thinking styles, which he metaphorically describes in terms of six coloured hats. Mediators should work to develop these types of thinking in themselves and should also develop skills that will help them encourage such thinking in disputing parties.

De Bono's "Six Thinking Hats" are discussed below.

White Hat: Information

White Hat thinking
traditional, logical thinking based on information that is known, available, or potentially discoverable

White Hat thinking is traditional, logical thinking based on information that is known, available, or potentially discoverable. It is useful during the stage just before brainstorming, especially if the collaborating parties share information. This kind of thinking has its limitations, though. For one thing, it is not particularly creative. But White Hat thinking can help curb excessive emotion. In many situations, certainly in conflict situations, parties have lost the ability to think rationally, and they begin to rely too much on emotion, especially negative emotion.

Red Hat: Emotion

When engaged in **Red Hat thinking**, parties look at problems using intuition and basic gut feelings, and they pay attention to their emotional reactions. When evaluating options after the brainstorming process, Red Hat thinking can help determine how acceptable the elements of an agreement may be. But too much Red Hat thinking means that emotions are dominating the process. In a conflict situation, these are likely to be negative emotions.

Red Hat thinking
thinking based on emotion and feeling rather than reason and logic

Black Hat: Critiquing

Black Hat thinking looks for the weaknesses in a suggestion or idea. It should dominate any process in which ideas are being evaluated for their durability and practicality. It should not, of course, enter the brainstorming phase itself; it is not a creative mindset. But in the post-brainstorming evaluation phase, Black Hat thinking discovers the weaknesses in an option so that the parties can either remove the option from the table, work to alter it, or develop a contingency plan to deal with its weaknesses. Black Hat thinking helps to make the elements of a final agreement tougher and more resilient.

Black Hat thinking
critical thinking that looks at flaws in or problems with a particular course of action

Yellow Hat: Optimism

Yellow Hat thinking is positive thinking. Effective mediators find they must use this type of thinking frequently during the early stages of mediation. After a while, they can encourage the parties to use the Yellow Hat themselves. The Yellow Hat and the Black Hat work well in tandem when parties are trying to decide which options will become part of their final agreement.

Yellow Hat thinking
positive thinking

Green Hat: Creativity

Green Hat thinking is creative thinking, which is the means of generating multiple options during the brainstorming process.

Green Hat thinking
creative thinking

Blue Hat: Process

Blue Hat thinking is the type of thinking needed to control a process. People who are chairing meetings, for example, wear the Blue Hat. In our context, the mediator wears the Blue Hat, being the process manager.

Blue Hat thinking
thinking that focuses on process rather than on content

The skills, techniques, and knowledge sets we have explored in this chapter will enable a mediator to guide the parties to discover, define, and decipher the causes of conflict and ultimately decide upon the best solutions for its resolution. A mediation process that follows the above pattern and ultimately generates outside-the-box options and then tests them for feasibility and durability is one that truly defines principled, integrative, win–win dispute resolution. Mediators who can encourage the parties to tell, interpret, and understand their stories; bring them to a place where they are able to see alternative interpretations of their own reality; and ultimately lead the parties to shift their own thinking styles in search of solutions as the situation dictates will be very effective.

KEY TERMS

active listening, 94

Black Hat thinking, 115

Blue Hat thinking, 115

brainstorming, 113

clarifying question, 103

closed question, 102

cognitive dissonance, 106

consequential questions, 103

convergent thinking, 113

divergent thinking, 113

expanding the pie, 113

externalizing conversations, 110

frozen words, 100

Green Hat thinking, 115

Hero's Journey, 107

"I" messages, 99

justifying questions, 104

latent content, 96

manifest content, 96

microskills, 94

narrative mediation, 104

open-ended question, 102

paraphrasing, 97

preferred story, 110

probing questions, 104

Red Hat thinking, 115

reflecting, 98

reframing, 98

summarizing, 97

totalizing descriptions, 110

White Hat thinking, 114

Yellow Hat thinking, 115

"you" messages, 99

REFERENCES

Campbell, J. (1972). *The hero with a thousand faces* (2nd ed.). Princeton, NJ: Princeton University Press.

Coon, D., & Mitterer, J.O. (2014). *Psychology: A journey* (5th ed.). Belmont, CA: Wadsworth Publishers.

Crisis Prevention Institute. (2017). *Non-violent crisis intervention manual*. Milwakee, WI: CPI.

De Bono, E. (2000). *Six thinking hats*. Toronto: Penguin Books.

Diamond, L. (1996). *Beyond win–win: The heroic journey of conflict transformation*. Occasional Paper Number 4. Washington, DC: Institute for Multitrack Diplomacy.

Egan, G. (2007). *The skilled helper* (8th ed.). Belmont, CA: Brooks/Cole.

Fisher, R., Ury, W., & Patton, B. (2011). *Getting to yes* (3rd ed.). New York: Penguin.

Fromkin, V., Rodman, J., & Hyams, N. (2019). *An introduction to language* (11th ed.). Boston: Cengage Learning.

Gibbs, J. (2003). *Reaching all by creating tribes learning communities*. Cloverdale, CA: CentreSource Systems.

Gowman, C.K. (2011). *The silent language of leaders: How body language can help or hurt how you lead*. San Francisco: Jossey-Bass.

Hansen, T. (2003). *The narrative approach to mediation*. Retrieved from http://www.mediate.com/articles/hansenT.cfm

King, T. (2003). *The truth about stories: A native narrative*. Toronto: House of Anansi Press.

LeBaron, M. (2002). *Bridging troubled waters*. San Francisco: Jossey-Bass.

Moore, C. (2014). *The mediation process: Practical strategies for resolving conflict* (4th ed.). San Francisco: Jossey-Bass.

Picard, C.A. (2016). *Practicing insight mediation*. Toronto: University of Toronto Press.

Rogers, C.R. (1959). *A theory of therapy, personality, and interpersonal relationships*. New York: McGraw-Hill.

Rubin, J.Z., Pruitt, D.G., & Kim, S.H. (2004). *Social conflict, escalation, stalemate and settlement* (3rd ed.). New York: McGraw-Hill.

Rule, W.R., & Bishop, M. (2006). *Adlerian lifestyle counselling: Practice and research*. New York: Taylor & Francis.

Shafir, R. (2000). *The zen of listening*. Wheaton, IL: Quest Books.

Winslade, J., & Monk, G. (2000). *Narrative mediation: A new approach to conflict resolution*. San Francisco: Jossey-Bass.

QUESTIONS AND EXERCISES

1. Change each of the following sentences into an "I" message that expresses how you might feel in each situation:
   a. Your teenage son comes home late, two hours after curfew.
   b. Your partner does not remember your birthday.
   c. Your client forgets to tell you something important.
   d. Your employer has said something negative about you.

2. Turn the following statements into factual descriptions.
   a. Your room is a mess!
   b. This office space is no good!
   c. That offer is outrageous!
   d. Your service was horrible!

3. Reframe the following statements so they meet the main criteria of positive communication, that is, they address underlying needs and eliminate blame.
   a. If we can't offer service to this client, then we might as well close up shop.
   b. Two thousand therapists in this city and I ended up with you.
   c. The student council representative is useless.
   d. You are a deadbeat dad!

4. Change the following closed questions to open-ended questions:
   a. Do you like having the children live with you?
   b. Do you plan on being in this same position in five years?
   c. Will you leave the house to your children in the will?

5. Review the following situation from the exercises in Chapter 1.

   George and Tang are from different cultural heritages. George was born in Canada and was raised in the Judeo-Christian ethic and belief system. From childhood he was taught to believe in creationism. His family has always sponsored involvement in music, because they believe music is the medium through which people are connected to the angels. Tang, on the other hand, was born in China. He learned at an early age that one approaches the eternal by stillness, through meditation. The two men are now attending the same university and live in adjoining residence rooms. Each night after studying, George likes to play the "Hallelujah Chorus" loudly in his room. This usually happens at 10 o'clock, just as Tang, next door, is settling in for meditation. Tang's culture also promotes a high

   degree of respect for others; it emphasizes allowing others to save face.

   Assume you are a mediator doing a pre-mediation with Tang.
   a. Create a clarifying question you might ask him.
   b. Create a justifying question you might ask him.
   c. Create a consequential question you might ask him.
   d. Create a probing question you might ask him.

6. Consider your own body language. Describe how you normally express non-verbally (for example, through body language, facial expressions, voice) the following emotions, then consider how someone who didn't know you might misinterpret those non-verbal cues.

	Usual Non-Verbal Expression	Alternative Interpretation
Frustration		
Confusion		
Sadness		
Indifference		
Anger		

7. Identify the cultural groups—for example, demographic (gender, age, ethnicity, educational level), citizenship, socio-economic status, religion, profession—to which the following people might belong:
   a. the current prime minister of Canada;
   b. a close friend of yours whose ethnic origin is different from your own;
   c. a professor you have for a post-secondary course.

8. Think of one or two stories or myths that may be important to each of the cultural groups you identified in the previous question.

9. Repeat the previous exercises with yourself as the subject. Take some time to consider your own cultural origin and self-defining stories.

10. Choose a popular and influential storyteller, for example, Hans Christian Andersen, Beatrix Potter, or even Walt Disney. Select one of their stories and choose

a hero and heroine from that story. Consider how the author's portrayal of these major characters, male and female, might have influenced the gender expectations of a youthful audience.

11. Write a brief paper describing a time in your past when you felt you had to challenge a social belief that was deeply held by your family or your society. Did turning away from the old belief require a journey deep into yourself, then a rebirth into a new level of awareness and understanding? Does every new generation of teenagers undergo some such process? Do people go through this when they move from their original culture to a new one?

12. What is your dominant thinking style? From a total of 30 points, assign a certain number of points to each of the six thinking styles depending on how likely you are to use it in a negotiation of some kind. Base your response on negotiating situations in which you commonly find yourself.

White Hat (information)	_____
Red Hat (emotion)	_____
Black Hat (critiquing)	_____
Yellow Hat (optimism)	_____
Green Hat (creativity)	_____
Blue Hat (process)	_____
TOTAL	30

Choose two or more of the hats for which you have a low score. Identify specific actions you could take to increase your facility with these thinking styles. How would you incorporate these behaviours into your usual negotiation and mediation practices?

13. With a partner, consider the following negotiation situations and identify the key interests that each party might have. For each interest, brainstorm with your partner until you have at least 10 ways of satisfying those interests. Use the four rules of brainstorming to guide the process (speak freely, do not criticize, produce as many ideas as possible, build upon and combine ideas). Remember, the ideas do not have to be realistic at this point; evaluation of ideas or strategies comes later in the process.

a. You are buying a new car and turning in your used one. You are negotiating the value of your trade-in. Here your concentration should be on alternative ways of maximizing the value of your used vehicle.

b. You are negotiating with your spouse over where to go for next summer's holiday. (For example, you might prefer to go mountain climbing while your partner might prefer relaxing at the beach—but you can create whatever scenario you like.) You need to consider such variables as the distance of the respective destinations and how the trips will be financed.

c. You are a member of a union negotiating the next collective bargaining agreement with management. Major union issues might include wages, seniority, training, pensions, and health-care benefits. Major issues for the company could include many of the same, plus cost control, productivity, new technology, and profits.

d. You are negotiating the sale of your house to people in the community you have known for some time. Issues here could include the price, the timeliness of the sale, the condition of the home, and your existing relationship with the potential purchasers.

e. You are negotiating the sale of your house to strangers.

Frame of Reference and Self-Image: The Origins of Cultural and Self-Awareness

LEARNING OUTCOMES

After completing this chapter, you will be able to:

- See how a person's world view is developed within his or her own frame of reference.

- Understand that ego- and ethnocentricity are the initial states of awareness for all people.

- Consider the prospects for changing a party's perceptions from within their own frame of reference.

- See how self-image is something the individual carefully guards and something that can be changed only slowly and carefully.

- Show that cultural differences reflect divergent but equally legitimate points of view.

- Practically apply, in questions and exercises, the concepts of frame of reference and cross-cultural understanding as they relate to mediation.

- Understand why an awareness of one's own negotiation and mediation style(s) is important.

- Define and understand emotional intelligence and empathy skills.

- With practical questions and exercises, develop self-awareness about personal strengths and weaknesses in negotiation.

Frame of Reference or Subjective Culture

Much work in the dispute resolution field has been done on how people construct reality. The mistaken assumption that we all share the same reality often causes miscommunication and conflict. The notion that every person has an individual **frame of reference**, or subjective culture, is something mediators need to understand.

frame of reference
a person's subjective reality, shaped by his or her particular experience and culture, and the basis for his or her perception of the world

Haney (1979), citing the *Dictionary of Behavioral Science*, defines the frame of reference as "a system of attitudes and values which provide a standard against which actions, ideas, and results are judged and which to some extent controls or directs action and expression" (p. 88). Kimmel (Deutsch & Coleman, 2000) refers to it as "categories, plans, and rules people employ to interpret their world and act purposefully in it" (p. 455).

Carl Rogers (1951) says several helpful things about frame of reference in connection with conflict resolution. The following four propositions are paraphrased from his work:

1. Every individual exists in a continually changing world of experience of which he or she is the centre.
2. The individual reacts to his or her world as he or she experiences and perceives it. The world he or she individually perceives is *reality* for that person.
3. The individual has one basic tendency and striving, which is to actualize, maintain, and enhance himself or herself.
4. The best vantage point for understanding another's behaviour is from within the person's internal frame of reference.

> Pray, don't find fault with the man that limps,
> Or stumbles along the road.
> Unless you have worn the moccasins he wears,
> Or stumbled beneath the same load.
>
> Just walk a mile in his moccasins
> Before you abuse, criticize and accuse.
> If just for one hour, you could find a way
> To see through his eyes, instead of your own muse.
>
> Source: Excerpt from Lathrap (1895).

In other words, an individual in any given culture views his or her own perception of reality as the correct one. This person's subjective culture, or frame of reference, is the standard by which he or she judges correctness of action, belief, and thought. A mediator dealing with intercultural conflict must get inside each party's frame of reference and change their particular perception of reality so that they can engage with each other.

The Concept of Frame of Reference: Benefits

The concept of frame of reference is useful to mediators for the following reasons:

1. It alerts us to the fact that each party's perception of the world is different from our own.
2. It reminds us that the greatest obstacle to understanding another's subjective world is our own frame of reference.
3. It enables us to see that no matter how alien, or apparently different from our own, another person's frame of reference is real to them and makes complete sense to them.
4. It encourages us to frame issues and determine needs and interests in a broader context than we might otherwise.
5. It reminds us, as mediators, of the very real need to be modest in offering our services and the conclusions of our own subjective culture and to accept graciously the realities offered by other cultures.

Self-Image

Another important concept for mediators who are dealing with intercultural conflict is **self-image**. As we have seen, every individual looks out at the external world and constructs an individual reality. In the same way, that person looks inward to determine who they believe they are. The result is the person's self-image.

self-image
the individual's subjective perception of himself or herself

The concept of self-image is related to the concept of personal and cultural identity. In disputes between different groups or between parties from different cultures, the polarizing element—the factor causing the parties to harden and grow rigid—is often self-image, or the parties' self-perceived identity.

Self-image develops as follows:

> As one grows from infancy and slowly evolves to a human personality … one creates internally an image of oneself. This image is a multifaceted, ambivalent, and increasingly complex self-concept. It is a self-definition, which is at least partly unconscious, formed out of the person's experience. (Haney, 1979, p. 92)

Self-image tells people who they are, what they believe, how they should react, and how they fit in and belong to the world around them. It grows out of the individual's own inward-looking experience and frame of reference. It is a part of the self that each person cherishes and protects. Haney (1979) describes it as "an enormously precious possession. One never leaves it behind—often protecting it at any cost. Some authorities assert that the most powerful drive of human beings is not self-preservation but self-image preservation" (p. 92).

Self-Image and Cultural Identity

People engaged in disputes that have an intercultural element often appear to be stubborn or closed-minded. Such people usually have a strong cultural identity—a kind of cultural self-image—that is shaping their outlook. This kind of identity can run very deep in a person. When we examined **value conflict** in Part I of this text, we talked about the many different religious beliefs, dress codes, or codes of social

value conflicts
conflicts that arise when people have different criteria for valuing ideas or behaviour or have goals based on mutually exclusive value systems

conduct that people may have. Parties to whom these distinctions have always been meaningful will have difficulty changing their orientation to the world. But sometimes the mediator, to keep hope in the mediation process alive, will have to believe that such change is possible.

Most parties believe, first and foremost, that their own culture is universal, incomparable, and the only valid one on Earth. This is the starting point for most people. When a party encounters cultural difference in another, they, of course, prefer their own culture and see it as superior. They may become aggressive or defensive. Such closed-mindedness can obviously be problematic within a negotiation. But these contradictory realities should inspire the mediator to explore, clarify, and understand.

Moving Away from Ethnocentrism

Milton Bennett (1991) describes how intercultural sensitivity develops. He says that the greatest obstacle to acknowledging another's culture, or frame of reference, is our own—in other words, our belief that our own culture is the only one in existence. If you are prepared to end what he calls "the disavowal of cultural difference," you can ascend the ladder of awareness to where "differences in modes of perception or expression are construed as cultural factors, rather than as examples of physical or moral defects" (p. 5). He outlines the mental stages people go through in moving from **ethnocentrism**—a mindset in which you believe your culture is the only valid one—to **ethnorelativism**, a mindset in which you accept that all cultures are valid:

ethnocentrism
a mindset in which one believes one's own culture is the only valid one

ethnorelativism
a mindset in which one accepts that all cultures are valid

1. An individual begins by denying the existence of other cultures.
2. When no longer able to deny that other cultures exist, the individual will attempt to preserve their own sense of culture and identity through self-isolation or by segregating members of the other culture.
3. When the other person's culture is too strong to ignore or isolate, the individual will try to defend against it by belittling it or claiming superiority over it.
4. As a last stand against the invasive awareness of the other culture, an ethnocentric person will claim a form of physical or universal denial. This is based on the idea that all cultures are really the same and there is no need to move out of one's own cultural comfort to a greater awareness of the other.

All these stages reflect a basic wish not to see the error of one's own ethnocentrism. A person with these attitudes wants to avoid the discomfort of mental growth and the uncertainty and pain of seeing things differently. Unfortunately, a person who remains ethnocentric won't be able to make new meaning with a person from another culture and won't be able to develop, with the other party, a perception of reality that accommodates both their points of view. Mediators should always expect to meet this type of ethnocentric thinking in the early stages of a mediation involving intercultural conflict.

Bennett's ethnorelative stages describe a movement toward an attitude of acceptance and accommodation. Once an individual has come to a willing awareness of the other culture's existence, three additional mental shifts are possible:

1. Acceptance of the other culture's behavioural and value differences, which are freshly perceived from within the other culture's frame of reference.
2. Personal adaptation to the other culture, together with a willingness to see differences in behaviour and values as vital and integral to that culture.

3. A willingness to assimilate or integrate the reality of the other culture into one's own mindset.

Bennett warns of the disorientation that such assimilation can cause. But if the process is undertaken slowly, and in a controlled way, this disorientation can be minimized. After all, accepting another culture's reality need not involve a rejection of one's own cultural reality. Rather, the other culture can have a broadening influence on one's own.

Not to know and be able to name one's own cultural preferences is to be controlled by them without realizing it. People controlled in this way are in a closed-minded state, and they will respond with bias and prejudice to anything they perceive as different or diverse.

Ethnocentrism and the Mediator

The mediator who is alert to the likely ethnocentrism of the parties in a mediation can do a number of things:

1. They can assure each side that the absorption of another's ideas and point of view is not fatal.

2. They can set an example for the parties with their own attitude of acceptance and integration. In other words, they can demonstrate the kind of attitude that allows people of varying cultures to live comfortably together.

3. They can make the parties' real interests and needs the focus of the mediation. This will help move them out of their rigid cultural positions. Keep in mind, though, that those interests and needs must be considered from within each party's own frame of reference.

4. They may, in questioning the parties, show an encouraging openness of mind and attentiveness in the face of unexpected or even unnerving answers. (But keep in mind that these answers, though unnerving to the mediator, make sense within the party's own frame of reference.)

It is important for the mediator to be attuned not only to differences in language but also to distinctions in non-verbal communication. Mediators must consider the possible significance of the parties' clothing and body language and must know about their different conceptions of time, personal space, and history. Remember, subjective culture is real to the one who has it; it is a complete, self-enclosed, meaning-making system. But no matter how different another's culture is from the mediator's own, the mediator can understand it if he or she makes the attempt with patience and an open mind.

The Mediator's Need for Self-Awareness

Self-awareness and self-knowledge are as essential for a practising mediator as microskills are. Mediators should recognize their own strengths and limitations, their favourite approaches to conflict, their cultural beliefs, and their personality types. This self-knowledge will allow the mediator to approach conflict situations with a neutral and open understanding.

Understanding Personal Conflict Style

yielding
resolving conflict by giving up one's own aspirations and accepting the other party's as more important

ignoring
pretending a conflict does not exist or suppressing conscious awareness of it instead of actively addressing it

contending
adopting combative techniques designed to fulfill one's own aspirations while thwarting those of the other party

problem solving
problem solving that integrates both parties' interests and seeks mutually beneficial solutions

Approaches to conflict are explained in Chapter 2. Individuals may use one of four approaches to conflict: **yielding**, **ignoring**, **contending**, or **problem solving**. One person, disliking conflict, may yield to an opponent at any prospect of it. Another person may have learned effective problem-solving skills as a child and used them consistently to deal with conflict. People tend to be consistent in their favourite approaches to conflict.

Many factors influence how we approach conflict:

1. how our parents approached conflict themselves,
2. how they taught us to approach it,
3. our temperament or personality style,
4. our education level, and
5. our personal experiences.

It is important for mediators to recognize and understand their natural style, or approach, where conflict is concerned; it will influence what they encourage their clients to do, what the focus of their session is, and how comfortable they are in the mediation session. One would assume that an effective mediator would believe in the problem-solving approach to conflict. This is generally the case, but certain situations or clients may cause them to revert, in spite of themselves, to a desire to yield or ignore. How do they handle a situation like that? Do they understand why they are reacting this way? What do they do about it? Consider the following case:

> Sherry met with two clients for their first mediation session, George and Joanne, both in their late 50s. They were divorcing. In the mediation session, George was being hostile and very abrupt. With his anger and bluntness, George reminded Sherry of her father, whom as a child she had feared. Sherry found herself feeling fearful of George and, with that fear, a childhood desire to yield to him as she always had to her father. A few times, she found it hard to manage the session due to this reaction. Sherry's own conflict style is to yield to extremely hostile individuals. She was self-aware enough to recognize this and asked a co-mediator to join her.

Mediators need to understand their own behaviour around conflict and to understand that certain conflict situations—those causing them to revert to an ineffective approach, such as yielding or contending—may be inappropriate for them to mediate. For these situations, a referral or a co-mediator may be necessary. Mediators need to make sure they have the skills and cognitive abilities, as well as the emotional capacity, to use problem-solving approaches to conflict. After all, this is what they are trying to help their clients do.

Understanding Negotiation Style

One person may naturally negotiate in such a way as to avoid or dismantle a conflict situation. But not all individuals can effectively negotiate in this way. Others have different negotiating styles. Recognizing what their style is can help them realize their strengths and make the most of their negotiating sessions. Parties in a negotiation may choose an agent because of that agent's particular approach.

The Rahim Organizational Conflict Inventory (Rahim, 1983) outlines five negotiation styles: avoiding, accommodating, compromising, competing, and collaborating. Each approach is based on a particular philosophy of negotiation, and each has its strengths. At times in a negotiation, depending on the situation, it may be necessary to adopt different approaches. This is where flexibility becomes a key skill in conflict resolution and negotiation.

Understanding Mediation Style

Mediators also need to be able to adapt their approaches to the client and the situation. They need to know the different styles and philosophies of mediation. (Review the earlier discussion of the evaluative, facilitative, transformative, and narrative styles of mediation.) Again, though, they will have their own dominant style, and recognizing what their style is will help them understand their behaviours, goals, and strategies. It will help clients, too, decide whether their services are the kind they need.

Assessing Personality Type

It is hard for people to assess their own personality; it takes time and effort to understand who we really are. However, when mediators are working with a *vulnerable population*—people who are undergoing stress and trouble in their lives—they need to have an understanding of their own personality type. This helps them understand how and why they interact with people the way they do, their needs and values, their strengths and weaknesses, their limitations and *buttons*. Having an empathic and understanding personality is crucial for mediators, who will encounter different personalities in their clients. A mediator may be challenged, tried, and pushed to their limits in a mediation session, and he or she may experience a positive or a negative reaction to the parties, but ethically the mediator is bound to treat them equally and without bias. Mediators need to maintain professional control at all time. We can think of mediators like practitioners in fields such as psychology, counselling, nursing, or social work; people are coming to them when their lives are full of trauma and chaos. These people need guidance and management from someone who can offer hope for the future. In fact, we might call a mediator *a seller of hope*.

Emotional Intelligence

Many researchers (Bradberry & Greaves, 2009; Goleman, 2006) claim that **emotional intelligence** is more important to success and happiness than general intelligence. Emotional intelligence can be defined as the ability to understand and manage our own emotions and the emotions of others in order to create and sustain positive relationships (Bradberry & Greaves, 2009). There are four key components to emotional intelligence: self-awareness, self-management, social awareness, and relationship management (Bradberry & Greaves, 2009).

emotional intelligence
the ability to understand our own emotions and the emotions of others

Mediators should have self-awareness, being aware of their own emotions and emotional reactions, along with personal limitations and strengths. Next, the mediator should have self-management in order to manage those emotions and reactions in a positive way. As stated earlier, mediators may be pushed to the limit by others, and they need to maintain professional control at all times. Without this ability, how can they possibly manage others' emotions in the mediation process? At the same time, the mediator must have social awareness—the ability to pick up on others' emotions, verbal or non-verbal, sent by clients in the mediation session. Such cues may indicate levels of comfort, areas of contention and confusion, or, more generally, whether the session is going well.

Relationship management requires the fourth and highest level of emotional intelligence. The mediator with this skill is able to manage relationships in a positive and productive manner based on his or her awareness of the parties' emotions. Conflict always involves heightened negative emotions, and managing them takes skill and patience. A mediator with emotional intelligence will be prepared to deal with these negative emotions as they appear.

Reflective Mediation Practice

retrospective reflection
looking back on inter-personal interactions and thinking critically about which behaviours worked well and which did not

At the end of a session, mediators need to consider retrospectively the interactions and behaviours of the parties at the table, and they need to determine how effectively they, as mediators, managed the process. **Retrospective reflection** involves going over what has happened and thinking critically about the process—about the outcome, about their performance as mediators, about the participants' behaviour, about what worked or did not work, and about what they would change given a second chance. This process allows them to constantly improve their skills. There may be times when certain strategies or sessions did not work, and they need to understand why. They should also reflect on sessions that went well so that they will have some idea of how to repeat the process in the future. A powerful tool for doing this is the **reflective journal**. In this journal, the mediator records his or her reflections on the day's session, asking questions like the following:

reflective journal
a journal that records how the day went with positive outcomes, challenges, emotional reactions, and insights; the journal can be reviewed to support behavioural and cognitive changes in one's life

- What worked well today and why?
- What did not work well today and why?
- What skills did I use effectively today?
- What added skills might have helped me today?
- What would I do differently next time?
- What am I proud of from today's session?

Remember, not all sessions will go perfectly or easily. Afterward, mediators may recognize mistakes they made and think of things they wish they had done or said. Keeping a reflective journal will help them make those changes and consolidate them for their future performances.

KEY TERMS

contending, 124
emotional intelligence, 125
ethnocentrism, 122
ethnorelativism, 122

frame of reference, 120
ignoring, 124
problem solving, 124
reflective journal, 126

retrospective reflection, 126
self-image, 121
value conflicts, 121
yielding, 124

REFERENCES

Bennett, M. (1991). Towards ethnorelativism: A developmental model of intercultural sensitivity. In M.R. Paige (Ed.), *Education for the intercultural experience* (pp. 4–11). Yarmouth, ME: Intercultural Press.

Bradberry, T., & Greaves, J. (2009). *Emotional intelligence: 2.0.* New York: Simon & Schuster.

Deutsch, M., & Coleman, P. (2000). *The handbook of conflict resolution: Theory and practice.* San Francisco: Jossey-Bass.

Goleman, D. (2006). *Emotional intelligence: Why it can matter more than IQ.* New York: Bantam.

Haney, W. (1979). *Communication and interpersonal relations* (4th ed.). Homewood, IL: Irwin-Dorsey.

Lathrap, M.T. (1895). *Judge softly.* Women's Christian Temperance Union of Illinois.

Rahim, M.A. (1983). A measure of styles of handling interpersonal conflict. *Academy of Management Journal, 26*(2), 368–376.

Rogers, C.R. (1951). *Client centered therapy.* Boston: Houghton Mifflin.

QUESTIONS AND EXERCISES

1. What is a frame of reference? Set out in your own words what a frame of reference is, how it is shaped, and why it is important to a mediator.

2. Understanding another's perception of reality is not the same as agreeing with it. But enabling parties to understand each other's perception of reality and to reflect that understanding back upon each other can be an important step in creating rapport between parties with very different interests. Why is this so? How can it be used as a tool in mediation?

3. How important is it for a mediator to understand how change occurs in people (for example, how the individual moves away from ethnocentrism, or how we transcend subjective culture, or how people change their minds) when mediating between parties of different cultures? Parties of different generations? Sexes?

4. What strategies would you consider most important for mediating between parties of diverse cultural or ethnic origins?

5. James was brought up in Montreal as part of a caring family. Throughout his youth and high school career, he was made fun of constantly because of his red hair and freckles. He became a very angry young man. Ultimately, he rejected his own family and background. He converted to Islam and travelled to Syria to join the Islamic State of Iraq and Syria (ISIS) to fight on its behalf for an Islamic state. Since the decline of ISIS, he has returned to Montreal. He sees his family and others around him as infidels. He feels his two sisters do not dress properly and therefore are *loose women*. He feels his parents do not understand true faith, but the imam at his mosque has indicated that James, now going by the name Abdul, should make peace with his family and give up his radical ways. He has therefore consented to enter into mediation with all or some of his family members. He admits he was radicalized and became an extremist while in Syria.

   Assume you are the mediator.

   a. Determine who from among the family should participate in the mediation.

   b. Do a self-assessment and examine your own understandings and attitudes in regard to the parties involved. Do you feel you have any inherent biases? What strategies would you employ to compensate for those biases?

   c. Finally, establish strategies and understandings that you feel will aid you in assisting the parties to create solutions that will enable them to move forward in peace and reunification.

6. Think about a negotiation experience you have had. Identify the factors that caused you to adopt one or more of the following styles:
   a. Yielding.
   b. Ignoring.
   c. Contending.
   d. Problem solving.

7. Which philosophies of mediation (evaluative, facilitative, transformative, or narrative) do the above negotiating styles translate into?
   a. Which style or philosophy of mediation is best suited to you?
   b. Do you have a backup or secondary style for situations where your primary style is ineffective?
   c. Give two examples of your using these approaches to help others through conflict situations.
   d. How did these approaches benefit the parties you were assisting?

e. Create a journal that reflects upon the two conflict situations you helped with. Assess the strengths and weaknesses of the styles and strategies you used. The reflective questions listed at the end of the chapter will help you with this.

8. Emotional intelligence includes self-awareness, self-management, social awareness, and relationship management skills. Reflect upon your strengths and weaknesses in each of these areas. Identify which of the four skill sets you are weakest in and devise a plan to develop that area.

9. Create a plan for a reflective journal that you would use after each mediation session. Make sure it includes all of the relevant areas discussed for reflective practice and make it personal to you.

Culture, Gender, and Power as Factors in Mediation

LEARNING OUTCOMES

After completing this chapter, you will be able to:

- Understand the differences between collective cultures and individualistic cultures with respect to conflict.

- Understand the mediator's need to view cultural difference from within each party's frame of reference.

- Understand the mediator's need to shift parties away from ethnocentrism to a more pluralistic approach to problem solving.

- Define *gender* and its impact upon mediation.

- Discuss how our perceptions of gender are created and how they may be changed.

- Define *power* in the context of mediation.

- Recognize the kinds of power that disputing parties may have.

- Understand how disputing parties try to use the power at their disposal.

- Understand that parties may or may not be aware of the power they possess and may or may not be inclined to use it.

- Understand how a mediator can manage the power dynamics in a mediation situation.

- In class discussions and exercises, practically apply new insights into culture, gender, and power.

- In a case study, assess the power imbalance between two disputing parties.

Cultural Differences

There are many ways of making meaning in this world. As we have said repeatedly, people have different ideas about what gives life value and what principles a person should live by. Individually and in larger groups, people have different cultures.

Cultures vary by region. For example, the cultures of Western Europe, North America, and Australia promote the rights of the individual over those of the group. Most other cultures in the world value the rights of the group over those of the individual. When people from different cultures confront each other, the result can be confusion, misunderstanding, and conflict.

Diversity Statistics

When mediators are conducting conflict analysis and resolution, they have to consider the role of culture—their own culture and that of others. This awareness and appreciation of other cultures and its role in conflicts is essential considering the changing world today (Laffier, Petrarca, & Hughes, 2017). People come from different cultures, religions, races, and social classes and speak different languages. In any relationship or setting, they bring with them their own sets of values, customs, and beliefs. Recently, Jeffreys (2016) referred to this as **cultural evolution**—the cultural growth and change within a society. It is predicted that by 2030, half of all US elementary school children will be children of colour. Countries around the world are seeing similar statistics. In Canada, this trend of diversification was referred to as the *mosaic effect* or the *mosaic culture* (Kalman, 2010). It is reported that more than 200 languages are spoken in the province of Ontario alone, and the number of households with English as their primary language is declining (Durham District School Board, 2011). Between 2001 and 2006, Ontario's visible minority population increased more than four times faster than the population as a whole. By 2017, about one-fifth of the Canadian population were members of diverse faith communities, including Islam, Hinduism, Buddhism, and Judaism, in addition to a growing number of individuals without a religious affiliation (Statistics Canada, 2010).

cultural evolution
the cultural growth and change within a society

CULTURE, GENDER, POWER

In April 2015, in France, Sihame Assbague started the hashtag #jeportemajupecommejeveux (I wear my skirt as I please). (Al-Solaylee, 2016, p. 237) This was in response to a teacher in a town in northern France who had sent home a 15-year-old Muslim student for wearing a long, black skirt, which, according to the teacher, was obviously demonstrating the girl's religious affiliation and thus was in violation of the country's official position on secularity.

Source: Al-Solaylee (2016).

Defining Cultural Competency

Cross (1988, p. 13) indicated that cultural competence is a "set of congruent behaviors, attitudes and policies that come together in an agency or professional and enable that agency or professional to work effectively in cross-cultural situations." Jeffreys (2016) adds that cultural competence is when a person in a position of care or support, whether that is policing, legal support, social work, therapy, or education, can provide culturally congruent care and there is a fit with the client's cultural beliefs, traditions, practices, and lifestyle. Providing this fit will be demonstrated through attitudes, beliefs, and actions. This may include: (1) valuing diversity, (2) being conscious of the dynamics inherent when cultures interact, (3) having cultural knowledge, and (4) having developed adaptations to service delivery reflecting an understanding of cultural diversity (Cross, Bazron, Dennis, & Isaacs, 1989).

However, cultural competency is not static; it changes in response to new situations, experiences, and relationships (Irish & Scrubb, 2012; Jeffreys, 2016; Livingstone, 2014). This suggests that a person can learn and improve his or her level of cultural competency. Take, for example, a police officer who has to work with the public on a daily basis and helps de-escalate conflicts. The more the police officer learns about another person's beliefs, values, and ways of communication, the more the officer can understand his or her approach to conflict and help find a solution. Besides direct interactions, other opportunities to develop cultural competency come from critical group discussions, educational courses, travel opportunities, cultural readings, and personal goal setting (Laffier et al., 2017). Personal reflection and opportunities for feedback on one's actions, attitude, and beliefs are important for the continued growth of cultural competency in professionals (Jeffreys, 2016).

Achieving cultural proficiency is important for all individuals, and it requires more than becoming culturally aware or practising tolerance. It is the ability to "identify and challenge one's own cultural assumptions, values and beliefs, and to make a commitment to communicating at the cultural interface" (Livingstone, 2014). In agreement with this view, Gorski (2010) stated that seeing other cultures as valuable resources for learning about a global community is foundational to address the **deficit ideology** that is so pervasive in society. However, a point to remember is that individuals and organizations may be at different levels of awareness, knowledge, and skills along the cultural competence continuum (Cross et al., 1989; Jeffreys, 2016). Furthermore, being culturally competent doesn't mean denying our own culture or

deficit ideology
the belief that inequalities result not from unjust social conditions, such as systemic racism or economic injustice, but from intellectual, moral, cultural, and behavioural deficiencies assumed

having to know everything about all cultures. Rather, it is about being willing to learn more about the cultural identities of the individuals in our personal or professional communities and using this knowledge to develop positive relationships, alternate world views, and meaningful learning experiences.

Conflict in Collective Cultures

collective cultures
cultures that value the group over the individual and emphasize the importance of harmonious relationships within the group

Collective cultures—cultures that value the group over the individual—tend to rely heavily on traditional values and traditional rituals; they take their bearings from the past. Rules of conduct and laws passed down through generations shape the identity of the group as a whole. The members of the culture follow these rules carefully for fear that social order and personal identity will be lost otherwise. These cultures value stability more than change. They have detailed codes of behaviour governing social interactions, events, and relationships. They prize age and experience above youthful ambition and energy. Time itself is viewed not as a medium of change but as a preservative element.

In these collective cultures, conflict is seen as social failure and is a source of guilt and shame to the disputants. Saving face by showing respect for the collective norms is a critical part of resolving conflict. Conflict is dealt with privately, out of sight of the whole community. The hope, in any conflict resolution process, is to restore the traditional community harmony, not to establish new meanings and values for the disputants. In collective cultures, an elder within the group, not an outside authoritarian figure, will be preferred as the engineer of peace.

Conflict in Individualistic Cultures

individualistic cultures
cultures that value the individual over the group and tend to prize such qualities as independence, creativity, freedom of thought and expression, and authority in decision making

In modern Western cultures, the individual is valued over the group. In other words, they are **individualistic cultures**. Independence, creativity, freedom of thought and expression, and authority in decision making are prized above conformity to group norms. Youth, wealth, and celebrity are preferred to age and wisdom. Group function is seen as the instrument of self-interest. One joins a club, for example, primarily to network and get ahead. Since individual success and mastery are the ultimate goals, time becomes a commodity to be saved, spent, and invested. In the workplace, we try to develop "efficiency measures" that save time, and "good time management" is viewed favourably.

stereotyping
assuming that people from a certain social category all have certain characteristics

In such cultures, authoritative third parties such as judges or arbitrators are entrusted with keeping social order; they resolve conflict case by case. Conflict, in modern Western societies, is often viewed negatively and with discomfort. But it is also seen as inevitable and as a potential source of growth and change. These individualistic societies tend to be future oriented, usually prepared to see change as something positive.

demonization
a disputant's use of stereotypes and falsifications to belittle, accuse, or attack the other side

Intercultural Conflict and Mediation

Cultures differ from each other in their values and interests, and a confrontation between them can easily produce conflict. **Stereotyping** occurs almost automatically in these cases, as does the **demonization** of differences.

intercultural conflict
conflict involving cultural differences between the parties—differences related to their frames of reference, values, myths, and stories

The mediator dealing with **intercultural conflict** needs to remember that no single culture has a monopoly on the truth. Each culture has its own frame of reference, its own assortment of values, myths, and stories. The mediator who grasps the cultural differences between the two disputants can help each get inside the other's frame of reference. This helps the parties feel respect and tolerance for each other's values and beliefs. This can lead, in turn, to their accepting new concepts of compatibility and new shared meanings as they work to resolve their dispute.

Mediating Intercultural Conflict

In mediating intercultural conflict, the mediator will try to understand the parties from within their own frames of reference. This involves being sympathetic toward their potential embarrassment and lack of confidence and their fear of being judged or of losing social or personal status. In the process, the mediator needs to be sensitive to both verbal cues and to non-verbal ones. There are also certain practical considerations for the mediator.

Controlling the Physical Space

When it comes to the physical conduct of a mediation that involves an intercultural factor, a mediator should consider the following measures:

1. Have the parties sit for conversations. For example, in some cultures, shorter people may feel intimidated talking to someone tall.

2. Be mindful of physical distances between the parties. Preferences can vary. People from Asian cultures, for example, may prefer to be at double arm's length from whomever they are conversing with. Preferred distances will vary depending on the parties' **gender** and culture but should always be considered by the mediator, especially if there's a chance of someone's personal space being violated.

   gender
   socially constructed notion of what is male and what is female

3. Create a comfort barrier—a table or desk or anything solid that masks portions of the body and creates a partial sense of privacy for the parties. If there is a need for the parties to stand while conversing, they should not face each other directly. Have them stand side by side instead. Again, this is for reasons of privacy. Standing side by side, neither party needs to feel the other's physical scrutiny.

4. Watch the parties' body language. This may tell you something about their comfort level. Watch out for physical behaviour that could be seen as intimidating. This will bring a defensive reaction from the other party; communication will be blocked, and listening will be suspended. Also, remember to maintain eye contact with the parties, but lower and modulate your voice to avoid being threatening yourself.

Regulating the Language

When it comes to regulating language matters in an intercultural mediation process, you might consider the following measures:

1. Encourage note taking. If you're dealing with a party for whom English is not a first language, you might consider having them take notes in their first language. In this case, though, you'll need to budget time for translating the notes and sharing their contents with others at the table.

2. Ask the parties beforehand for permission to slow the pace of dialogue and to ask them to repeat material if necessary.

3. Explain, summarize, and give feedback with the following rules of thumb in mind:

   a. Reduce matters to point form—simple, short sentences with clear, single points. This helps separate thoughts for easier understanding.

   b. Be prepared to explain those elements of communication that a non-native speaker of English might miss—for example, idioms (peculiarities of usage), the special meanings conveyed by tone, and the presence of sarcasm.

   c. Assist the parties with their word choices where meaning and clarity are important. Don't be too quick to do this, though; it may seem patronizing.

   d. Allow time for transitions between ideas, sources of information, and issues.

   e. Make sure parties are aware when the discussion shifts from ideas to numbers; ideas and numbers are processed differently in the brain, and a person new to the language will need time to adapt to the shift.

   f. Use written handouts for key goals, rules, concepts, or terminology. These will help the parties' awareness and understanding and will help them retain meanings.

4. For information that one party may, for cultural reasons, find difficult to understand or accept, consider written, as opposed to spoken, disclosure. This can allow the party to feel private at a difficult time.

5. People for whom English is a second language may often nod rather than repeat a question or ask for clarification. After you say something, watch for the quick nod and then the breaking off of eye contact, followed by a silent downward look. This may indicate that the party hasn't understood what you have said but is reluctant to ask you to clarify; they are too embarrassed. Watch for the sideways glance followed by the return of eye contact; this can indicate thought and comprehension.

6. Use silence as a tool to enhance communication and learning. Be patient, kind, and discriminating in cutting short silences.

It is important to remember that good mediating techniques and a willingness to understand are often the surest guides to dealing with the cultural factor in mediation. After all, people can be made to understand that their private realities are not truth itself but products of conditioning and environment. When they understand this, their perceptions of reality can be shifted. This is a crucial step in resolving conflict and creating peaceful relationships.

Transcending Subjective Culture

The individual's drive to understand other people is based partly on a desire to predict what these people will do. Such knowledge enables the individual both to protect their self-image and to maintain, enhance, and actualize the self. Haney (1979, p. 96) suggests that we form images of others because we need or want to predict their behaviour—or their reaction to our own behaviour. This, in turn, should enhance our ability to (a) cope or deal with them in whatever manner is required by the situation and (b) satisfy our needs in respect to the relationship. Needs are defined broadly here as including the kinds of needs you satisfy when you do very selfless or altruistic things, as well as needs that are more self-centred.

Predictability and control are important for protecting self-image. Radical, sudden, uncontrolled changes in a person we are dealing with can have a threatening effect on our self-image and sense of well-being.

What do Haney's theories mean for mediation in intercultural situations? The mediator knows that people develop within their own frame of reference and have a very deep-seated self-image. Self-image—in which culture plays a very important role—is a cherished possession that will be guarded from sudden, drastic, and uncontrolled change. Around this self-image is a comfort zone—a protective layer shielding the individual's self-image from environmental challenges. This protective buffer can be pierced, however, by radical change, positive or negative, and the results are painful and disorienting for the individual. Consider, for instance, a Muslim woman who is used to having her head and face covered being forced to remove her veil in public or a person from an Asian culture for whom "saving face" is of primary concern suddenly being called a liar before his or her peers. The mediator must be sensitive and gracious enough to respect the vulnerability of each party's self-image.

Haney (1979) maintains that the self-image of a person can be productively changed so long as the change occurs "in small, gradual, and above all self-controlled increments" (p. 94)—in other words, so long as the party can perceive themselves to be in charge of the process of change.

Cultural Awareness and Conflict Resolution

Too often, we see conflict resolved through *artifact redistribution*, that is, through the redistribution of money, resources, or goods. But such solutions are merely a quick fix, conveniently measurable. They don't address the underlying causes of conflict. Conflict resolution theory has at least moved us away from zero-sum, win–lose thinking and toward win–win thinking. The reality is that material considerations are bound up with considerations to do with relationship and symbol. Consider the emancipation of the slaves in the United States during and after the Civil War. Simply freeing slaves by purchasing their freedom produced a change, but it has taken centuries to ensure that symbols of freedom and equality apply uniformly to all the people, as dictated by the US Constitution. Change in one dimension will necessarily bring about changes in the others. Only when we see all three operating together, interrelated in time and space, do we develop the kind of awareness that enables us to bring true and durable change to self-image or cultural image that enables new direction or perception.

As mentioned in Chapter 1, Ferguson (2009) has identified four basic ways in which we change our minds. Review Ferguson's descriptions in more detail in Chapter 1, but now, for clarity, they are:

1. by exception,
2. by incremental change,
3. by pendulum swing, or
4. by paradigm shift.

Dealing with an intercultural dispute, a mediator can control the speed and intensity at which the parties change their minds. They can bring about slow, incremental shifts in awareness, knowing that parties can move only so far from the subjective culture where their reality is rooted.

Remember, the best vantage point for understanding another's behaviour is within that person's internal frame of reference.

A mediator must reach the parties where they are, within their own frame of reference. This must be their starting point—the place from which they can expand their awareness. They need to maintain their sense of control over this change. Conflict resolutions that involve imposed criteria or authoritative commands do not offer this control; they remain unconnected to the parties' realities and will most likely produce artificial, unsustainable results.

The Gender Factor

What is gender's relevance to mediation? This is really a twofold question. First, do our notions of gender—and, perhaps, our gender preferences—affect our view of how intergender conflicts should be resolved? Second, does an understanding of gender differences help a person mediate intergender conflict?

Shifting Views on Gender

power
in a dispute situation, the ability to make the other party think, believe, or behave in a way they would not voluntarily

As a factor in negotiation and mediation, gender is bound up with the factors of culture and **power**. Sex is biologically determined, but gender is socially constructed. For this reason, ideas about what is male, what is female, or what may constitute alternative or non-traditional definitions of gender vary across cultures and even across generations within a single culture.

The young learn about gender roles from their parents and from the cultural heritage they are born into. In Western culture, young boys tend to have blue rooms, young girls to have pink ones. Young girls read about princesses being swept off their feet and protected by handsome princes. They are expected to play with dolls and indulge in nurturing behaviour and fantasies of motherhood. Boys are expected to be rough and tumble. They play with guns and fancy themselves warriors. They are expected not to cry or show emotion.

gender expectations
culturally determined notions of how men and women are supposed to behave

In Western society, several developments have brought strong challenges to these traditional **gender expectations**. Since the Second World War, women have been a significant part of the labour force. Feminism has challenged male dominance and privilege in society. There has been a general movement toward equality between the sexes. Our understandings of gender and of gender-appropriate dress, activities, occupations, and attitudes have become much more flexible. Other cultures remain far more rigid and traditional in their views on gender.

Gender in Mediation

Mediators trying to promote change must understand that while a person's ideas about gender can be deconstructed and his or her different elements identified, these ideas are often deeply entrenched in the individual psyche, bound up with that person's most intimate convictions and beliefs. A party's thinking about gender must be understood from within their own frame of reference—in other words, in terms of their own culture and the stories that define them.

Kolb and Putnam (1997) have considered a different aspect of gender and mediation. Are gender biases built into negotiation and conflict resolution techniques? Kolb and Putnam agree with the principle mentioned above—that gender (unlike biological sex) is socially constructed, not hard-wired. According to this principle, we should not stereotype what is male and what is female because these things are, to some extent, flexible, not fixed. Nevertheless, Western culture continues to see certain qualities as typically male, others as typically female. Some of these gender-specific attributes are *socially empowered*—in other words, seen in positive terms within a society. Kolb and Putnam's concern is that, in a patriarchal or male-dominated society, positive female attributes don't play as large a part as they should in approaches to conflict resolution.

Positive qualities that Western culture normally views as male are "individuality, independence, competitiveness, objectivity, analytic and rational thinking, instrumentality, reasoning from universal principles, strategic thinking" (Kolb & Putnam, 1997, p. 89). Positive qualities that Western culture views as female are "community, dependence, cooperation, subjectivity, intuition and emotionality, expressivity, reasoning from the particular, and ad hoc thinking" (Kolb & Putnam, 1997, p. 89). Though they are socially constructed, these ideas about "male" as opposed to "female" approaches to problem solving can be useful to negotiators and mediators.

It has been suggested that men view certain matters quite differently than women do: the value of rights versus the value of relationships; equality versus equity; short-term goals versus long-term goals. Some people claim that high-powered men, compared with high-powered women, tend to be very aggressive in conflict situations and to adopt absolute, take-it-or-leave-it positions. Such men tend to be focused on their own goals. High-powered women tend to be less aggressive and exclusive in their behaviour and more inclusive and supportive in their actions.

Consider the following claims in the light of your own experience:

- Women tend to be more collaborative and relationship oriented than men. They care more about building and preserving relationships. They also tend to be more willing to accommodate others' actions and more inclined to take others' responses into account when planning strategy.
- Men are more focused on their own positions than women are and therefore more adversarial in nature. They place principles and rules ahead of the need to understand other people in a relationship.
- Men's tactics tend to be more position oriented and rigid than women's tactics are; women tend to be more flexible and supportive.

Whatever your response to these claims, you'll probably agree that someone mediating between men and women needs to be prepared for different orientations. Gender is an important factor in conflict resolution.

Power in Mediation

What Is Power?

When mediating a dispute, the mediator needs to be able to identify the types of power that might influence the process. Mediators also need to know how much power each party has and how much power each thinks the other has.

In a dispute situation, power can be defined as the ability to make the other party think, believe, or behave in a way they would not voluntarily. Like conflict itself, power is not, by definition, either negative or positive, and it may be a positive or negative factor in mediation.

Power Plays and How to Deal with Them

escalation

the growth of a conflict in intensity, complexity, and size

At the outset of a dispute, through the **escalation** period, and even in the early stages of mediation, parties often try to use power to achieve their ends. It is an overrated strategy and rarely successful. As has been discovered with the United States imposing tariffs on steel and aluminum on Canada in 2018, other parties are often forced to respond with strength or power by imposing their own tariffs. The result is that no one wins trade wars (Department of Finance Canada, 2018).

The two sides in a dispute may have more or less equal amounts of power, or, as is often the case, there may be a marked imbalance of power. The mediator needs to identify what kind of power each party has and how much.

At any point in the mediation process, one party may try to impose their power on the other side. They often do this by taking rigid positions. The mediator needs to be on guard against this and to be skilled enough to lead the parties away from positions and back toward interests. A party may overestimate their own social power or economic superiority and use bluffs to threaten the other party with social isolation or economic shutdown. In cases like this, the mediator might ask the party to explain exactly how they would ensure that their opponent was going to run out of money or allies. Parties will often threaten and try to bluff each other in dispute situations, claiming to have more power than they really have. For instance, one party may say to the other, "You can't win against me—I'll bleed you dry financially." In a case like this, the mediator may find the kinds of questions outlined in Chapter 7—clarifying, consequential, and probing questions—useful for defusing the situation. For example, the mediator might ask the party to explain exactly how they would ensure that their opponent ran out of money first. Sometimes identifying the sources of power in a dispute can be helpful. Making parties better aware of their own and the other side's power (in all its variations and types) can help them focus on interests. Power loses its "punch" when it is brought out of the shadows and exposed to both parties.

Power doesn't exist in isolation. It only exists within the context of a relationship between people, when certain things are important and valuable to both. Parties in a dispute, confronting each other over interests that seem mutually exclusive, have this kind of relationship.

Power dynamics in a dispute tend to be fluid, changeable. A good mediator recognizes this and is able to manage these dynamics in such a way that the parties stay focused on identifying and satisfying interests.

Power Imbalances

Power imbalances between the parties within a mediation can significantly alter the process. Disputes involving a significant power imbalance are never easy. A mediator will sometimes determine that these imbalances are so acute that they should not mediate, on professional and ethical grounds.

It might be expected that, in an unbalanced situation, the party with much greater power would usually achieve their goals at the less powerful party's expense and be satisfied with the result. In fact, a significant power imbalance increases the likelihood of threats, resistance, violence, and a solution satisfactory to neither party.

Lord Acton famously stated that "power corrupts, and absolute power corrupts absolutely." What this means is that an individual with power often develops a taste for more power, to the point of becoming tyrannical. In mediation, the mediator sometimes finds that the converse is also true: Too little power can corrupt as well. That is, a person without any power may react to his or her situation with violence and despair. A more powerful party that resorts to power tactics may be reducing the possibilities for creative, mutually satisfactory solutions since their tactics will provoke a defensive, hostile reaction from the other side. Once again, a mediator who can shift the parties from a power focus to an interest focus greatly increases the chances for a strong, durable agreement.

Manifestations of Power in the Mediation Process

How might different kinds of power come into play in the dispute-resolution process? The most common, and least effective, kind of power is **distributive (either/or) power**. Here, the focus is on one party's winning against—or gaining power over—another party. A distributive orientation to power tends to characterize win–lose, zero-sum approaches to managing conflict.

An alternative to distributive power is integrative power. **Integrative (both/and) power** is power used with, rather than against, another party. It is produced when the disputants join forces to achieve mutually acceptable goals. In other words, each party uses its power to achieve desirable outcomes for both parties. Integrative power tends to characterize win–win approaches.

Another kind of power is **designated (given) power**. This is power that one party gives to another party or gives to the relationship itself rather than keeping it for themselves. This kind of power is often found in modern workplaces. Any *employee empowerment* initiative is an example of designated power. Managers are using designated power when, instead of exercising their **legitimate power** to supervise their subordinates, they trust them to do a good job. Designated power also characterizes win–win approaches.

Real and Pretended Power

It often appears that one party in a dispute has more power than the other, but this may or may not actually be the case. Sometimes appearances are deceiving. One party may want to appear to have more power than the other side; they see this illusion as advantageous—a way of intimidating the other side. Parties in conflict often go to great lengths to deceive their opponents in this way.

Real or imagined, power exists and is a factor in dispute situations. There are different kinds of power exercised by parties in a dispute, and the mediator needs to be aware of them.

Other Kinds of Power

Power may come from a variety of sources. One type of power is legitimate power— power that is based on one party's formal authority over another party in a social

---

distributive (either/or) power
power aimed at controlling and defeating the other party

integrative (both/and) power
power used with, rather than against, another party, to the end of mutual gain

designated (given) power
power that one party gives to another party or gives to the relationship itself rather than keeping it for themselves

legitimate power
power that is based on one party's formal authority over another party in a social structure

structure. It is the kind of power, for example, that a manager has over a subordinate. Each higher-level manager within an organizational hierarchy has more legitimate power than the employees ranked below them do. Courts, judges, police, and other specially authorized figures have legitimate power over ordinary citizens. Parents have more legitimate power than their children.

Following are some other types of power (French & Raven, 1959) you might find in a dispute situation:

1. **Expert power** is based on special skills and abilities one party may have that are in short supply or that the other party in the dispute does not have.

2. **Coercive power** is based on punishments or undesirable consequences that one party can inflict on another if the other party doesn't comply with their wishes. It often takes the form of threats—"I can hurt you if you do not do what I want."

3. **Reward power** is based on rewards or desirable consequences that one party has to offer the other party—"I can give you something if you do what I want."

4. **Referent power** is based on personal characteristics that one party has that may cause the other party to like or admire them. This kind of power may seem unlikely in a dispute situation, but it very often exists.

5. **Network power** is based on who you know, how well you know them, and how their power (real or imagined) may be able to influence the dispute situation.

6. **Information power** is based on something you know—special information of some kind—that is not widely known and that the other party in the dispute does not know.

7. **Resource power** is based on some resource you have, such as time or money, that is not equally available to the other party.

Power is an important factor in mediation and negotiation. Each party to a conflict will try to use their power, real or illusory, to give them an advantage over the other side. A mediator who wishes to bring disputing parties to a place where their interests can be satisfied must understand power in its various forms and be able to manage it.

Summary: Culture, Gender, and Power

A mediator dealing with a dispute needs to find out if either party has culture-based assumptions or ideas about gender that may stand in the way of creative change and resolution. Ideas about gender can be deeply entrenched in the individual, and the mediator needs to be respectful in this regard. Remember, the parties in a dispute undertake the heroic journey toward conflict resolution in the face of deep-seated fears about personal chaos and the loss of identity. The greatest challenge for the mediator is to see beyond stereotypes and help the parties do the same. To accomplish this, the mediator needs to understand each party's personal reality. This is best done by seeking—and encouraging—understanding, not forcing agreement. The mediator can help parties bound by cultural or gender biases to understand their rights to independent determination and choice. The mediator, through his or her ability to sense the presence and use of power imbalances, can also help the parties to release their rigid positions and refocus their thoughts and discussions on interests. By recognizing the different types of power, the mediator can name, clarify, and demonstrate potential problems in the abuse or misuse of different kinds of power.

KEY TERMS

collective cultures, 132

cultural evolution, 130

deficit ideology, 131

demonization, 132

designated (given) power, 139

distributive (either/or) power, 139

escalation, 138

gender, 133

gender expectations, 136

individualistic cultures, 132

integrative (both/and) power, 139

intercultural conflict, 132

legitimate power, 139

power, 136

stereotyping, 132

REFERENCES

Al-Solaylee, K. (2016). *Brown: What being brown in the world today means (to everyone)*. Toronto: HarperCollins.

Cross, T.L. (1988, Summer). Services to minority populations: What does it mean to be a culturally competent professional? *Focal Point, 2*(4), 1–5.

Cross, T., Bazron, B., Dennis, K., & Isaacs, M. (1989). *Towards a culturally competent system of care*. Washington, DC: Georgetown University Child Development Center.

Department of Finance Canada. (2018). *Countermeasures in response to unjustified tariffs on Canadian steel and aluminum products*. Retrieved from https://www.fin.gc.ca/access/tt-it/cacsap-cmpcaa-1-eng.asp

Durham District School Board. (2011). Guidelines for inclusive language. Retrieved from https://www.ddsb.ca/AboutUs/EquityInclusiveEducation/Documents/Guidelines_Inclusive_Language.pdf

Ferguson, M. (2009). *The Aquarian conspiracy*. Los Angeles: TarcherPerigee.

French, J.R.P., & Raven, B. (1959). The bases of social power. In D. Cartwright (Ed.), *Studies in social power* (pp. 150–167). Ann Arbor, MI: University of Michigan Press.

Gorski, P.C. (2010). *Unlearning deficit ideology and the scornful gaze: Thoughts on authenticating the class discourse in education*. Virginia, MA: George Mason University.

Haney, W. (1979). *Communication and interpersonal relations* (4th ed.). Homewood, IL: Irwin-Dorsey.

Irish, C., & Scrubb, M. (2012, November 12). Five competencies for culturally competent teaching and learning. *HR Insights*. Retrieved from http://uichrinsights.blogspot.com/2012/11/five-competencies-for-culturally.html

Jeffreys, M.R. (2016). *Teaching cultural competence in nursing and healthcare* (3rd ed.). New York: Springer Publishing.

Kalman, B. (2010). *Canada: The land*. Ottawa: Crabtree Publishing.

Kolb, D., & Putnam, L. (1997). Through the looking glass: Negotiation theory refracted through the lens of gender. In S. Gleason (Ed.), *Workplace dispute resolution*. East Lansing, MI: Michigan State University Press.

Laffier, J., Petrarca, D., & Hughes, J.M. (2017). The need for promoting and developing cultural competency in future teachers. In L. Leavitt, S. Wisdom, & K. Leavitt (Eds.), *Cultural awareness and competency development in higher education* (pp. 148–167). Hershey, PA: IGI Global.

Livingstone, R. (2014, July 10). *What does it mean to be culturally competent?* Retrieved from https://wehearyou.acecqa.gov.au/2014/07/10/what-does-it-mean-to-be-culturally-competent

Statistics Canada. (2010). *Canada's ethnocultural portrait: The changing mosaic*. Retrieved from http://publications.gc.ca/pub?id=9.562362&sl=0

QUESTIONS AND EXERCISES

1. Consider the following scenario: A father of the Muslim faith, living now in Canada but born in the Middle East, has recently come into conflict with his teenage daughter over her refusal to wear in public the headgear appropriate to his religion and tradition. She is part of a Canadian peer group with values quite unlike her father's, from a generation of young Canadians inclined to question their parents' beliefs. The father has threatened to turn her out of the house unless she dresses in the way he thinks appropriate.

   Consider what types of power are operative in the above scenario. Does the father have legitimate power? Does the power of social pressure have an impact?

   Imagine that father and daughter are willing to pursue mediation and that you are to be the mediator. What strategies will you use to help them understand, if not agree with, each other's point of view? How will you manage the power dynamic between the parties to ensure a balanced discussion? How will you help them assess the risks of non-agreement?

2. In a society that is male dominated (that is, patriarchal), do we tend to see male qualities as preferable and a path to success? Are female qualities devalued accordingly? How might we address this problem and enrich both negotiation and mediation in the process?

3. How can assessing the disputants on the basis of culture and gender help in the pre-mediation process of conflict analysis?

4. Are female mediators likely to approach the process of mediation differently than their male counterparts do? In what ways are their techniques likely to be different? What are likely to be the strengths and weaknesses of each gender's approach?

5. Consider how interests, in the context of negotiation and mediation, may vary according to the culture of the disputant. For instance, Western culture highly values freedom of expression; another may see modest dress as all important. A culture of religious fundamentalism will regard the freedom of religion prized in the West as a bad thing. How could a clear understanding of the deep cultural differences between two disputants help you prepare for a negotiation or mediation?

The Mail-Order Bride

Costancia Reyes, 22 years of age, has been married to Arthur Stratton, 57, for the past six years. Costancia is what is often referred to as a *mail-order bride*. She was born and raised in the Philippines and had not been outside of her native country until her family and the agents working on Arthur's behalf arranged for her to emigrate to Canada in order to become his wife. The two had never met prior to their marriage. Arthur is a successful insurance broker and has many friendships and interests outside of work. Costancia is, for the most part, excluded from that part of Arthur's life. Arthur expects her to be what he approvingly terms a *traditional wife*. This means that she cooks, cleans, manages the household, and caters to Arthur as he sees fit. They do not have any children.

Recently, Costancia has considered leaving Arthur. She finds her situation intolerable. Her financial dependence upon him is total. She lives in a suburb of Toronto, near Arthur's office, that has no Filipino community. Costancia has friendly relations with a couple of neighbours but no close friends and certainly no Filipino friends. Her Roman Catholic faith has sustained her during her difficult times, but Arthur, who has no religious affiliations, is not supportive of her attending mass and she is rarely allowed to, much to her dismay. Her faith and her allegiance to her family in the Philippines, who arranged her marriage in the hope that it would bring her a better life, have contributed to her staying with Arthur longer than she might have otherwise. But while she believes she has a moral and familial duty to stay with Arthur, she is unhappy to the point of desperation. About a year ago, she confided to her sister in a letter that she was thinking of leaving. She has not heard from any of her family members since.

Power Analysis

At first glance, it may appear that there is a significant power imbalance between Arthur and Costancia. Is this, in fact, the case? Try to determine how much of the various types of power each party possesses.

Assuming a total of 10 points for each type of power, allocate the appropriate number of points to Costancia and Arthur. Total the two columns at the bottom of the sheet.

	Costancia	Arthur
Legitimate power	_____	_____
Expert power	_____	_____
Coercive power	_____	_____
Reward power	_____	_____
Referent power	_____	_____
Network power	_____	_____
Information power	_____	_____
Resource power	_____	_____
TOTAL	_____	_____

Consider the following:

1. Is there an insurmountable imbalance of power between Arthur and Costancia?

2. Does one party have more of some types of power than the other does?

3. How would you, as a mediator, create a better balance of power between Arthur and Costancia? Is this possible?

4. What skills would you use to shift the focus of the parties from power to interests?

PART IV

Professional Applications

Having said much about the philosophy, techniques, and art of mediation, we will end this text on a practical note. Our last chapters will examine mediation as a professional practice. It is currently the case that mediators, unlike lawyers, paralegals, and doctors, are not governed by legislation and licensing requirements. The attorney general of Ontario has indicated that this situation is unlikely to change any time soon. But mediation is a rapidly growing profession and it needs to have professional standards.

The Canadian Bar Association has created codes of conduct that set ethical standards for mediators. These codes of conduct, while not legally binding for all mediators, have been adopted by the attorney general of Ontario for certain practitioners—namely, the mediators who are included on the mandatory mediation lists for dealing with civil litigation cases. These codes of conduct serve as an excellent guide for all mediators. They offer guiding principles for a mediator's conduct and decision making. They give the public a means of protecting itself from practitioners who lack the necessary skills and knowledge to mediate effectively. And, from a public relations standpoint, these codes of conduct promote confidence in mediation as a valid process for resolving disputes. Other interested organizations, such as the Ontario Association of Family Mediators, also have clear standards that prospective mediators must meet to gain their certifications. Standards of this sort help to establish a consistent level of professional performance and also to educate practitioners about liability considerations, especially those involving conflict of interest, bias, and confidentiality. These considerations, and other considerations related to ethical codes of conduct, are the subject of Chapter 14.

The following chapters will examine some other practical requirements for mediators: for example, the need to create a precedent for your contract to mediate and the need to be covered by errors and omissions insurance. These chapters will also examine the growth of mediation in our society. Mediation is increasingly popular both as a peaceful, cost-efficient means of settling disputes and as a source of meaningful careers. This part of the discussion may be useful to those planning a career in mediation.

Lastly, these chapters will examine some of the professional bodies now emerging to represent and direct the developing profession. Organizations such as the ADR Institute of Canada or the Ontario Association of Family Mediators may soon be crucial in establishing guidelines for professional development and certification and in giving members the opportunity to network within the profession.

Community Mediation

10

LEARNING OUTCOMES

After completing this chapter, you will be able to:

■ Define and identify communities.

■ Assess the causes of community disputes.

■ Understand the importance of identifying the legitimate stakeholders in community disputes.

■ Understand how to prepare for a community mediation.

■ Understand how to select the appropriate dispute-resolution process for a community mediation.

■ With questions and class exercises, practically apply the principles of community mediation.

Mediation in Communities

Community mediation is on the rise. The notion that community disputes can be handled in a win–win fashion, inexpensively and non-adversarially, is attractive. This idea is particularly attractive when we define communities in a broad sense and see the many areas where mediation might be useful. That is, the term *community* can apply not only to neighbourhoods but also to schools, campuses, residential condominiums, service clubs, or faith communities. The ordinary workplace, too, can qualify as a type of community whose conflicts may be served by mediation.

Community is not strictly limited to a group represented or connected by a physical place or space as those noted above. Many of them are; however,

> the conception of community extends beyond locality (with its spatial or geographic communities) and embraces a multiplicity of groups and networks to which, it is believed, we all belong. This conception of community, which is argued to be more in keeping with contemporary social life, does not rely upon a fixed assumption of where a community will be found. Rather, it develops upon the notion of "communities of care"—the networks of obligation and respect between the individual and everyone who cares about him or her the most, which are not bounded by geography. (Bazemore & Schiff, 2001, p. 135)

Backgrounds

retributive justice system
our society's main system of justice, which treats illegal behaviour with punishment alone

Community conflicts used to be seen as the concern of the **retributive justice system** alone. In other words, crimes and disputes in communities were the domain of lawyers, judges, and the legal system. Justice was imposed by a third party. This system emphasized due process, formal rules, and the retrospective determination of facts. Punishment was based on guilt, blame, and the need for retribution.

Alternatives to this retributive form of justice have existed in many societies for centuries. In Ontario, alternatives began to appear in the 1970s. In Kitchener, Ontario, two Mennonite probation officers suggested to a judge that two youths responsible for extensive property damage might—rather than be sentenced in the normal fashion—face their victims directly and work out with them a solution based on apology, forgiveness, action, and compensation. The judge permitted this, and it proved to be a successful solution.

This event made people aware that the participants themselves could resolve problems and conflicts in the community in very positive ways, with lasting benefits to the community. Dealt with in the conventional ways—handed off to the justice system or ignored—conflicts within the community simply escalate. People began to understand this and to believe that communities should take responsibility for resolving their own conflicts and should reap the benefits of doing so. People began to question the law enforcement perspective on community conflict—that it is simply a matter of a broken rule or a broken law. They began to accept that communities could resolve their problems peacefully and, in doing so, increase understanding and communication between community members.

Forms of Community Mediation

Community mediation has taken many forms, including government-sponsored mediation services and volunteer neighbourhood boards. The value of these services is widely accepted, but their growth has been limited by two factors: the need for funding and the need for codes of ethics and a system of uniform practices. There has been a lack of consistency in how mediation is practised and taught. This is because many of the people practising it and teaching it are volunteers who lack formal training themselves. Despite these minor problems, mediation's role in resolving community disputes is growing.

In its wide-ranging effects, community mediation brings to mind Bush and Folger's (2004) radical view that mediation can transform our whole society. Boulle and Kelly (1998) note how mediation's role has grown in our communities:

> The various community dispute resolution services deal with a wide variety of matters. There was an initial focus on interpersonal neighbourhood disputes involving such matters as overhanging trees, noise and other disruptions of the peace, personal abuse, and troublesome pets. Broader neighbourhood issues, such as community behavior and housing estates or re-planning of residential areas, have also been mediated. There have also been many mediations and facilitation within community organizations, including schools, parents and friends associations, and voluntary support groups. A growing area of interest and application is in the school context where training of children and teenagers to be peacemakers and peer mediators, as young as kindergarten age, is taking place using various means such as storytelling, role-playing and traditional drama. (p. 232)

For community mediation to work, you need to identify who the actual **stakeholders** are. Knowing who should be a part of the process, what their interests are, what their role in the process should be, what type or types of conflict are present—this knowledge is as important in community mediation as it is in other kinds of mediation; you need this knowledge in order to design and develop strategies for an effective mediation process. In fact, community mediations often require elaborate, multi-party processes. Designing such processes is one of the challenges that community mediators face.

stakeholders
the people who have a stake in the outcome of a dispute

Multi-party negotiation and mediation differ from two-party disputes in a number of ways (Lewicki, Barry, Saunders, & Tasa, 2011). The most obvious one is that there are more parties at the table. However, mediators must also consider informational and computational complexity (more issues, perspectives, and overall information), social complexity (greater impact of interpersonal and group dynamics), and procedural and strategic complexity (managing who is at the table and when, who speaks for whom, etc.). Many of these issues are preliminary in nature and must be decided before actual entry into negotiation or mediation.

IN THE NEWS

BALTIMORE RISING

Baltimore Rising is a 2017 documentary film showing multi-party community negotiations between such diverse groups as activists, police, community leaders, citizens, and gang members to bring stability to Baltimore in the wake of protests and riots that occurred following the 2015 death of Freddie Gray while he was in police custody.

Defining Community

community
a gathering of people
who have something in
common—physical space,
beliefs, values, or interests

Community is never just a place. Communities give people their sense of identity and of belonging, their sense of being at home in the world. To understand what a person's community is, you need to look beyond physical context and consider ideology as well—belief systems, notions of authority, ideas of proper relationship and protocol.

In a community mediation, as in any other kind of mediation, the mediator's role is to help people modify their thinking. (How people think determines how they act.) To do this, the mediator first needs to *understand* their thinking. Listening to people's stories in an open-minded way can help the mediator accomplish this.

When dealing with a community dispute, the mediator may find it useful to think—and have the disputants think—in terms of a *community story*. Questions like the following may help move the parties toward mutual understanding and help encourage a shift in thinking: "What is missing from your community story?" "Are you listening respectfully to the other party's story?" "What are the assumptions that each of you has about the other party's intentions?"

Types of Communities

Let's consider how people in two typical communities—religious organizations and neighbourhoods—see themselves, and let's consider how each of these communities might shape its members' beliefs, values, and relationship concerns. These are the kinds of things a mediator needs to know.

Religious Organizations

Religious affiliation is often inherited and unquestioned. The positions taken by a disputant from this kind of community may be based on unchallenged dogma or on questionable assumptions about the universe. The mediator needs to tread carefully; he or she needs to step back and view the situation objectively. Gathering information, considering alternatives, and promoting respectful listening are critically important. One advantage the mediator has in this context is that most religions prize peaceful relationships. The prospect of amicable relations and mutually beneficial solutions will usually appeal to a religious person.

value conflicts
conflicts that arise when
people have different
criteria for valuing ideas
or behaviour or have
goals based on mutually
exclusive value systems

When dealing with **value conflicts**—that is, disputes over ethics or beliefs or between parties with very different value systems—the mediator should not pretend to have all the answers to faith-related questions. The best approach is to address value questions in an open and honest way and to seek common ground between the parties (for example, try to think of transcendent goals they might share). The mediation process itself will often create a shift in the parties' feelings about each other, causing anger to ebb and hearts to heal.

Neighbourhoods

Neighbourhoods vary. Neighbourhoods in small towns may be closely knit, and the people within them may have much in common, including a sense of pride in their community. Neighbours in larger communities, such as major urban centres, may not know each other at all; they may be neighbours based on physical proximity alone. On the other hand, urban neighbours will always have something in common: a desire for safety, for privacy, and for public facilities (for example, parks and recreation centres) they can all share.

The mediator who is dealing with community conflict at the neighbourhood level needs to know who the actual stakeholders are—needs to know, in other words, that the parties with actual interests in the dispute are present at the table. Sometimes, parties with no real stake in the dispute get involved along the way. These hangers-on need to be removed from the process or kept out of it until their presence is appropriate. Mediation for neighbourhood disputes needs to be carefully designed. Should the process include stakeholders only? Or should it also include—and at what point—others who want to be part of the process?

Another issue is that of excluded stakeholders. One of the dangers when mediating a neighbourhood dispute is in "failing to define, demarcate and distinguish 'community', resulting in inconsistent, unmanageable, and unprincipled practices" (Bazemore & Schiff, 2001, p. 328). An additional consideration is that there may not be a ready-made or pre-defined community: "In other words, the question is not so much whether community does or does not exist, but rather *at what stage of development is the community and how much direction and assistance does it need*" (p. 312).

Coltri (2004) discusses how groups or individuals who feel they should be part of a community mediation but have been left out can seriously impede the mediation's progress toward a workable outcome. Excluded groups or individuals often dislike any settlement that is being considered and may actively attempt to sabotage the process.

Types of Neighbourhood Conflicts

The mediator of a neighbourhood dispute must keep in mind that he or she is dealing with people's private homes and lives. The strong territoriality that people feel in their own homes can create real friction over such basic things as the placement of a fence, the condition of a hedge, or the availability of parking spaces. Children's behaviour—for example, their noisiness or their trespassing—can create profound problems between neighbours. Unequal access to commodities of some kind or to local facilities (for example, community centres, libraries, golf courses) can also be a source of conflict. Neighbourhood disputes occur over predictable matters.

In neighbourhoods where people are divided across racial, faith, or gender lines, value-oriented problems can arise. These kinds of conflicts often involve stereotyping and prejudice, and they escalate quickly. They often lead to some person or family being singled out and identified as *the problem*. Racism and intolerance can result in conspiracies to exclude, restrict, and evict these *problem* people.

Neighbourhood conflicts can also have less obvious causes. Sometimes there are old relationship grievances—betrayals or broken friendships—underlying a dispute. Sometimes these prior grievances are what the current conflict is really about. Sometimes there is a recreational quality to these disputes; people eagerly take up sides and proclaim their loyalties rather than actually work to resolve the problem. Some people would rather assert their dominance over their neighbours than try to help the community. The mediator's job is to be aware when these kinds of things may be happening and to return the parties to a positive sense of community and common ground.

In dealing with neighbourhood disputes, the mediator should also be aware that mental health problems can surface in the parties involved—paranoia, for example, or dementia in older people. Where these conditions arise, the mediator may need to add psychological procedures and qualified professionals to the process.

ARBITRATION IN THE COMMUNITY

In 1986, a Muslim community in Toronto "purchased a small Protestant church in a modest residential neighbourhood" (Isin & Siemiatycki, 2002) and converted it into a mosque with only minor modifications. By 1996, the congregation had grown too large for the building and they sought to expand and redesign the structure. Resistance from neighbourhood residents was significant and included claims that the proposed structure would alter the existing character of the neighbourhood, parking spaces in the community would be overwhelmed, and property values would decline. This resistance lasted until the Ontario Municipal Board (a provincial arbitration tribunal) decided in favour of expanding the mosque, albeit with modifications, in 1997.

Community Mediation Service Providers

convenor
the representative of a mediation service who makes initial contact with the disputing parties in order to determine whether mediation is an appropriate means of resolving their conflict

Community mediation service providers are often brought into a conflict by referral. One of the disputing parties will contact a mediation representative by phone or in person. The representative, often called a **convenor**, will enter into discussions with the disputant to determine if mediation is an appropriate process for that conflict. If the situation involves special factors, such as psychological problems, the convenor may simply refer the party to a specialist, such as a mental health professional.

But, if the situation is appropriate, and the disputant remains interested in mediation, the convenor will send a mediator to meet with the party and educate them about the nature of mediation. The mediator will attempt to determine if mediation or negotiation or some other dispute-resolution process would be most appropriate. If the initial party still wants to proceed with mediation, the mediator will contact the other disputant and request to meet with them. The mediator's visit to the other party will determine whether mediation is going to be the way of resolving this dispute. If it is, the mediator will gather the information he or she needs and begin the planning process. If the mediation involves only two parties, mediation may proceed face to face or by way of shuttle mediation. In a **shuttle mediation**, there is no face-to-face contact between the disputants; the mediator *shuttles* back and forth between the parties until they reach agreement. If the conflict involves more than two parties, the next step will be to design a process to accommodate all of them.

shuttle mediation
a mediation process in which there is no face-to-face contact between the disputants; the mediator "shuttles" back and forth between the parties until they reach agreement

Other Communities

What beliefs and values and goals a community has will depend on what kind of community it is—a post-secondary school, a service club, a distinct ethnic group, a family, or even a particular workplace. Each of these will have a particular relationship to authority and a certain preference for how conflict is settled. Even within one of these communities, the belief systems and orientations of members will vary.

As a mediator, your job is to assess what beliefs, positions, or processes are causing a particular conflict and then intervene to help the parties find a solution. Careful investigation and preparation will help with this.

Preparing for a Community Mediation

Community mediation can be complex. The conflict may involve many parties and issues and may have a substantial history. When this is the case, the process for intervention needs to be carefully designed. A number of things need to be considered.

1. Community Expectations

Approaches to conflict vary in communities as they do elsewhere. **Power-based approaches** are sometimes favoured. The expectation in work environments or religious communities, for example, is that people in positions of authority—managers, officers, religious leaders, boards of directors—will impose their power in resolving disputes. All community members will expect this. In some cases, they will also expect a **rights-based approach**. That is, the parties will expect to be able to present their case before an authoritative third party who will decide on a winner according to established criteria. In other community disputes, people will expect interest-based methods for problem solving. They will favour healing processes and integrated solutions for everyone involved.

The community's preferences will obviously affect what kind of intervention is chosen for a dispute. Different types of problem solving may be used at different stages of the process. For example, one approach may be used for selecting which community members will take part in the mediation, another for establishing the issues to be addressed, and another for determining the order of presentation during the process. For large disputes, you need to determine early on who will represent the different parties at the table and how much authority these representatives will have. And you need to determine the process they will use to report back to their constituent groups for direction, confirmation, or approval.

In short, the mediator needs to gather information about the community's dispute-resolution preferences and build them into the mediation's design.

power-based approach an approach to conflict resolution whereby people in positions of authority—managers, officers, religious leaders, boards of directors—use their power to resolve disputes

rights-based approach an approach to conflict resolution that allows the disputing parties to present their case before an authoritative third party who will decide on a winner according to established criteria

2. Assessing the Community's Goals

As a mediator, you need to look into the purposes and goals of the parties you are dealing with. You will learn about these things, and about their values and preferences, by listening to the parties in a respectful way. You can also learn whether they would prefer a distributive solution or an integrated one. This knowledge will help you design the process. Your respectful listening will also show them how they ought to behave themselves.

3. Assessing the Type of Conflict Involved

In Chapter 3, following Moore's (2014) categories, we listed the five types of conflicts: relationship conflicts, data conflicts, interest conflicts, structural conflicts, and value conflicts. Preparing for a community mediation, the mediator needs to determine which type of conflict is involved. This knowledge will help you determine the most appropriate intervention. Has the conflict arisen from data problems, with one or more of the parties misinformed in some way or lacking access to needed information? Are there relationship problems or value problems within the group? Is there a structural or hierarchical problem within the group? Are there group members whose interests are not being acknowledged or respected? Assessing such things will help you determine which issues should be dealt with first, what information you need before beginning the process, and who the actual stakeholders are.

4.   Assessing the Stakeholders

Assessing the stakeholders means determining who actually needs to be involved in the process. Are the parties who are most deeply concerned in the dispute coming forward? Do they have the authority to make decisions? Are there people missing? Are there people present who should not be? In complicated community mediations, you sometimes need to determine exactly what issues and interests are involved before you can determine who the real stakeholders are. Do people really represent who they say they represent? Are their interests really the same as those of the people they represent? Are they really part of the group they seem to belong to? How should each of the groups be defined, established, and represented? Is there a need to educate some or all of the parties about the dispute-resolution process? Should there be a mechanism built into the process so that the representatives can consult their groups at various stages? These kinds of assessments will help produce a mediation process that is inclusive, representative, and fair.

5.   Determining Methods and Stages

Keep in mind the various dispute-resolution processes available: negotiation, mediation, arbitration, and litigation. These are all valid responses to conflict. Consider each option with regard to timing, costs, process, and likely consequences. Matching the process to the expectations of the community may require using different approaches at different stages. For example, some stakeholders will use negotiation to decide on their representatives and to determine their issues and goals. Then they will call on some third-party authority or authoritative internal member to help them decide which issues should be retained. Perhaps they will need to use some simple form of arbitration in determining which members will represent them at the table or—in a case where issues or interests are unclear—in selecting agenda items.

As you try to decide on an appropriate process, always keep in mind the issues of time, costs, and access. And be flexible, at any stage of the process, about allowing members of the group to reconsider a previous stage or to communicate with members outside the group if they need something clarified.

Community disputes are really just another area where mediation can be usefully applied. Remember, though, that this type of mediation can run from straightforward two-party disputes to multi-issue, multi-party disputes with much at stake and many stakeholders. A successful intervention is based on thorough investigation, research, planning, and design at the pre-mediation stage.

KEY TERMS

community, 148
convenor, 150
power-based approach, 151

retributive justice system, 146
rights-based approach, 151
shuttle mediation, 150

stakeholders, 147
value conflicts, 148

REFERENCES

Bazemore, G., & Schiff, M. (2001). *Restorative community justice: Repairing harm and transforming communities.* Cincinnati: Anderson Publishing.

Boulle, L., & Kelly, K.J. (1998). *Mediation: Principles, process, practice* (Canadian ed.). Toronto: Butterworths Canada.

Bush, R.A.B., & Folger, J.P. (2004). *The promise of mediation: The transformative approach to conflict.* San Francisco: Jossey-Bass.

Coltri, L.S. (2004). *Conflict diagnosis and alternative dispute resolution.* Upper Saddle River, NJ: Pearson.

Isin, E.F., & Siemiatycki, M. (2002). Making space for mosques. In S.H. Razack (Ed.), *Race, space, and the law: Unmapping a white settler society* (pp. 185–209). Toronto: Between the Lines.

Lewicki, R.J., Barry, B., Saunders, D.M., & Tasa, K. (2011). *Essentials of negotiation* (Canadian ed.). Toronto: McGraw-Hill Ryerson.

Moore, C.W. (2014). *The mediation process: Practical strategies for resolving conflict* (4th ed.). San Francisco: Jossey-Bass.

QUESTIONS AND EXERCISES

1. Think about a dispute in your neighbourhood that fell short of being a matter for the justice system but that led to increasing antagonism between the groups involved. Who was involved, how did it escalate, and how might it have been converted to a positive experience for the community?

2. Describe the distinctions you see between the court system and the mediation process for dealing with community disputes. What considerations should determine which of these processes is chosen?

3. Consider the fact that courts have adopted or approved of mediation for many purposes: They prescribe mandatory mediation in civil matters; it is used to work out family agreements; and for criminal matters, it is part of the victim–offender negotiation involved in sentencing. Given these now official roles for mediation, is there a possibility of its being co-opted and compromised by the formality of the court system?

4. Consider the following situation. In a given neighbourhood, there has been long-standing antagonism between dog owners and people who don't own dogs. The latter group complains about the noise the dogs make, the threat they pose to children, and, of course, the scoopable messes they leave on people's lawns. Over time, the two groups have become polarized and are now hostile to each other. A few times, people have almost come to blows over the presence of a dog in the wrong place at the wrong time. The neighbourhood consists of approximately 40 households. Half the people in the neighbourhood want dogs to be kept out of the area entirely. The other half sees it as an issue of basic freedom for dogs and dog owners.

    Assess the above situation to determine how the problem should be dealt with. Which parties should be involved, in what capacity, and what strategies should be used in setting up a mediation?

5. For the situation described in the previous question, develop a presentation explaining to the two parties why mediating their conflict might be preferable to ignoring it or to allowing it to escalate until the police have to step in.

Workplace Mediation 11

LEARNING OUTCOMES

After completing this chapter, you will be able to:

- Understand how conflict is usually dealt with in business organizations.

- Understand some of the most common types of organizational conflicts.

- Understand how an organization's structure and culture affect how it deals with conflict.

- Compare the relative effectiveness of power-based, rights-based, and interest-based approaches to conflict in the business world.

- Apply the principles of workplace mediation in role-playing exercises.

Business Organizations as Communities

In the previous chapter, we examined community mediation. We mentioned there that business organizations are essentially communities, each having its own internal structure, culture, rules, regulations, and procedures. Although we tend to see businesses as highly rational institutions driven purely by the bottom line, the truth is that they are as prone to conflict as any community.

In this chapter's discussion of workplace mediation, we will take a broad view of what a business is; we will include in that category any organization that exists to achieve a set of goals. This category includes volunteer organizations, charities, public and private sector businesses—all for-profit and not-for-profit organizations.

As in any community mediation, a workplace mediation may involve multiple stakeholders (individuals or groups) with competing interests. Identifying these stakeholders and their varying interests is very important.

Typical Workplace Disputes

Dispute situations in the workplace are as varied as dispute situations anywhere. In many cases, these disputes have little to do with the work being done. Certain conflict situations are typical:

1. Sometimes conflict develops between equal co-workers—in other words, between people with equal power in the workplace. One party may become resentful because they feel the other is not *pulling their weight*. Interestingly, the other employee often feels the same resentment toward the accuser.

2. Sometimes a power differential does exist between the parties in conflict. A manager has more **legitimate power**, or position power, than a subordinate and may be in conflict with them. For example, let's say a senior manager asks one of their junior managers to work overtime. The junior manager receives no extra compensation for this, and there is no formal requirement that they be given any. The junior manager feels they have been asked to do this far too often and are starting to resent the fact that the senior manager can require it of them. They complain to the senior manager, who orders them to work the overtime and refuses to discuss the matter further.

3. Sometimes workplace conflicts are between employees and outside parties—for example, between a customer and a customer service representative. Let's say a customer attempts to return a product to the store where it was bought. The warranty for the product expired the day before, so the customer service representative refuses to accept the returned item. The customer complains that they were unable to return the product the day before because the store closed earlier than usual. They get into a shouting match, and the customer is escorted from the store by security personnel.

4. Conflicts in the workplace are sometimes between competing groups, teams, or departments within the organization. For example, the accounting and marketing departments in a large company may be in conflict over how much money should be spent on a new advertising campaign.

5. Sometimes conflicts occur in unionized environments where **collective agreements** exist. A collective agreement is a contract between the management of a business and its unionized workers. It is achieved through a

legitimate power
power that is based on one party's formal authority over another party in a social structure

collective agreement
a contract between the management of a business and its unionized workers, achieved through a process of collective bargaining

process of collective bargaining between the two parties. It contains various terms and conditions that regulate the employment relationship between the workers and management. Where a collective agreement is in place, certain dispute-resolution mechanisms, such as formal grievance procedures, may already exist. Typically, collective agreements contain provisions for grievance handling that may lead to arbitration proceedings.

6. Collective agreements have begun to incorporate mediation into the grievance-handling process. There is growing recognition that mediation is cheaper than arbitration. It is also less time consuming. The productivity of a business is likely to suffer during the period between the submission of the grievance and the arbitration ruling—any unresolved conflict is disruptive.

7. Mediation is also useful for handling grievances because it addresses the parties' underlying interests. Arbitration processes, which are rights based, do not do this.

IN THE NEWS

MEDIATION SUCCESS RATE IN THE FEDERAL PUBLIC SERVICE

The Federal Public Service in Canada uses mediation as a workplace dispute-resolution option. The success rate for mediation in this context is impressive:

> The Tribunal's mediation services offer stakeholders the opportunity to resolve staffing complaints based on an interest-based model of dispute resolution. From April 1, 2014 to October 31, 2014, 61 mediations were conducted, resulting in 131 complaint files being processed and 110 complaints being settled. This represented an overall success rate of 84%, with similar rates whether mediations were conducted by telephone, by videoconference or in person. Since 2005, 1,531 files were processed during mediation sessions, with an average success rate of 84 percent. (p. 4)

Source: Public Service Staffing Tribunal (2015).

The Five Kinds of Conflict

The five kinds of conflict—structural, relationship, interest, data, and value (Moore, 2014)—occur in the workplace as they do elsewhere. In the workplace, they *may* look something like the following:

1. *Structural conflicts.* For example, let's say a supervisor requests that a subordinate spend more time working on projects within their department. The organization has recently moved from a traditional hierarchical structure to a so-called matrix structure in which employees typically work on a variety of projects under the supervision of many different team leaders. In other words, the employees are shared among the team leaders. When deadlines approach, the various team leaders often call on the employees, whom they regard as *their* team members, to devote more time to the projects they lead. Team leaders often feel they are in conflict with one another and with their team members. The organizational structure, then, has been a contributing factor to the conflicts that emerge.

2. *Relationship conflicts.* For example, two project team members disagree about the goals of the project they are working on together. As deadlines approach, their communication breaks down, tensions escalate, and, ultimately, the project stalls and the deadline is missed.

3. *Interest conflicts.* For example, two employees on a work project have very different interests in terms of the outcomes they desire from the project. One seeks recognition from senior management, hoping for a promotion. The other is interested in the quality of the project itself and disapproves of what they see as the other employee's concern about personal gain.

4. *Data conflicts.* For example, recent cost pressures have caused senior leaders to consider reducing the number of employees. One member of the senior leadership team claims that the organization is on the verge of bankruptcy and has no alternative but to lay off employees immediately. Another member claims that the organization is financially sound and can easily survive until business conditions improve.

5. *Value conflicts.* For example, the two senior leaders from the previous example have fundamental philosophical differences about downsizing as a strategy. One considers it to be a betrayal of employee trust and believes it should never be done. The other considers it an acceptable business decision and feels that employees and their trust are not factors to be considered at all.

Organizational Structure, Power, and Mediation

We have emphasized that interest-based mediation can bring closure and satisfactory outcomes to a variety of conflict situations. This certainly applies to workplace conflicts. You might think, then, that business organizations would embrace mediation as an attractive approach to conflict management. Business organizations have compelling reasons to keep their employees satisfied in this respect: Highly valued employees are more likely to leave an organization that they perceive to be unfair and ineffective in conflict management. Businesses are starting to use mediation, but it is still not generally used. Why not? To answer this question, we must consider the nature of organizations and consider how their structure and culture determine their approach to conflict.

Traditional Approaches to Conflict in Organizations

Managing conflict in organizational settings has traditionally relied on rights-based or power-based mechanisms.

How do power-based mechanisms work? Typically, the manager or employee with more legitimate power decides what to do about a conflict situation. This is the case for a conflict involving a manager and a subordinate as well as for a conflict between co-workers of equal legitimate power. Even if the manager is not directly involved in the conflict, they typically decide what happens. McShane, Steen, and Tasa (2015) refer to this strategy as the **inquisitional approach**. Managers typically find this to be the quickest and easiest approach to conflict, at least in the short term.

inquisitional approach
an approach to workplace conflict whereby the manager uses his or her authority to settle a dispute between two co-workers

And it is perfectly consistent with the concept of **managerial prerogative**, that is, with the idea that managers have the right to make decisions. However, unless the conflict situation is fairly simple, employees usually dislike a third party's imposing a *solution* on their situation. Inquisitional approaches typically do not involve any thorough investigation into the true nature of the conflict, the real interests of the parties, or the circumstances surrounding the conflict.

managerial prerogative
the manager's right to make decisions

Rights-based mechanisms are another option for handling conflict in organizational settings. These approaches focus on interpreting organizational policies and procedures, legal statutes, terms of collective agreements, or other contracts. But for many conflict situations, the business organization has no policy, statute, or contractual term that is relevant. When this happens, the usual response is to default to a power-based approach. Another feature of rights-based approaches, as we have noted elsewhere, is that they tend to produce winners and losers. In some cases, the parties accept these decisions, but in others, they do not.

Both power-based and rights-based mechanisms often have secondary, escalating effects if the parties are unhappy with the outcomes. Coltri (2004) refers to these as meta-disputes. These are disputes over the way the initial, or primary, dispute has been handled or mishandled. For example, two project team members are in conflict over their respective roles in the team. Their manager attempts to resolve the issue by reprimanding both employees and removing both of them from the project. The employees were hoping for role clarification but have been punished instead. The conflict is not only unresolved but has in fact worsened.

Interest-based approaches need to fill the vacuum left by inadequate power- and rights-based systems.

Organizational Culture and Mediation

Regarding the resistance to mediation in workplace environments, we need to consider that any organizational culture itself, as it now exists, may be a barrier to mediation processes. **Organizational culture** refers to the beliefs, values, and assumptions shared by an organization's members. The existing culture tends to be very conservative and highly resistant to change of any kind—even to clear improvements. It may be opposed to interest-based conflict management principles, preferring power-based or rights-based processes. In fact, even organizational cultures that explicitly state that they are open, creative, and innovative, or those that explicitly state their belief in egalitarianism and open communication, may resist new thinking regarding their existing policies and practices.

organizational culture
the beliefs, values, and assumptions shared by an organization's members

---

IN THE NEWS

SILICON VALLEY TECH FIRMS' GENDER DISCRIMINATION

Silicon Valley, or broadly speaking, the "tech" industry, has recently been shown to have a significant gender bias within a white male–dominated culture even though these companies speak of themselves as meritocracies.

Sources: Corbyn (2018); Kolhatkar (2017).

In some cases, individual managers and employees within an organization may want mediation processes to be introduced. But they come up against a deep resistance to change. This resistance can exist even where almost everyone in the organization seems to agree a change is in order. Where does this resistance come from?

Organizations, according to Kurt Lewin (Costantino & Merchant, 1996), exist most of the time in a state of stasis or equilibrium. Forces of change may act upon the organization, but they are resisted by the existing status quo—the static force that keeps the organization in a stable state. In other words, organizational cultures are naturally resistant to change. Even when employees and managers are unhappy with existing conditions, they tend to hang onto them because they are used to them.

Conflict Management Systems

Employees expect the organization they work for to handle conflict effectively, fairly, rationally, and according to just principles. Satisfying employees in this respect is crucial to retaining them, and retaining employees is necessary if the organization is to continue to be healthy and effective in the long term.

Ury, Brett, and Goldberg (1988), followed by Costantino and Merchant (1996), have done foundational work in designing dispute-resolution systems. Both recommend a durable system, based on a formalized set of procedures and structures, that allows the parties to develop their own solutions, solutions that satisfy their various interests. However, as we have seen, organizational cultures are resistant to change. In an organization, implementing an interest-based system for resolving conflict is much easier than it sounds.

Costantino and Merchant (1996) identify a few key considerations for people who are trying to introduce an interest-based conflict management system into a business organization. These people need to understand, first, that the existing system, no matter how ineffective and dysfunctional it may be, will be difficult to dislodge simply because it is a system. Second, they need to involve the various stakeholders in the introduction process. The stakeholders' involvement will help overcome the existing power structure's resistance to the new initiatives. Third, every effort must be made to change the existing organizational culture to one that accepts conflict as inevitable and encourages choice in how it is managed.

By way of summary, Costantino and Merchant (1996) state the following:

> It is not enough to continue to tinker at the edges of conflict, with interventions that are limited, slow, and unintentional. … The once-dominant image of individuals and small exclusive groups unilaterally determining the future and direction of their organizations is fading. Instead, organizations are turning to collaborative efforts with stakeholders and organizational participants, because these groups have the innovative ideas … so key to organizational survival, effectiveness, and growth. (pp. 218–219)

KEY TERMS

collective agreement, 156

inquisitional approach, 158

legitimate power, 156

managerial prerogative, 159

organizational culture, 159

REFERENCES

Coltri, L.S. (2004). *Conflict diagnosis and alternative dispute resolution*. Upper Saddle River, NJ: Pearson.

Corbyn, Z. (2018, March 17). Why sexism is rife in Silicon Valley. *The Guardian*. Retrieved from https://www.theguardian.com/world/2018/mar/17/sexual-harassment-silicon-valley-emily-chang-brotopia-interview

Costantino, C.A., & Merchant, C.S. (1996). *Designing conflict management systems: A guide to creating productive and healthy organizations*. San Francisco: Jossey-Bass.

Kolhatkar, S. (2017, November 20). The tech industry's gender-discrimination problem. *The New Yorker*. Retrieved from https://www.newyorker.com/magazine/2017/11/20/the-tech-industrys-gender-discrimination-problem

McShane, S.L., Steen, S.L., & Tasa, K. (2015). *Canadian organizational behaviour* (9th ed.). Toronto: McGraw-Hill Ryerson.

Moore, C. (2014). *The mediation process: Practical strategies for resolving conflict* (4th ed.). San Francisco: Jossey-Bass.

Public Service Staffing Tribunal. (2015). *Annual report of the Public Service Staffing Tribunal 2014–2015*. Retrieved from http://pslreb-crtefp.gc.ca/about/reports/2014-2015/PSST/documents/PSST_Annual_Report_2014-2015-eng.pdf

Ury, W., Brett, J.M., & Goldberg, S.B. (1988). *Getting disputes resolved: Designing systems to cut the costs of conflict*. San Francisco: Jossey-Bass.

QUESTIONS AND EXERCISES

1. This chapter described some typical workplace disputes in connection with Moore's five types of conflicts. Choose one of them. Identify the interests of the parties involved. In groups of three, role-play a mediation in which one member is the mediator and the other two are the parties to the dispute.

   Consider who else in the organization might be stakeholders in any of these hypothetical disputes. What might their interests be, and how would you deal with them?

Restorative Justice

12

LEARNING OUTCOMES

After completing this chapter, you will be able to:

■ Become familiar with restorative justice programs, including victim–offender reconciliation and sentencing circles.

■ Understand the social and legal conditions in which victim–offender reconciliation programs and sentencing circles came into being and understand how these programs have been integrated into the justice system.

■ Understand how victim–offender reconciliation programs and sentencing circles actually work.

■ In specific case studies, assess whether restorative justice has been appropriately used and whether it has produced appropriate outcomes.

■ Practically apply restorative justice by role-playing a victim–offender mediation.

Alternative Dispute Resolution and Criminal Justice

The criminal justice system is one of the many areas where alternative dispute resolution has been effective. *Restorative justice*, as it is known, operates through a variety of social and community-based programs dealing with victim–offender relationships, the rehabilitation of criminals, and the treatment of community injuries that result from criminal acts. It involves a number of processes, including victim–offender reconciliation programs (also known as victim–offender mediation) and sentencing circles.

These innovations to criminal justice seem to have been occurring not only in Canada but across the world. More and more, individual communities want to have input at the grassroots level into the way criminal acts are responded to. Restorative justice initiatives have grown steadily in number in the past 30 years, gaining government funding and promotion along the way. In Ontario, for instance, the Ministry of the Attorney General and the Ministry of Community Safety and Correctional Services have established directives and provided funding for a number of community-based restorative justice programs.

What Is Restorative Justice?

restorative justice
a model of justice that treats crime as a violation of relationships and aims to restore the victim, the offender, and the community, and, ultimately, to prevent a recurrence of the crime

What does the term **restorative justice** mean? Correctional Service Canada (2012) defines it in the following way:

> In the face of crime and conflict, restorative justice is a philosophy and an approach that views crime and conflict principally as harm done to people and relationships. It strives to provide support and safe opportunities for the voluntary participation and communication between those affected (victims, offenders, and community) to encourage accountability, reparation, and a movement towards understanding, feelings of satisfaction, healing, safety and a sense of closure.
>
> Restorative justice is a non-adversarial, non-retributive approach to justice that emphasizes healing in victims, meaningful accountability of offenders, and the involvement of citizens in creating healthier, safer communities.

Bazemore and Schiff (2001) state that "restorative justice's focus on repairing harm to individual victims, with a concern for respectful treatment of the offender, is a response to the perceived failure of criminal justice systems and agencies to pay adequate attention to these needs" (p. 27). They continue by stating that the restorative justice technique "until very recently has been a process primarily focused on the dialogue between the individual victim and the offender, mediated by a third party and aimed particularly at meeting victims' needs for information, input, reparation and healing" (p. 27).

restitution
compensation the victim receives from the offender for the losses suffered because of the offender's crime

The Centre for Justice & Reconciliation (2018), a program of Prison Fellowship International, says the goal of restorative justice is a society "that emphasizes repairing the harm caused by criminal behaviour." Our society can reach this goal by allowing broader participation in the justice process and by creating unorthodox opportunities for **restitution**. In this way, the restorative approach to criminal justice differs from the traditional **retributive justice system**. The latter treats crimes as offences against the state and treats victims of crime quite impersonally; they become mere evidence that a crime was committed (Cooley, 2002).

retributive justice system
our society's main system of justice, which treats illegal behaviour with punishment alone

Of course, it is not only the direct victims of crime that the criminal justice system in Canada disregards. The broader community, even though it is sometimes deeply affected by a crime, is barely involved in the workings of justice. A few community members may provide evidence or serve on a jury, but that is all. The impact of a crime on the community is barely acknowledged.

A consultation paper prepared by the Canadian Resource Centre for Victims of Crime (2011) asks the following question: "If we were to start from scratch and build an entirely new criminal justice system, would it resemble our current system" (p.1)? For those in Canada who understand how little connection there is between victims, communities, and notions of fair and meaningful justice, the answer to this question would certainly be *no*.

Origins of Restorative Justice

The Canadian Mennonite community is responsible for adding restorative principles to the justice system. Inspired by their religion to look for a better way of healing the effects of crime, they introduced **victim–offender reconciliation** in the 1970s (Boulle & Kelly, 1998). The story is told by the Abbotsford Restorative Justice and Advocacy Association (2007):

> After two young offenders vandalized 22 properties in a small Ontario town, the assigned probation officer, Mark Yantzi, and a Mennonite prison support worker, Dave Worth, asked the judge for permission to arrange for the two offenders to meet with the victims of the vandalism in order to see if reparations could be made. News of the success of this new (yet centuries old) approach quickly spread. Soon, Victim Offender Reconciliation Programs were being created across Canada.

This trend has continued. Since 1974, victim–offender mediation programs have grown rapidly worldwide. In 2001, it was reported that more than 1,300 programs had sprung up in 18 countries (Umbreit, Coates, & Vos, 2001). Some Canadian programs experienced huge early success. For example, a program in Winnipeg, Manitoba was seeing over 1,000 referrals and mediating over 400 cases per year by the mid-1990s (Cayley, 1998).

The rebirth of **sentencing circles** as a part of Canada's justice system also started with a single case. Judge Barry Stuart of the Yukon called together a sentencing circle in 1991, in the case of *R v Moses* (1992). Stuart's goal was to increase the community's participation in the justice system and to ensure that the root causes of crime were being addressed; he wanted something more than the usual dispensing of *Criminal Code* punitive measures (Libin, 2009). After the use of the sentencing circle in *R v Moses*, this Indigenous method of restorative justice became more widely used in Indigenous communities in the 1990s. The *National Post* reported that the use of sentencing circles in Saskatchewan, with its large Indigenous population, reached its peak in 1997, with 39 sentencing circles, and that the use of circles in subsequent years, though less, was still substantial (Libin, 2009).

Victim–Offender Reconciliation Programs

A victim–offender reconciliation program, also known as victim–offender mediation, involves a mediation process led by specially trained (and usually volunteer) restorative justice mediators. These people bring offenders face to face with their victims in order to personalize the offence. As with most other forms of mediation—the exception is the mandatory mediation process in certain civil courts in Ontario—participation in victim–offender mediation requires the consent of both victim(s) and offender(s). Once at the table, the participants are encouraged to speak their minds, to reveal their interests, and to express (and confront) their feelings about the offence.

victim–offender reconciliation
a form of mediation that works to reconcile victim and offender by having the latter make reparations for the harm done to the victim

sentencing circles
a meeting of victims, offenders, their families, and concerned community members, who gather in a circle at the post-conviction phase to discuss the impact of the crime and to work together—along with members of the legal community—to recommend a restorative sentencing

restitution agreement
the settlement that emerges
from a mediation between
a victim and an offender

The goal of the process is for offenders, who are typically first-time offenders or young people charged with relatively minor offences, to learn the human consequences of their actions and, ultimately, to take responsibility for their misdeeds, often by way of a **restitution agreement** or some other form of mediated settlement. For victims, the process promotes healing through a couple of means. It allows them to confront their fears by facing the offenders and to express their thoughts and emotions. Also, the mediated settlement may call for the restoration of the victim's property or for some other form of repayment by the offender, monetary or symbolic, that meets the victim's stated interests. Often, though not always, a successful victim–offender mediation session can bring not only restitution for the victim but a criminal discharge or a suspended sentence for the offender.

The success of victim–offender reconciliation programs depends upon a number of things. First, it is essential that the offender is willing to take full responsibility for his or her actions. Beyond this, it is important to understand that it is not the victim's job to rehabilitate, reform, or retrain the offender, unless, of course, he or she chooses to help in doing so. It is essential within the system that victims have as much information as possible about the case, the offence committed, and the offender. Victims need to understand their role in the program, along with its potential benefits and risks, and be perceptive enough to identify and articulate their needs.

Clearly, this approach to restorative justice creates a new vision and version of justice for victims. Properly managed, and based upon true understanding of offences committed, it can bring consideration to the consequences of the act, both for the healing of the victim and the redirection of the offender.

Sentencing Circles

It is a traditional view in many Indigenous communities that crime is a symptom of a broken society. They generally view crime as a cancer. They also believe that such an illness can only be cured through community participation in the healing process. The ancient healing circles in Indigenous communities served as the models for the sentencing circles of today. In a sentencing circle, victims, offenders, their respective families, and concerned community members—including the elders and leaders of the community—meet together in a circle. These people, in consultation with official criminal justice representatives (that is, lawyers and judges), discuss the impact of the crime and work together to recommend a community-centred, restorative sentencing.

With respect to timing, a sentencing circle is convened at the post-conviction stage (that is, during the sentencing portion of a criminal trial). It is convened at the trial judge's request, often on the recommendation of the affected communities and the lawyers involved. Sentencing circles are not empowered to alter the court's determination of innocence or guilt. Rather, they are designed to help the court, after it reaches a verdict of guilt, provide appropriate, meaningful, restorative sentencing—in other words, sentencing that is proportionate to the offence and that addresses the most important interests of the people affected by the offence. Sentencing circles expand community involvement in sentencing by including the following groups in the process:

1. *The justice committee.* This group works outside the actual circle process but has various responsibilities. It is responsible for determining—initially and throughout the process—whether a sentencing circle is appropriate for the situation. It is responsible for contacting potential participants (for example, the victim, the offender, their support groups, as well as community members and elders) and for determining whom to include in the process and whom

to appoint keepers of the circle. The justice committee is also responsible for certain administrative duties, such as the scheduling of meetings.

2. *The offender.* This is the person who committed the crime and who must, for the sentencing circle to work, be willing to take responsibility for his or her offences. The offender must also have a support group of family or friends who can help him or her through stages of remorse and healing on the path to reformation and redemption. These supporters will help the offender conform to the circle's imposed obligations. The offender will create a plan for sentencing, with the assistance of their support group. This plan will include the offender acknowledging the harm caused by the offence, taking responsibility for his or her actions, and reconciling with and compensating the victim(s). By these means, and with the assistance of the community, the offender can achieve genuine rehabilitation.

3. *The victim.* This is the person against whom the offence was committed. A willing participant in the circle, the victim establishes their own support group and gives direction to the Crown and to the rest of the circle about their interests or needs.

4. *The Crown and/or police.* These participants object or give consent to the use of a circle and work with the justice committee to ensure the ongoing appropriateness of the circle. The Crown also keeps in contact with victims to ensure that their interests and needs have been expressed and are being met.

5. *Court workers, duty counsels, or agents.* These participants in the sentencing circle may be lawyers, agents of the court (for example, duty counsel), or agents of another kind, such as paralegals. One of them represents the offender during the circle process and another represents the victim. The offender's counsel offers the client advice about legal rights, guides them through the circle process, and helps establish a balanced support group. Victims' representatives prepare their clients for participation in the circle and help them translate their intentions into actions.

6. *The judge or justice of the peace.* The judge's or JP's role is to review the reports of proceedings from the justice committee, the Crown, and the support groups. The judge will obtain from the keepers of circles the list of upcoming cases, decide if a record of circle proceedings needs to be kept, and, if necessary, develop their own awareness of the circle process. The judge will also provide guidelines for sentencing. Ultimately, a judge will impose a sentence after considering the recommendations of the circle.

7. *The keepers of the circle.* These participants establish that all requirements for the circle have been met. They see to the exchange of all preliminary documents and verify that the victim, offender, support groups, and other necessary persons are prepared to participate. They are responsible for arranging the physical space in which the circle will operate. This includes ensuring that all tools to be used in the circle—for example, the talking stick, the feather, or the stone—are available. (These tools are a device for allowing all members of the circle to speak freely, without interference from other members. Whoever holds the talking stick, feather, or stone must be permitted to speak without interruption.) During the circle process, the keepers welcome and seat elders in the circle. They remove participants who are disrespectful to the process or who hinder its success. They will select a person to lead the circle in prayer, and they will welcome, introduce, and answer questions about the circle process (Macfarlane, 2003).

The Sentencing Circle Process

Once the circle is convened, its members, under the direction of the keepers of the circle, take turns discussing the various aspects of the offence, including its effects on the people involved. The group works toward a consensus on sentencing recommendations, trying to balance the gravity of the crime committed and the need for retribution against the need to heal the victim, the offender, and the community. Consideration may extend to those members of the offender's own family and community who will experience the negative consequences of the offence, for example, the children who will be deprived of an incarcerated parent. The court will take the recommendations of the circle into account when deciding how to sentence the offender.

In the mainstream criminal justice system, the victim and the community tend to be removed from the process. They are left bearing only the scars of their injuries. It is a system that processes the offender using a standard set of rules. There is no concern about whether the offender may have acted out of desperation or injury or may be a broken person in need of healing. This system denies victims and communities the opportunity to reclaim what they have lost through the offence, and it denies offenders a chance to take real personal responsibility for the damage they have done. Sentencing circles, by contrast, remove the spotlight from the past and place it on future healing. They consider all of the circumstances when deciding what needs to be healed, repaid, repaired, or replaced. They will also consider what can be learned from the crime and what can be strengthened or supported—in the victim, the offender, and the community—in order to prevent such crimes from occurring again (Macfarlane, 2003).

Judge Barry Stuart, mentioned above, states the following:

> The principal value of Community Sentencing Circles cannot be measured by what happens to offenders, but rather by what happens to communities. In reinforcing and building a sense of community, Circle Sentencing improves the capacity of communities to heal individuals and families and ultimately to prevent crime. (Bazemore & Schiff, 2001, p. 134)

Conclusion

A 2002 report prepared for the Law Commission of Canada (Cooley, 2002, p. 19) tells us that restorative justice programs, compared with traditional justice responses such as incarceration, probation, or court-ordered restitution, are more effective in bringing satisfaction to victims and offenders, in persuading offenders to comply with restitution, and in reforming offenders.

Another significant benefit of restorative justice programs—apart from offering a holistic approach that benefits all the parties involved in a crime—is that they provide less costly alternatives to the existing criminal justice system. That alone will drive their continued growth in this country.

KEY TERMS

REFERENCES

Abbotsford Restorative Justice and Advocacy Association. (2007). *The history of restorative justice*. Retrieved from http://www.arjaa.org/history-of-restorative-justice

Bazemore, G., & Schiff, M. (2001). *Restorative community justice: Repairing harm and transforming communities*. Cincinnati: Anderson.

Boulle, L., & Kelly, K.J. (1998). *Mediation: Principles, process, practice* (Canadian ed.). Toronto: Butterworths Canada.

Canadian Resource Centre for Victims of Crime. (2011, March). *Restorative justice in Canada: What victims should know*. Retrieved from http://www.crcvc.ca/docs/restjust.pdf

Cayley, D. (1998). *The expanding prison: The crisis in crime and punishment and the search for alternatives*. Toronto: House of Anansi Press.

Centre for Justice & Reconciliation. (2018). *Tutorial: Introduction to restorative justice*. Retrieved from http://restorativejustice.org/restorative-justice/about-restorative-justice/tutorial-intro-to-restorative-justice

Cooley, D. (2002). *Restorative justice in Canada: Lessons learned*. Ottawa: Law Commission of Canada.

Correctional Service Canada. 2012. *Restorative justice factsheet*. Retrieved from http://www.csc-scc.gc.ca/restorative-justice/003005-0004-eng.shtml

Libin, K. (2009, February 27). Sentencing circles for Aboriginals: Good justice? *National Post*. Retrieved from http://www.nationalpost.com/news/Sentencing+circles+aboriginals+Good+justice/1337495/story.html

Macfarlane, J. (2003). *Dispute resolution: Readings and case studies* (2nd ed.). Toronto: Emond Montgomery.

R v Moses, 1992 CanLII 12804, 3 CNLR 116 (YT Terr Ct).

Umbreit, M.S., Coates, R.B., & Vos, B. (2001). The impact of victim–offender mediation: Two decades of research. *Federal Probation, 65*(3), 29–35.

QUESTIONS AND EXERCISES

1. A young person has been charged with the criminal offence of vandalism—specifically, writing obscene messages in spray paint on one of the outside walls of the high school he attends. He is willing to admit his guilt and atone for what he has done.
   a. Consider and list the factors determining whether an offender should be sentenced through the traditional court system or should be a candidate for a restorative justice program.
   b. List the ways that a restorative justice program can benefit the victims of crime.

2. In recent years, sentencing circles have been used in some very high-profile criminal matters. Some of you probably recall the tragic story of Christopher Pauchay, a Yellow Quill First Nations man whose small children froze to death after he became severely intoxicated and took them out underdressed into a frigid January night. The sentencing circle in this case was made up of elders, family members, community members, mental health and addictions professionals, a probation worker, a police officer, and others. Its recommendations were rejected by the court in favour of a prison sentence. Those recommendations included a conditional sentence, to be served at home, and a lifetime of ceremonial service to Yellow Quill elders—that is, an ongoing commitment to traditional spiritual practices. These recommendations also provided for Pauchay to be reconnected with the mother of his children and with his remaining child. Consider this case and discuss whether you feel the recommendations of the sentencing circle were fair. Did the court make the right decision in rejecting those recommendations?

3. Bill and Ted are two college students on their way home from a night of drinking at the local pub. Getting rowdy in their intoxicated state, they start throwing stones around in the campus parking lot. One of these stones happens to strike and smash the window of a parked car belonging to a law professor, Mr. Darrow. Bill and Ted flee the scene, unaware that security cameras have

captured their images. Both are arrested and charged. Meanwhile, Mr. Darrow arrives to find that his vehicle has been damaged. This is very inconvenient for him. He has to pay the out-of-pocket deductible expenses in order to have his insurance replace the broken window. Also, he has to spend a lot of time dealing with his insurer, with the auto shop that is fixing the window, and with the police who are preparing charges against Bill and Ted.

Then Mr. Darrow receives an invitation to participate in a victim–offender mediation session at the local community justice centre. It seems that Bill, who threw the stone that broke Mr. Darrow's window, wishes to speak with his victim and negotiate possible compensation for the damage. Recognizing that one night of tomfoolery could have lifelong implications for Bill, Mr. Darrow, though very angry, accepts the invitation.

In groups of three, role-play the mediation between Mr. Darrow and Bill.

Mediation Across Disciplines

LEARNING OUTCOMES

After completing this chapter, you will be able to:

- Explore how mediation skills are utilized in different professions and fields.

- Investigate how mediation is a life skill for all ages.

- Explore the overlap between mediation and social work, policing, psychology, and teaching.

Introduction

Mediation is more than a process found in legal fields. Mediation is a skill that benefits all individuals, as well as a process found in a range of professions. Various professions require elements of mediation for conflict resolution and collaboration. This includes teachers, police officers, social service workers, customer service workers, and therapists. In fact, one could argue that the job of *parenting* requires constant mediation skills! In this chapter, we explore how mediation, viewed as both a skill and a process, is used and is beneficial in fields and professions such as education, policing, psychology, and social work.

Education

Schools and teachers utilize mediation in myriad ways. Currently, students are taught components of mediation skills as part of the education curriculum in Canada (Ministry of Education, 2018). School boards use mediation to deal with teacher, parent, and community conflicts. Teachers use mediation skills to manage classrooms. In addition, many schools use peer mediation to address student conflicts. This use of mediation benefits the education system and contributes to the success of students.

Schools across Canada now teach basic elements of mediation to children as young as five years old in kindergarten (Ministry of Education, 2018). In 2014, the Harvard University Advanced Leadership Initiative Think Tank (2014) released a report that discussed the skills children need to be successful in the 21st century (see Figure 13.1). These seven skills included critical thinking/problem solving, creativity/innovation, collaboration, question formulation, global awareness, communication skills, and technology skills.

Figure 13.1   Education for the 21st Century

1. **Critical thinking and problem solving.** Businesses don't feel that many students enter the workforce with skills related to non-routine thinking and solving complex problems. From the perspective of employers, these are key skills for high-skilled, high-paid jobs.

2. **Creativity and innovation.** Employers want individuals who think outside of the box and develop new solutions to complex problems. While such skills are extremely important, they can be hard to measure.

3. **Collaboration.** The workforce of the future will be diverse and globally distributed. Individuals must be able to collaborate.

4. **Question formulation.** Ideal employees can formulate and ask appropriate questions, which show higher-order thinking. Some schools have begun adopting pedagogy that includes working with students to develop skills to formulate questions.

5. **Global awareness.** In the past, students have been somewhat isolated. Going forward, employers want students with a sense of global awareness.

6. **Communication skills.** Thinking and problem solving are critical, but solid oral and written communication skills are also essential and often lacking today.

7. **Technology skills.** All students need to be comfortable with and able to use technology.

Source: Harvard University Advanced Leadership Initiative Think Tank (2014).

Three of these skills are directly related to mediation: critical thinking and problem solving, collaboration, and communication. Communication skills are needed in mediation to effectively present positions, needs, and options for resolutions. Collaboration skills are required to come to an agreement in mediation and understand that all perspectives are worthy. Students understand that differences can be discussed, examined, and understood respectfully (Kelly, 2014). Additionally, students are taught to think critically and assess problems. Problem solving and critical thinking are essential in mediation to determine the parties involved, the type of problem, and each person's position and needs. O'Reardon (2011) indicated that education and mediation meet *through* the aspect of critical thinking. Critical thinking requires one to consider consequences and examine alternatives. The act of mediation demonstrates to students that being in conflict is not a negative sign, but what distinguishes us as human beings is the way we *engage* in it.

Schools also rely on mediation and restorative justice practices to address community- and school-based concerns. For example, schools may use the mediation process to come to an agreement on school policies, student discipline processes, or school versus community concerns. A case example is Oakland's Ralphe Bunch High School, a continuation school for over 250 students. In an effort to increase success and peace, the school promoted spaces for dialogue via mediation, restorative conversations, circles, family group conferences, and community conferences (Gross, 2016). Aspects of mediation were even used in teacher and student meetings. The school reported a reduction in suspensions by half. Citing the positive impact of restorative justice approaches, one staff member stated:

> I had the opportunity to participate in a teacher–student mediation that restored peace in the class and healed a fraught teacher–student relationship. The student and I temporarily stepped out of our prescribed roles and artificial hierarchy to express concerns and to collaborate toward a resolution. This was a deeply humanizing process for both my student and me, one that prevented a possible suspension for my student + increased my joy and effectiveness in the classroom (Gross, 2016, p. 9).

Mediation is also a key approach to addressing student versus student conflicts. Unresolved and lingering conflict frequently leads to violence, interfering with productivity and the quality of life in schools and the community (Trevaskis, 1994). Schools have attempted to manage interpersonal conflicts among students, teachers, and administrators by various models of discipline, such as referrals to the principal's office, detention, suspension, and **expulsion**. However, these methods do not teach the students the problem-solving and conflict resolution skills they need in life to resolve conflict in a productive, non-violent way (Trevaskis, 1994). Dissatisfaction with traditional processes established to settle disputes has led educators and others to try new ways of conflict resolution, such as mediation. Students who are taught the skills of mediating disputes learn political skills, which can be used beyond the classroom: listen effectively, summarize accurately, and think critically (Parsons, 1991).

Schools, especially secondary schools, may also use peer mediation practices. Peer mediation involves one or two trained student mediators assisting two disputants through a structured process to reach resolution of a dispute (Trevaskis, 1994). School staff benefit from a system whereby less time is spent dealing with minor issues and fewer conflicts flow into classrooms. Peer mediation is also used in higher education settings (see box). However, peer mediation is only suitable for minor disputes. Major disputes, such as assault and serious bullying, are not suitable for this process (New South Wales Department of Education, 2011).

expulsion
removing a student from the school due to behavioural or criminal concerns

IN THE NEWS

A COLLEGE PEER MEDIATION PROGRAM

Durham College in Oshawa, Ontario, Canada has a graduate certificate in mediation. Students in this program are training to go into the mediation field. In order to give them experience in mediating, they become peer mediators for all other college students. Campus Conflict Resolution Services was established and an official process was designed whereby students or their professors could be referred to the centre. This gives the mediation graduate students experience in the field, adds support for students, and reduces professors' need to focus on classroom management problems.

Source: Durham College (2018).

Sometimes mediation is used to address teacher discipline problems. A mediator may be tasked with determining the consequences of a teacher's behaviour, or a formal arbitration process may be required. In these cases, the arbitrator has the power to determine the outcome, and the school board or teacher would have to agree to the outcome. There have been complaints that this process is flawed because arbitrators do not understand the psychological impact on children, the role and influence that the teacher has, or the roles of schools and curriculum. In some legal cases, the teacher was permitted to return to teaching very quickly, and this concerned parents and staff (Treveskis, 1994).

Arbitration practices such as this are also used in higher education settings. If an employee is unhappy with aspects of their job, including pay, duties, or benefits, an arbitration process may be used to settle the issue. For example, a professor may not be happy with their workload, and no agreement can be made between the university or college and the faculty association. There has been an increase in mediation and arbitration in higher education, especially concerning women and equity (Hughes, 2018).

Policing

At the very core of policing is the ability for conflict resolution. Present research illustrates how many alternative forms of dispute resolution (for example, mediation) available to patrol officers are consistent with the pragmatic realities of policing (Cooper, 1998). Mediation is a methodology for addressing social interaction disputes, for example, public disputes, community-based disputes, and interpersonal disputes (Cooper, 1998). On a daily basis, police officers are faced with conflict situations and are expected to make difficult conversations work on the spot. They use mediation skills, such as active listening, that are beneficial in establishing communication, building rapport, defusing emotions, collecting information, and helping the parties to move on (Volpe, 2016). Other techniques and skills common to mediation and police work include caucus sessions, bias awareness, handling power imbalances, keeping an open mind, handling emotions, dealing with impasse, addressing ethical issues, and bringing sessions to closure. Police officers can use guidelines for respectful discourse to encourage parties to share their concerns, explore options, and perhaps walk away with a better understanding of what transpired. However, mediation is unacceptable for police officers to use in certain types of situations, such as domestic violence or child abuse (Cooper, 1998).

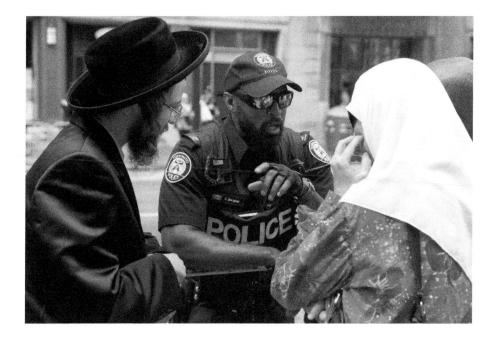

In his research with police officers, Volpe (2016) found that those officers who felt comfortable playing the role of mediator routinely did so quite naturally, usually by using their intuition and without specific mediation training. They used natural communication and problem-solving skills. Volpe also found anecdotal evidence from the growing number of officers who have been trained in mediation programs and academic coursework that they feel better prepared to engage the public and more confident in their interactions.

Sgt. Brenden Kennelly from Durham Regional Police Services Police Education pointed out that many police services want to hire new recruits who demonstrate natural negotiation and mediation skills. During the hiring process, potential recruits can be provided with case studies to show how they would de-escalate a conflict. This can demonstrate problem-solving and mediation skills that are desired by the hiring agency (B. Kennelly, personal communication, Sept. 2018). Some aspects of mediation are taught to new recruits in their police college training, a three-month intensive program to prepare them for life as a police officer (Kennelly, 2018).

Many police scenes are amenable to resolution through non-conventional dispute-resolution methodologies such as mediation (Cooper, 1998). For example, when different police departments show up to the same scene, there may be a dispute over territory and decision-making powers. Officers may have to engage in informal mediation to determine the role of each department and the common goal.

Police services are always looking for ways to build community relationships. Many of the proposed solutions to improve police–community relations focus on building rapport and trust between the police and members of the local communities they protect. One such method of building trust is using mediation to address community concerns, including police complaints. There is a growing presence of mediation programs handling civilian complaints against the police. Civilians and police have an opportunity to discuss what happened, how each perceived it, clarify any miscommunications and misunderstandings, and move on with a better understanding of what occurred. Bartels and Silverman (2005) studied levels of satisfaction for citizens and police officers who participated in police complaint mediation. A two-page questionnaire of multiple-choice and open-ended questions was sent to the sample population (N=285) of officers and complainants who either had their cases mediated or fully investigated. Complainants who participated in mediation were significantly more satisfied with the police complaint procedure (Bartels & Silverman, 2005).

Social Work

Social workers use mediation skills to resolve conflicts, negotiate agreements, and mediate truces between family members on a daily basis (Kelly, 2014). There are five general types of services that social workers provide related to mediation and conflict resolution (see Figure 13.2): prevention, reconciliation, decision-making, procedural assistance, and substantive assistance (Kelly, 2014).

Because social workers are trained in areas such as identifying and analyzing underlying interests, developing resources, and generating options, they are well suited to handle issues related to mediation and conflict resolution. After documenting the congruence of mediation and social work in terms of purpose, objectives, interventions, and values, Barsky (2001) proposed mediation as a specialization of social work practice. The goal of every intervention in both social work and mediation is to further the self-sufficiency of the clients served (Howard, 1987). Mediation in social work focuses on family-led decision-making that empowers families and wider support networks of friends and family to find solutions. Clients are also encouraged to gain power and efficacy to negotiate problem resolution; this is an empowerment-oriented strategy in social work practice (Parsons, 1991).

Figure 13.2 The Congruence of Mediation and Social Work

Mediation   Social Work

1. prevention
2. reconciliation
3. decision-making
4. procedural assistance
5. substantive assistance

Source: Kelly (2014).

Teaching clients to negotiate and mediate for themselves may result in mutually agreeable solutions and growth on the part of the clients. Research has shown that better outcomes for families and fewer family breakdowns can be achieved if a social worker has had training in mediation and negotiation (Barsky, 2001). However, Barsky is careful to point out that while social workers have much to contribute, particularly in the area of family mediation, mediation is a distinct profession with its own values, techniques, approaches, and professional persona.

Psychology

The field of psychology is based on the concept that individuals are faced with conflicts in life, and this causes emotional and **cognitive** distress. These conflicts may be at a personal level (conscious or unconscious), social level, or intimate level. For example, a person may have conflicting personal feelings about a family member, his or her job, or even his or her past actions. Sometimes a person is aware of these personal conflicts, but in some situations, the distress one experiences comes from unconscious conflicts. For instance, imagine a young girl who witnesses a terrible bullying incident at school. She does nothing to intervene out of fear. Months later, she starts experiencing nightmares and anxiety and stops sleeping, but she is unclear why this is happening. She may be experiencing a cognitive conflict over her actions at a subconscious level.

People may also become distressed over personal conflicts with family, friends, or spouses. Cloke (2008) indicates that such conflicts can only be resolved through emotional processing skills, skills that require the guidance of experts in the field of psychology. In fact, Cloke (2008) believes mediators should receive more training in this area. The author notes that, when interviewed, many mediators identified the following topics as lacking, but needed, in their education:

1. ways of using **brief therapy** and similar psychology-based techniques in mediation;
2. methods for increasing emotional intelligence; and
3. ways of discovering what people think or want subconsciously and of bringing them into conscious awareness.

Several aspects of understanding conflict resolution relate directly to psychology (Bader, 2010). Dissecting conflict requires self-awareness, understanding of social dynamics, and knowledge of healthy versus unhealthy systems. In *The Psychology of Conflict* (2016), Randolph states that psychology is increasingly perceived by lawyers as a vital tool for resolving conflicts in the litigation environment, whether the dispute is a commercial one or related to family, community, or employment. With an ever-growing demand for mediators across international borders, the psychologically informed mediator can even provide much-needed facilitation in peace negotiations.

Both the therapist and the client would benefit from psychology theories to engage in the mediation process. Clients would benefit from developing self-esteem and empowerment. The therapist could help the client achieve these in order to engage in the mediation process in a more equitable and constructive manner.

The therapist would use mediation skills to help solve clients' social and personal conflicts. For example, a psychologist would rely on mediation skills when conducting family therapy or couples counselling. Psychologists require mediation skills when put into situations dealing with divorce or family dysfunction (Diamond, 2011). These sorts

cognitive
relating to the mental processes of perception, memory, judgment, and reasoning

brief therapy
is short-term and focused on helping a person to resolve or effectively manage a specific problem/challenge or to make a desired change

of conflict may be related to psychological issues (for example, substance abuse, trauma, etc.). Family/marriage therapy often requires resolution of long-standing issues. The average mediator does not understand complex issues such as this (Diamond, 2011).

conflict resolution therapy
models of conflict resolution are used in therapy with families or couples

In fact, there is a form of therapy called **conflict resolution therapy**, developed by psychologist Susan Heitler (2010). In 1990, Dr. Heitler began using conflict resolution techniques found in the legal field and embedded them into her psychotherapy practice with couples. Conflict resolution therapy focuses on what clients most often want from their treatment. In addition, the treatment method is focused, fast moving, and efficient. It incorporates techniques for rapid exploration of family of origin sources of dysfunctional patterns. At the same time, it emphasizes coaching the communication and conflict resolution skills that enable couples to sustain a positive relationship (Heitler, 2010). Mediators and psychologists may differ in their approach, however. Mediator styles tend to skew toward the evaluative; that is, they help participants evaluate their legal position and the costs and benefits of pursuing legal remedies versus a mediated settlement. Psychologists tend to use a facilitative style. They are trained to closely follow a client's narrative, matching affect, language, and pacing when appropriate.

In either case, the art of mediation and psychology are closely intertwined and offer plenty of opportunities for supporting individuals.

Bader points out that the psychological process of understanding the self is very important in mediation. Issues of self and identity raise profound and often painful questions about who we are (Bader, 2010). This can sometimes lead to unhealthy behaviours such as poor eating, substance use, isolation, risk behaviours, fighting with family, negative relationships, or even self-harm. Parties in mediation are often forced to consider aspects of themselves: their needs, wants, and sense of self-esteem and self-efficacy. Bader suggests that on a psychological level, parties in mediation typically move through a cycle of narcissistic inflation, deflation, and then, hopefully, realistic resolution. He calls this the IDR cycle (Bader, 2010). This process demands strength of self on a basic, simple, healthy ego level, especially at the outset. Parties strive to be equal to the task. However, during critical moments of the resolution stage, parties who wish to reach resolution may have to release their psychological investments in the outcome of the negotiation. They have to reassess their positions, which often require them to reassess their self and relation to their world. The capacity to *let go* is also a critical aspect of the psychology of mediation. (We may recall Elsa singing "Let It Go" in the movie *Frozen* at this moment!)

The mediator's own issues of self and identity will also arise during mediation. During critical moments, the mediator, too, may have to release the sense of narcissistic self-investment in the outcome (Bader, 2010). Thus, our usefulness as mediators will often depend on the extent to which we have learned to deal with issues of self and identity, not only in others, but also in ourselves. Therefore, the topic of psychology is extremely important to the mediation field. Psychologists who are knowledgeable in the area of the self, including identity and esteem, are well equipped to use this knowledge to support parties through the mediation process. They can especially help when clients may feel that they are losing face by compromising on their positions or not getting all of their perceived needs met.

Psychologists also use the practice of mediation at times. For example, during a victim–offender reconciliation process, the psychologist may arrange for the victim to meet with an offender or perpetrator in order to support their therapy for healing and closure. Psychologists for serious crimes do not use this method, however. The victim and offender may meet under supervised care, with the therapist walking them through the mediation and healing process.

CASE STUDY #1

Katie is 21 years old. Throughout high school, she bullied another girl. She now feels tremendous guilt over her actions. She would like to meet with her victim from years ago, apologize, and explain her actions. Katie's therapist encourages Katie to reach out to the girl. Katie does and asks the other girl to meet, perhaps with Katie *and* her therapist. The girl agrees, and the therapist conducts a mediation session with the two girls, allowing both to begin a new healing process.

CASE STUDY #2

Geoff, aged 16, is the youngest of six boys. Over the years, Geoff has been harassed and picked on by his siblings. In fact, they have injured him on a number of occasions, and he feels victimized. His therapist chooses to do a mediation session with the whole family to allow Geoff to express his thoughts and feelings to his brothers and give them an opportunity to talk as well.

CASE STUDY #3

Betty is 54 years old. Her house was burglarized by two local teens she knows well. She feels violated and embarrassed that she trusted them. The two boys are going through a restorative justice practice with the courts that involves community hours. The therapist who works with Betty conducts a victim–offender meeting. The goal is to mediate an agreement for the community hours and how they will continue to live as trusting neighbours.

Family therapy involves many aspects of mediation, and the two practices of family therapy and family mediation heavily overlap. Family mediation focuses on resolving a dispute, is usually present and future focused, and is shorter in length. For example, a family may engage in mediation to resolve a dispute over a will or finances. Family therapy focuses on resolving unhealthy relationships and structures in the family system. It is often focused on the past to understand how the unhealthy systems came to be. For example, a family may come to therapy to deal with the substance abuse of family members or help them work through a difficult period, such as the death of a family member. Both practices of therapy and mediation are focused on the future and creating healthy relationships and peace.

Favaloro (1998) points out that some types of family therapy are more aligned with mediation than others. However, both

- are solution-task oriented;
- look for exceptions;
- emphasize: if it works, do more of it;
- emphasize: if it's not broken, don't fix it; and
- are brief.

The following case study was provided by Favaloro (1998) in his article and is a good example of how the problems presented by clients sometimes go beyond mediation and demonstrate the need for family therapy. The case study presents an ethical question: At what point is a mediator no longer qualified to conduct a mediation session because it has moved into *therapy* territory? Alternatively, can the mediator continue if he or she has expertise and training in therapeutic mediation practice, a slightly different practice than straight mediation?

CASE STUDY #4

This case involves a father and his fifteen-year-old daughter. The client's presenting issues centred around the daughter's refusal to go to school, subsequent arguments, and disciplinary clashes. The mediation process involved both of them expressing their concerns, and my role was to facilitate communication of feelings and to future-focus parties. The parties became positional, with dad wanting his daughter to attend school, daughter not wanting to go. The parties could not agree, or agree to disagree, and an impasse persisted. In exploring the issues further, I found that dad held strong emotions of hurt and anger around his responsibilities to his daughter, fueled in part by resentment toward his recently divorced former wife and her actions and attitudes toward him and their daughter, as well as from residual effects from abusive incidents in his childhood. The daughter expressed bitterness and hatred toward her mother and had had thoughts of suicide. She recognized, after exploring it, that refusing to go to school helped her cope and was also a way of expressing her anger. Exploring these factors satisfactorily was considered beyond the contract of mediation as originally understood. Early on in the process, the clients were offered options. They were asked whether they wished to be referred elsewhere, to work in a more therapeutic fashion, to make limited agreements at this time, or to continue at some other time. The parties chose to continue working on their deeper issues. Sessions were videotaped, with consent, to assist in supervision. There were a number of individual sessions during which the parties were very distraught and emotional.

These sessions proved invaluable in assisting the clients to become more focused in the present and to help them clarify issues for future negotiations. Therapeutic intervention was seen to occur both in the individual sessions and when clients were together. As mentioned, this involved more of an exploration of emotional states. When the clients were together and became antagonistic toward each other, and when it wasn't clear what the issues were, then a mediative process was entered into. The mediative approach helped the clients focus. I have found mediation is most useful when clients are overly hostile because it offers a structured method of containing conflict. The rule of thumb I often work with is: the higher the conflict the more structured the (mediation) approach. As a mediator, I am the "chairperson" of the meeting and call the shots, in terms of process. When families are really stuck and uncommunicative, I may need to call on other strategies. For families such as these, therapeutic problem solving most clearly represents the process they are involved in. In the above case example, because the clients chose to examine the emotional background to their dispute individually, it meant that my role changed, that I needed to act more as a therapist than as a mediator. It could be suggested that I was involved in therapeutic mediation. Introducing techniques to help client's express unresolved emotions was certainly a departure from the original mediation contract. It was fortunate that, in this case and at that time, the funding organization supported such therapeutic sessions; that I had the skills; and that the parties were clear about [trying] and motivated to try different approaches.

Source: Favaloro (1998).

In this chapter, we reviewed how mediation is used and why it is important to other fields. In education systems, mediation is used by students, teachers, and school boards to resolve conflicts. Students are taught the basics of mediation skills, such as communication, critical thinking, and collaboration, to encourage their success. Police use mediation skills on a daily basis when interacting with the public. In addition, mediation has been used to help settle community complaints and concerns. The fields of social work and psychology integrate the mediation process when helping clients and their families. It is evident that mediation as both a process and a skill is a key to success for many professions.

KEY TERMS

brief therapy, 177   conflict resolution therapy, 178   expulsion, 173
cognitive, 177

REFERENCES

Bader, E. (2010, January). The psychology of mediation, part I: The mediator's issues of self and identity. Retrieved from https://www.mediate.com/articles/baderE2.cfm

Barsky, A. (2001). Understanding family mediation from a social work perspective. *Canadian Social Work Review, 18*(1), 25–46.

Bartels, E.C., & Silverman, E.B. (2005). An exploratory study of the New York City Civilian Complaint Review Board mediation program. *Policing: An International Journal of Police Strategies & Management, 28*(4), 619–630. Retrieved from https://www.emeraldinsight.com/doi/abs/10.1108/13639510510628703

Cloke, K. (2008, October). Building bridges between psychology and conflict resolution: Implications for mediator learning. Retrieved from https://www.mediate.com/articles/cloke7.cfm

Cooper, C. (1998). Patrol police officer conflict resolution processes. *Journal of Criminal Justice, 25*(2), 87–101. Retrieved from https://www.sciencedirect.com/science/article/pii/S0047235296000530?via=ihub

Diamond, I. (2011, March). The value of a psychologist mediator. Retrieved from https://www.mediate.com/articles/diamondi1.cfm

Durham College. (2018). Campus conflict resolution services. Retrieved from https://durhamcollege.ca/academic-schools/school-of-justice-emergency-services/about-the-school/campus-conflict-resolution-services

Favaloro, G.J. (1998). Mediation: A family therapy technique? *Conflict Resolution Quarterly, 16*(1), 101–108.

Gross, O. (2016). *Restore the respect: How to mediate school conflicts and keep students learning.* Retrieved from http://archive.brookespublishing.com/documents/what-is-teacher-student-mediation.pdf

Harvard University Advanced Leadership Initiative Think Tank. (2014). *Education for the 21st Century: Executive summary.* Cambridge: Harvard Advanced Leadership Initiative.

Heitler, S. (2010, September). Conflict resolution therapy. Retrieved from http://www.therapyhelp.com/conflict-resolution-therapy

Howard, D.A. (1987). *Mediation and social work: A study of form, fit and future* (Doctoral dissertation, University of Pennsylvania, Philadelphia, PA).

Hughes, J. (2018). Women in STEM: Addressing equity through universal design [Keynote address]. HEIT Conference, Ireland. https://docs.wixstatic.com/ugd/c416fd_235673d41aa645f3bfaddfb913a2add1.pdf.

Kelly, D.R. (2014). Social work and mediation/conflict resolution: The benefits, challenges, and practitioner improvements associated with the use of mediation/conflict resolution in social work practice (Master's thesis, University of Texas at Arlington, Arlington, TX).

Ministry of Education (Ontario). (2018). The Ontario curriculum: Elementary. Retrieved from http://www.edu.gov.on.ca/eng/curriculum/elementary/grades.html

New South Wales Department of Education and Communities. (2011). Peer mediation for secondary schools. Retrieved from https://education.nsw.gov.au/student-wellbeing/media/documents/attendance-behaviour-engagement/behaviour/secondary-whole-package.pdf

O'Reardon, D. (2011, July). Mediation in the classroom: How critical thinking can facilitate conflict resolution. Retrieved from https://www.mediate.com/articles/oReardonD4.cfm

Parsons, R.J. (1991, December). The mediator role in social work practice. *Social Work, 36*(6), 483–487. Retrieved from https://www.researchgate.net/publication/21400715_The_Mediator_Role_in_Social_Work_Practice

Randolph, P. (2016). *The psychology of conflict: Mediating in a diverse world.* London, UK: Bloomsbury.

Trevaskis, D.K. (1994, December). Mediation in the schools. Retrieved from https://www.ericdigests.org/1995-2/mediation.htm

Volpe, M. (2016, November). Mediation in the future of policing. Retrieved from https://www.mediate.com/articles/VolpeFutures.cfm

QUESTIONS AND EXERCISES

1. Look up your local Ministry of Education curriculum documents and see what is taught about conflict resolution, negotiation, and mediation to children.
   a. What would you add based on what you have learned from this book?
   b. Design your own one-hour mediation class for a public or high school class. Consider what you would teach children about mediation.

2. Find a case in the news where a police officer or police used or did not use mediation skills with the public or internally.
   a. What was done that demonstrates the theories you are learning about in this course?
   b. What could have been done differently?

3. How could police use mediation with the following types of complaints?
   a. Two neighbours are having a dispute over noise.
   b. A teenager keeps running away, and the parents are angry.
   c. A fight breaks out over a parking spot in a crowded mall.

4. Make up a family feud scenario and discuss how mediation can be used in family therapy.

Professional Practice and Ethical Considerations

14

LEARNING OUTCOMES

After completing this chapter, you will be able to:

- Familiarize yourself with basic ethical practices for mediators.

- Identify the prominent codes of conduct for mediators.

- Become aware of the legal duties and responsibilities of a mediator.

- Consider from a practical standpoint, through hypothetical ethical dilemmas, some ethical questions commonly faced by mediators.

- Become familiar with common areas of mediation practice.

- Understand professional practice considerations in the areas of professional associations, insurance, and fees.

- Understand the basic elements of an agreement to mediate.

- Form a practical plan for pursuing a career in alternative dispute resolution.

Qualifications for Mediators

The vast majority of people who become mediators do so from a genuine desire to promote peaceful dispute resolution. But even those with the best intentions may sometimes find themselves facing ethical dilemmas or find themselves in situations where, without realizing it, they are incapable of providing the services required due to a lack of experience or necessary expertise in a particular field. For these, and other, reasons, professional bodies like the ADR Institute of Canada (ADRIC), and Family Mediation Canada, as well as government-operated programs such as the **Ontario Mandatory Mediation Program** (OMMP) or the BC Human Rights Tribunal, have developed or adopted various **codes of ethical conduct** for mediators.

A *Toronto Star* article by Linda Diebel (2008) entitled "Unqualified mediators prey on broken families" gave pause to many people, including highly trained and qualified mediators. Diebel made the point that "anybody can hang a shingle and plunge into a highly sensitive area of working with divorcing couples and their children at a time when most are financially and emotionally vulnerable." This statement is true but, with growing memberships in various ADR practice organizations, such as those mentioned above, it is a safe bet that most professional mediators take their role very seriously. Very few are as irresponsible as Diebel's phrasing suggests.

Self-Regulation

Currently, mediation as a profession is self-regulated (Diebel, 2008). There is no legal requirement—nor can we expect one any time soon—that a mediator in private practice has earned particular qualifications from some governing body. The situation is different should a mediator wish to join—or obtain a specific designation from—a professional association or to register on a **mediators' roster** at the courts. In such cases, the regulations around professional training and qualifications are often quite strict.

The lack of formal regulation to which Diebel refers is something the profession may deal with in the future. For now, the practice is largely self-regulating. Marg Bruineman (2017) wrote in the *Law Times* that the lack of formal regulation, combined with the growth of professional organizations like ADRIC, "has led to self-regulation, which is supported by market forces—if a mediator doesn't prove their worth, further work is unlikely to follow."

David McCutcheon, a mediator and arbitrator and past-president of ADRIC and its Ontario branch, quoted in Bruineman's (2017) article, states:

> By and large, mediators have become a pretty solid professional group. In the early days when qualifications were a little less rigorous and there weren't codes of ethics, I think the people actually had a pretty broad range of behaviours. I think as the mediation profession has matured, the bad apples have been pretty much taken out of the profession.

We are now in a place where the field of mediation has developed in such a way that there are many highly qualified private mediators to choose from. Currently, family and civil courts are, where appropriate, directing disputants—applicants and respondents—to experienced and professional private mediators. Mediation associations are doing their part, too, to promote the professionalism of the practice

Ontario Mandatory Mediation Program
a court-annexed mediation program under which parties involved in certain kinds of civil action are required to attend at least three hours of mediation in a bid to resolve their dispute without the court's involvement

codes of ethical conduct
sets of rules that apply to members of a body or organization

mediators' roster
a list of approved professionals who offer mediation services to participants in a particular program, such as the Mandatory Mediation Program

of mediation, in **civil mediation** generally and **family mediation** in particular. They have, for example, established accreditations based on minimum standards of training and experience and, in some cases, on professional examinations. And it is not just mediation that is getting the industry self-regulation treatment. Professional organizations like ADRIC offer training, certification, rules, and codes of conduct for arbitrators as well. Professional associations and their training standards will be covered later in this chapter.

Codes of Conduct for Mediators

Codes of conduct for mediators serve four primary purposes. First, they are meant to guide practising mediators. Second, they are meant to inform the client parties about the mediation process. Third, they are meant to protect the mediating parties from harm caused by lax standards or unknowledgeable, unskilled, and unethical mediators. Last, these codes of conduct are meant to promote public confidence in mediation as a viable option for the resolution of conflicts and disputes.

There are a number of professional bodies and government programs with codes of conduct. These codes are different, but they share many of the same standards. Most of these codes are publicly accessible. For the purpose of illustration, we will look more closely at one of them, the *Canadian Bar Association of Ontario—ADR Section Model Code of Conduct for Mediators* (CBAO Code of Conduct). This code of conduct is used in the OMMP and can be found on the website of the province's Ministry of the Attorney General (MAG) at https://www.attorneygeneral.jus.gov .on.ca/english/courts/manmed/codeofconduct.php.

Codes of Conduct: Typical Contents

The following discussion draws extensively, but not exclusively, on the CBAO Code of Conduct for mediators. For a precise account of that code's definitions and rules of practice, please consult the CBAO Code of Conduct directly.

The Ministry of the Attorney General provides for local mediation committees to administer the CBAO Code of Conduct in each county where the OMMP exists. On its website, the ministry directive immediately preceding the CBAO Code of Conduct states that "mediators selected for the roster under the MMP will be expected to conduct themselves in a manner consistent with the policies of the MMP" (MAG, 2008–2016) and goes on to list a number of commitments required of every mediator. In addition, "mediators are expected to observe the spirit as well as the letter of the Code of Conduct."

The aim is to ensure that MMP mediators:

1. are competent to render the mediation services that the nature of the dispute requires;
2. will conduct mediations under Rule 24.1 and Rule 75.1 appropriately and limit themselves to the role of mediator (that is, not provide other professional services in addition to mediation);
3. will provide mediation services in a timely manner; and
4. will use only approved terminology in advertisements and promotional materials.

civil mediation
any mediation dealing with civil law disputes between individuals (for example, contracts, torts)

family mediation
mediation that deals with matters affecting the family, including divorce, custody and access, and the division of family property

Objectives

The CBAO Code of Conduct, which is used by the OMMP, is meant to provide guidelines for professional conduct, to protect the public, and to promote confidence in the mediation process.

Definitions

The CBAO Code of Conduct defines mediation as a process of facilitated negotiation by an impartial third party, who helps the parties in dispute reach a mutually acceptable, voluntary agreement. It defines a *mediator* as

> an impartial person whose role in mediation is to assist and encourage parties to a dispute:
>
> - to communicate and negotiate in good faith with each other;
> - to identify and convey their interests to one another;
> - to assess risks;
> - to consider possible settlement options; and
> - to resolve voluntarily their dispute.

The word *impartial*, according to the CBAO Code of Conduct, means that a mediator must be—and must be seen to be—"unbiased toward parties to a dispute, toward their interests and toward the options they present for settlement" (MAG, 2008–2016).

The Principle of Self-Determination

self-determination
the parties' right to make decisions for themselves

The CBAO Code of Conduct defines **self-determination** as the right of the parties to make decisions for themselves throughout the mediation process. The parties' right to self-determination means that mediators must:

- provide sufficient information about the process and about themselves, including an explanation of the principle of self-determination;
- not provide legal advice; and
- advise unrepresented parties to obtain independent legal advice where appropriate.

Impartiality

impartiality
the principled neutrality that prevents the mediator from taking sides or giving preferential treatment in a negotiation

The CBAO Code of Conduct rules concerning **impartiality** require that mediators provide services "only in those matters in which they can remain impartial" and that they "remain impartial" throughout the process. Should they "become aware of their lack of impartiality, they shall immediately disclose to the parties that they can no longer remain impartial and shall withdraw from the mediation."

Conflict of Interest

conflict of interest
a case where the mediator cannot be impartial or stands to gain personally at the expense of one of the parties in the mediation process

The CBAO Code of Conduct says that mediators must disclose to the parties any known **conflict of interest** as soon as possible. The mediator shall then withdraw from the mediation process, unless the parties consent to continue using that mediator's services despite the acknowledged conflict of interest. Likewise, the Code forbids professional relationships outside of the mediation itself between a mediator (or their partners or associates) and any of the parties involved in the mediation, unless the parties unanimously consent to such outside relationships. Finally, mediators shall not allow "pressure or influence from third parties … to compromise the independence of the mediator."

Confidentiality

Mediation relies upon the principle of **confidentiality**. Mediators have a responsibility to inform the parties of the confidential nature of the process. Generally speaking, mediators should not disclose information or documents included in the mediation to parties who are not included in the process. This rule may be waived in the following circumstances: when the parties give their written consent to disclosure; when the court orders it, or disclosure is required by law (as in **open mediation**, for example, where the judge requires the mediator to report on the proceedings, or in cases of abuse); when the disclosure reveals a threat to human life; or when that information is anonymous, or *non-identifiable*, and used for statistical research or purposes of that kind. With respect to caucusing and confidentiality, mediators shall inform the parties that any discussion occurring in caucus will be kept in strict confidence unless all the parties involved consent to disclosure. In other words, despite the general rule, where a mediator feels it would be helpful to disclose to the other party something discussed confidentially in caucus, the mediator ought to seek permission to make said disclosure. Finally, with respect to the storage and disposal of files, mediators shall exercise the utmost caution to maintain confidentiality.

confidentiality
the duty of the mediator and of the parties in mediation not to disclose details of the process to people not directly involved in it

open mediation
a mediation process requiring that the mediator report details of the proceedings to a judge; a non-confidential mediation

Quality of the Process

The CBAO Code of Conduct rules concerning quality of the process are meant to ensure that mediators provide a superior mediation process for the parties. Mediators are required to educate the parties properly about the process before it commences and to ensure that the parties have fair and equal opportunity to participate. Mediators are also required to inform the parties that mediation is most successful when they—the parties—have full authority to settle and are willing and able to put in the time and effort to accomplish this. Another rule is that mediators who are lawyers shall not represent their mediation clients in a court proceeding. This follows from the rule that mediators shall not provide other professional services to their mediation clients. Finally, mediators have a responsibility to update their education continually in order to remain current in their professional skills and abilities.

Advertising

The rules concerning advertising are intended to protect the public and to ensure that the practice of mediation is promoted in an honest and straightforward manner. These rules require that any written promotional material or oral presentation advertising mediators' services include accurate information about the mediator's education, background, and professional experience. These rules also require mediators to "refrain from guaranteeing settlement or promising specific results" (CBAO, pt. VIII).

Fees

Fees are not covered in the CBAO Code of Conduct but are included in a regulation under the *Administration of Justice Act* (1990) and Part 3 of the OMMP's code of conduct. This text will discuss fees later in this chapter. Let us say here, though, as a general rule, that it is good professional and ethical practice for mediators to be upfront about their fees and to provide sufficient information about them in writing and that mediators should not accept fees for services other than mediation, including contingency or referral fees.

Agreement to Mediate

agreement to mediate
the contract, executed at the outset of mediation, that establishes the rules of the process, the parties' good-faith commitment to it, the mediator's neutrality, the confidentiality of the process, and the mediator's compensation

One way to ensure that the parties understand the process and terms of mediation is to include those terms in an **agreement to mediate**, which is then forwarded to and signed by the parties. Such an agreement need not be comprehensive or cover all the terms of mediation. According to the CBAO Code of Conduct, the agreement should cover, but not necessarily be limited to, the following matters:

- confidentiality of communications and documents;
- the right of the mediator and parties to terminate or suspend mediation;
- fees, expenses, retainer, method of payment, and what, if any, fee there is for cancellation, lateness, or delay; and
- the fact that the mediator is not compellable as a witness in court proceedings by any parties to the mediation.

Termination or Suspension of Mediation

Mediators shall terminate or suspend mediation for any of the reasons previously listed in the code (for example, conflict of interest or reasonable apprehension of bias) or if one or more of the parties request it. Furthermore, the mediator shall terminate or suspend the process if he or she perceives that the process will be unfair or imbalanced—if, for instance, one of the parties is using the process inappropriately (for example, to gain information for use in litigation or some other process), or is unduly delaying the process, or is not acting in good faith, or is persistently behaving counterproductively. Mediators may attempt to address and correct any of the situations described above but are required to terminate the process should those situations or actions continue.

Other Conduct Obligations

The CBAO Code of Conduct for mediators does not replace, supersede, or alienate any ethical standards prescribed or imposed upon a mediator by virtue of another professional calling he or she may have.

Other Legal Duties and Responsibilities

We may consider the ethical practice considerations covered in the CBAO Code of Conduct as general minimum standards for mediators. There are other ethical considerations specific to particular areas of practice, such as family mediation.

The Ontario Association for Family Mediation (OAFM) and Family Mediation Canada (FMC) are two associations for qualified family mediators. Each has its own code of conduct and its own practice standards.

FMC requires mediators to work with participants to create a client-centred process that takes into account the participants' age, culture, gender, and education, as well as their emotional, financial, and psychological circumstances. Mediators for family disputes must also consider issues of power imbalance and abuse. Guidelines for dealing with abuse have been developed for mediators in this practice area. These guidelines may also apply to issues—bullying, for example—that come up in certain areas of community mediation practice.

Dealing with Abuse

In a paper for the University of New Brunswick, Neilson (2001) noted that a mediator faced with an abusive situation

> must do more than ensure a lack of abusive actions during or between sessions. The mediator must also ascertain: whether the victim's fears and apprehensions about safety and well-being will affect his or her ability to participate fully; whether such fears or apprehensions can be addressed while mediation is being conducted; whether abuse that occurred in the past has affected the abused person's ability to communicate and negotiate with the former partner on an equal footing; whether the abused person's ability to obtain, assess and analyze information pertinent to the matters being discussed has been affected; and whether the abused person's ability to withstand settlement pressures and delays has been affected. (p. 141)

It is widely understood that abuse, even if it has ceased, may be ongoing in terms of its psychological impact and the power imbalance it creates. That is why Family Mediation Canada takes special care in training its mediators to recognize and deal with it. Among the principles it teaches is that "the proper course of action is always to assume that face-to-face, facilitated mediation will be inappropriate in cases involving past or present abuse and to err on the side of caution" (FMC, 2003, p. 15). Because abuse can have profound effects and can seriously affect a mediation, it must be monitored and assessed throughout the process.

The general rule regarding abuse is that it is "the mediator's first priority [to] ensure the safety of all participants and their children" (2003, p. 16). Moreover, "mediators should inform all participants that mediators are not neutral in issues of abuse or safety and have a legislative duty to report [to police] past and present child abuse ... and threats of future abuse or harm" (2003, p. 16). Mediators also have a duty "to step out of a neutral role and to act to protect the vulnerable if a formerly abusive partner engages in intimidation or abuse during a mediation or shuttle negotiation process" (2003, p. 16). Family Mediation Canada recommends that "usually, such behaviours will result in ending the mediation or shuttle negotiation and referral to a service or process that offers additional protection" (2003, p. 16).

A solid working knowledge of relevant legal and ethical codes is crucial for practising mediators. Such knowledge will help protect both the mediators and their clients. Professional codes and guidelines for mediators help instill public confidence in the process. They discourage unethical practitioners. The laws and regulations governing mediation are complex and ever changing and they vary according to practice area, and mediators are responsible for maintaining current knowledge of them. Because of this **duty of care**, mediators are encouraged—and in some cases

duty of care
a legal obligation to act with reasonable prudence when performing acts that may harm others

required—to carry insurance to protect themselves and their clients from unintentional ethical breaches.

For precise information about ethical codes of conduct and legal standards in specific areas of mediation, please consult directly the professional associations that issue them.

Careers in Mediation

Some of you may have begun to ask, "Where do I go from here?" or "What options exist for me if I want to have a career as a mediator?"

Mediation is an ever-more popular means of resolving disputes, and it is becoming a viable career. Traditionally, many mediators have been lawyers. They have also been psychologists, therapists, social workers, and spiritual or faith community leaders. But there is a growing number of professional mediators whose primary career from the outset is mediation. Many mediators enter private practice, often specializing in one or two practice areas, such as family mediation, community mediation, workplace mediation, or commercial mediation. Other mediators are finding full-time employment with government organizations, including administrative tribunals and commissions, as well as with private firms, schools, and school boards.

Government-based commissions, departments, and tribunals where mediation is practised include the following, among many others: the Department of National Defence (Canada); human rights commissions (federal and provincial); the Landlord and Tenant Board (Ontario); the Federal Public Service Labour Relations Board (Canada); and various provincial boards governing workplace safety and worker's compensation. Many post-secondary institutions are also using mediators to help resolve disputes between students and between students and staff. The family court clinics in each jurisdiction of the Ontario Family Court employ mediators to assist in bringing non-judicial resolutions to family conflict, particularly when the conflict centres on divorce, custody and access, and support matters. Indeed, family mediators are available through various programs throughout Canada. For example, Family Justice Centres in British Columbia offer mediation through family justice councillors who are trained and certified in mediation. Another example is Quebec, which offers family mediation services. The Quebec program has published very encouraging statistics about the success of family mediation in their program:

> In 2017, the Ministère de la Justice asked the enterprise SOM to conduct a survey of parents after they had used family mediation services. The survey results show that
>
> - 84 percent of parents reached an agreement with their former spouse during the family mediation process;
> - 81 percent of parents were satisfied with the services obtained, among other things because the process was easy (97 percent) and because mediation took the interests of their children into account (90 percent);
> - 90 percent of respondents would use the services again if needed. (Justice Quebec, 2017)

A growing number of private organizations, including not-for-profit organizations, also use mediators. In many medium and large corporations, human resources departments are often responsible for conflict resolution. Not-for-profit organizations that are privately run, including community groups and faith communities or churches, frequently employ dispute-resolution professionals as well.

These organizations often provide the following: mediation services for community conflicts and for disputes involving children and youth; anti-bullying programs; and rehabilitative and restorative justice initiatives.

IN THE NEWS

SOCIETY FOR HUMAN RESOURCE MANAGEMENT (SHRM)

Competencies include:

In team settings, HR professionals who are adept at using their relationship management skills foster collaboration and open communication among colleagues. They help to establish an organizational environment that values and promotes teamwork. Effective HR professionals are also able to identify potential sources of conflict, and encourage parties in conflict to stay positive, respectful and task-related.

In the case of counterproductive conflict, competent HR professionals work to identify root causes and mediate disputes in an impartial and respectful manner.

Source: SHRM (2018, p. 18).

Types of Disputes Requiring Mediators

Mediators may be generalists or they may be specialists in specific practice areas. Mediators connected to the government and private organizations listed above, as well as mediators with other affiliations, can be found practising in the following areas:

- banking and real estate disputes;
- civilian interaction with police;
- community and neighbourhood conflict;
- contractual disputes;
- criminal and restorative justice initiatives;
- environmental assessments;
- family law areas;
- human rights complaints;
- immigration and refugee claims;
- insurance claims;
- land use planning and development;
- landlord and tenant disputes;
- organizational and workplace disputes;
- schoolyard and student conflict;
- separation and divorce, custody and access, family obligations and support, wills and estates, intergenerational conflict; and
- trade and commerce.

There will always be mediators in private practice, of course, who choose to work in the above-listed areas. Many of these mediators will hope to be put on the civil and family court mediation rosters, including Ontario's Mandatory Mediation Program through the Superior Court of Justice. For these mediators, accreditation is very important, as are continuing education, marketing their practice, and finding and maintaining appropriate office space. Membership in professional associations is becoming essential for success as a mediator, especially for those in private practice.

Professional Associations

As noted earlier in this chapter, mediation is not a regulated profession. Also, there is a number of professional bodies that represent mediators, arbitrators, and other ADR professionals They assist mediators with advertising, continuing education, practice insurance, professional networking, and, ultimately, professional credibility. Many of these professional bodies are connected to specific practice areas, such as family mediation; others are more general in nature. In all cases, professional associations are an excellent resource for all practising mediators.

We will briefly examine two such Canadian organizations here: the ADR Institute of Canada and the Ontario Association for Family Mediation. For further information regarding these organizations and how to join them, please refer directly to the organizations themselves.

ADRIC

The ADR Institute of Canada (http://www.adric.ca/) is a national professional association that provides accreditation, education, and networking opportunities for mediators. It operates in association with its seven regional affiliates in British Columbia, Alberta, Saskatchewan, Manitoba, Ontario, Quebec, and the Atlantic Provinces.

IN THE NEWS

THE ADR INSTITUTE OF CANADA

The ADR Institute of Canada (ADRIC) is recognized as Canada's preeminent alternative dispute resolution (ADR) professional organization.

ADRIC sets the standard for best practices for ADR in Canada. We support conflict resolution through arbitration, mediation and other forms of ADR, and provide leadership, value and support to our member.

ADRIC's mission is to advance the practice and profile of ADR across Canada. We provide education and certification, promote ethical standards and professional competency, and advocate for all forms of ADR for public and private disputes.

Those seeking an ADR professional can choose an ADRIC member with confidence.

More than two thousand ADR practitioners across the country belong to ADRIC through affiliates in British Columbia, Alberta, Saskatchewan, Manitoba, Ontario, Quebec, and the Atlantic Provinces.

Source: ADRIC (n.d.).

Professional Designations

ADRIC offers four professional designations: two for mediators (Chartered Mediator [C.Med]; Qualified Mediator [Q.Med]) and two for arbitrators (Chartered Arbitrator

[C.Arb]; Qualified Arbitrator [Q.Arb]). All four designations involve stringent education and experience requirements, as well as the payment of an application fee and an annual maintenance fee, for which the national organization bills members every year. Experience requirements for the C.Med designation include a minimum of 80 hours of mediation training, 100 hours of related study (for example, in the areas of psychology and communication), and a minimum of 15 paid mediations in which the applicant acted as the sole or lead mediator. To continue to hold one's designation, one must remain a member in good standing with ADRIC, carry practice insurance, and adhere to the institute's practice standards, including ongoing training requirements.

For more information on the requirements for each of the offered designations, please consult the ADR Institute of Canada directly.

The Ontario Association for Family Mediation (OAFM)

Another professional body is OAFM (www.oafm.on.ca). OAFM, like ADRIC and its regional affiliates, is not an official regulatory body; rather, it is a not-for-profit association that promotes family mediation for separating couples and for families in conflict. The organization has been in existence since 1982 and provides a number of benefits to its members, including professional development, a members' referral service, professional accreditation, and—as with ADRIC—preferred professional insurance rates.

Professional Designation

OAFM offers one designation for highly experienced members: the Accredited Family Mediator, or Acc.FM, designation. As of July 1, 2014, the requirements for obtaining this designation include, among other educational and experiential requirements, the completion of the following OAFM courses:

1. Introduction to Mediation (20 hours);
2. Family Law (21 hours or equivalent experience as a mediator or practising family law lawyer);
3. Family Mediation (40 hours); and
4. Screening for Domestic Violence and Power Imbalances (21 hours).

Members also must carry at least $1,000,000 of mediator professional liability insurance, while adhering strictly to the ethical code of conduct for members. As with other professional bodies, application, maintenance, and membership fees apply.

Professional Insurance for Mediators

Insurance coverage exists for the protection of both the mediator and the client. Mediators are encouraged, and in some cases required, to carry professional liability insurance. Insurance exists to cover any damages to the client that may occur through the mediator's error. Mediators need to carry insurance to protect their personal assets in case a client chooses to pursue a court action against them.

One of the many benefits of membership in a professional association is the access it gives to liability insurance coverage at a preferred rate. As mentioned above, accreditation with professional bodies often requires a mediator to carry a minimum amount of liability insurance, though mediators should carry such insurance whether required to or not.

The insurance plans offered through ADRIC and the OAFM are by no means the only ones available. Mediators and other ADR professionals should make the insurance coverage decisions that work best for their type of practice and that adhere to any requirements placed upon them by any professional or regulatory bodies to which they may belong.

Mediators' Fees

For mediators who practise privately, fees will be determined by what the market will bear. In other words, as with most other businesses, mediators' fees will usually correspond to those of other mediators in their practice area and geographical region. However, mediators who are practising as part of a roster or list—through the court system, for example—must adhere to the fee structure put in place by government regulations.

For example, the OMMP fees for a three-hour mediation session under Rule 24.1 are set out in Ontario Regulation 451/98 of the *Administration of Justice Act* (1990), as follows:

> 24. (1) The mediator's fees for the mandatory mediation session shall not exceed the amount shown in the following Table:

Table 14.1   Mandatory Mediation Fees

Number of Parties	Maximum Fees
2	$600 plus GST
3	$675 plus GST
4	$750 plus GST
5 or more	$825 plus GST

It is only after the mandatory mediation session time has been completed that the mediator has some autonomy regarding his or her fee. Under section 4(3), the regulation states the following:

> After the first three hours of actual mediation, the mediation may be continued if the parties and the mediator agree to do so and agree on the mediator's fees or hourly rate for the additional time.

Other mediation organizations, such as church groups, may have their own fee structures, and their mediators must adhere to them. Anyone interested in these fee structures should consult the relevant associations and organizations. A mediator's fees, whether set by themselves or by an organization, should be fully disclosed to clients prior to the start of mediation. This is standard practice. It is a very good idea to set the fees as part of the agreement to mediate.

The Agreement to Mediate

The importance of the agreement to mediate has already been discussed in this text. Presenting the agreement to clients before the mediation process begins is ethically sound and is a requirement in many codes of conduct. This presentation symbolizes the start of mediation and ensures that all parties involved are approaching it with similar expectations.

The Agreement to Mediate: Core Elements

Generally, an agreement to mediate will clarify and define the following:

1. the purpose of mediation;
2. the mediator and the parties,
   a. who they are,
   b. what their role is;
3. confidentiality,
   a. the proscription against requiring the mediator to testify,
   b. the issue of open versus closed mediation;
4. self-determination;
5. rules of the process,
   a. that ground rules will be in place;
6. full disclosure;
7. issues to be mediated;
8. structure of the process,
   a. length and location of meetings,
   b. caucusing;
9. fees and other costs;
10. role of lawyers and independent legal advice;
11. termination of mediation.

Conclusion

The major premise of this text has been that something beneficial occurs when we approach disputes not as adversaries trying to win a contest but as co-creators of new, shared meaning, working cooperatively to resolve conflict. The practice of mediation, as we have seen, involves not only a collaborative philosophy but also a fundamentally new perspective on problem solving. It creates opportunities for people to generate win–win solutions for problems that might at first seem inevitably adversarial. Once we accept the fact that conflict is everywhere, in every relationship, and that it contains the seeds for growth and new understanding, our choices in how to approach it are clear. In the face of conflict, we can continue to ignore, to yield, or to contend. Or we can benefit from the new directions offered by negotiation and mediation and learn the processes and practicalities of cooperation.

KEY TERMS

agreement to mediate, 190
civil mediation, 187
codes of ethical conduct, 186
confidentiality, 189
conflict of interest, 188

duty of care, 191
family mediation, 187
impartiality, 188
mediators' roster, 186

Ontario Mandatory Mediation
Program, 186
open mediation, 189
self-determination, 188

REFERENCES

Administration of Justice Act, RSO 1990, c A-6, O Reg 451/98.

ADR Institute of Canada (ADRIC). (n.d.). About us. Retrieved from http://adric.ca/about-adr

Bruineman, M. (2017, April 17). Focus: Mediators largely unregulated in Canada. *The Law Times*. Retrieved from https://www.lawtimesnews.com/article/focus-mediators-largely-unregulated-in-canada-13294

Diebel, L. (2008, January 14). Unqualified mediators prey on broken families. *The Star*. Retrieved from http://www.thestar.com/article/293746

Family Mediation Canada (FMC). Practice, certification and training standards. (2018). Retrieved from http://www.fmc.ca

Justice Quebec. (2017). Family mediation—negotiating a fair agreement. Retrieved from https://www.justice.gouv.qc.ca/en/couples-and-families/separation-and-divorce/family-mediation-negotiating-a-fair-agreement

Ministry of the Attorney General (Ontario) (MAG). (2008–2016). Code of conduct. Retrieved from http://www.attorneygeneral.jus.gov.on.ca/english/courts/manmed/codeofconduct.php

Neilson, L.C. (2001, March). *Spousal abuse, children and the legal system: Final report for Canadian Bar Association, Law for the Futures Fund*. University of New Brunswick. Retrieved from https://www.unb.ca/fredericton/arts/centres/mmfc/_resources/pdfs/spousalabuse.pdf

Society for Human Resource Management (SHRM). (2018). *The SHRM body of competency and knowledge*. Retrieved from https://www.shrm.org/certification/Documents/SHRM-BoCK-FINAL.pdf

QUESTIONS AND EXERCISES

1. Imagine you are the mediator for a divorcing couple. During the course of the mediation, the parties ask if you will ask their children which parent they want to live with. What do you do? You decide to meet with the children, and they tell you that one of their parents gets angry a lot and hits them and locks them in their room. What do you do? Why?

2. A person who has gone through a divorce mediation process complains of having been *bulldozed* by their spouse: "By the end of those twelve hours, I was sobbing and couldn't talk. I couldn't understand what had happened, or what I had agreed to. Now my lawyer is telling me that I should not have signed anything, and that the mediator should have known better."

   Does this person have any legal recourse against their former mediator? To whom or to what body can this mediator be reported, if any?

3. You are a mediator in a personal injury case. In caucus, the injured party discloses that their injury is not as serious as they are claiming. They also disclose that their lawyer is aware of this and has arranged for a doctor to provide the false evidence needed for their claim. As a mediator, what should you do? Why?

4. You are a mediator in a personal injury case. In caucus, the representative of the insurance company tells you that they have no intention of settling and that they are just there to gather information about the other party, to use in subsequent litigation. As a mediator, what should you do? Why?

5. Draft an agreement to mediate that you could use as a professional mediator. Be sure to include all the key elements of the agreement that were mentioned in the chapter.

6. Research at least five professional associations for mediators. For each one, create a list of the benefits that membership would give you, including any accreditations offered. Then create a list of qualification requirements both for membership in the association

and for the accreditation, if any, that it offers. Lastly, set up a T-chart to compare and contrast the benefits and the costs of membership and accreditation (if applicable) for each association.

7. Where do you see yourself as a mediator a year from now? In two years? In five years? In 10 years?

   a. Contact a professional mediator from a Canadian professional mediators' association of your choosing. Interview that mediator about their training and experience, as well as about professional practice considerations (for example, employment, private practice, roster qualification).

   b. Create a plan of action for your professional development as a mediator. Take into account your research of professional associations and your interview of the mediator. Be sure to include the education and training you will need and the experience requirements you may need to meet. Consider, as well, the costs and time requirements involved in your chosen career path, whether as a mediator in private practice or as a mediator in some other capacity.

8. In civil litigation, we now have something known as *mandatory mediation*. Given that mediation is a voluntary process driven by individual self-determination and a willingness to cooperate, how can it be a *mandatory* process? In your estimation, is mandatory mediation a valid concept and, if so, how do you justify it? And if it is embedded in our justice system, is it still an alternative form of dispute resolution?

Glossary

active listening a way of listening that involves giving the other party our full attention, showing them in every way that we are trying to understand

ADR alternative dispute resolution—a broad term for forms of dispute resolution that are alternatives to court or other rights- and power-based systems (e.g., mediation)

adversarial assumption a disputing party's assumption that they are locked in battle with the other side and can only win at the other's expense

agreement to mediate the contract, executed at the outset of mediation, that establishes the rules of the process, the parties' good-faith commitment to it, the mediator's neutrality, the confidentiality of the process, and the mediator's compensation

argumentation the second stage in an aggressive negotiation, where a party presents their own case in the best light possible while emphasizing the weakness of the other side's case

argumentative approach an approach to conflict based on the traditional Western notion that we arrive at truth through a competitive clash of ideas

aspirations the particular hopes and desires that arise from our underlying interests

authority to settle the power to resolve all issues fully and finally at the table

bargaining range the range of solutions acceptable to a negotiating party, from most to least acceptable

BATNA the best alternative to a negotiated agreement; a course of action the negotiating party might adopt should the upcoming negotiations break down or come to deadlock

Black Hat thinking critical thinking that looks at flaws in or problems with a particular course of action

Blue Hat thinking thinking that focuses on process rather than on content

both/and thinking assuming that there are many possible solutions to a problem, not just one

brainstorming generating a wide variety of ideas without worrying about which are feasible

brief therapy is short-term and focused on helping a person to resolve or effectively manage a specific problem/challenge or to make a desired change

caucusing separating the parties and meeting with them privately, away from the table

change by exception the mental change that occurs when a person with an absolute view of something acknowledges an exception to the rule

change by pendulum swing the change of mind that occurs when a person abandons one closed and certain system for another

civil mediation any mediation dealing with civil law disputes between individuals (e.g., contracts, torts)

clarifying question a question that is used to bring out more information or to clarify a point someone has made

closed question a limiting question that requires only a "yes" or "no" response

codes of ethical conduct sets of rules that apply to members of a body or organization

cognitive relating to the mental processes of perception, memory, judgment, and reasoning

cognitive dissonance a condition in which a person holds two contradictory ideas simultaneously and is driven to reduce "dissonance" by changing his or her attitudes, beliefs, and behaviours

collaborative or cooperative problem solving problem solving that integrates both parties' interests and seeks mutually beneficial solutions

collective agreement a contract between the management of a business and its unionized workers, achieved through a process of collective bargaining

collective cultures cultures that value the group over the individual and emphasize the importance of harmonious relationships within the group

community a gathering of people who have something in common—physical space, beliefs, values, or interests

compromise give up parts of your claim and move closer to the other party's position

concession the yielding of some part of one's position

confidentiality the duty of the mediator and of the parties in mediation not to disclose details of the process to people not directly involved in it

conflict a state that exists when one party's aspirations are incompatible with those of another party

conflict of interest a case where the mediator cannot be impartial or stands to gain personally at the expense of one of the parties in the mediation process

conflict resolution therapy models of conflict resolution are used in therapy with families or couples

consequential questions questions that ask a party to consider the possible consequences of a prospective course of action—for example, to assess risks and likely outcomes of current decisions or actions

contending adopting combative techniques designed to fulfill one's own aspirations while thwarting those of the other party

contradiction the principle by which our minds favour either/or thinking and assume that only one of two conflicting notions can be correct

convenor the representative of a mediation service who makes initial contact with the disputing parties in order to determine whether mediation is an appropriate means of resolving their conflict

convergent thinking a type of thinking that uses logical, rational processes and focuses on a specific goal, solution, or way of doing things

cooperative approach a creative approach to conflict resolution that aims to create win–win solutions for the parties involved

cooperative problem solving focusing both on one's own and on the other party's aspirations, with a view to finding a solution that satisfies both

crisis the stage in a competitive negotiation where further concessions are needed but neither party is willing to make them

cultural evolution the cultural growth and change within a society

data conflicts conflicts that occur over information (for example, disagreements over what information is relevant or how that information should be collected and interpreted)

deficit ideology the belief that inequalities result not from unjust social conditions, such as systemic racism or economic injustice, but from intellectual, moral, cultural, and behavioural deficiencies assumed

demonization a disputant's use of stereotypes and falsifications to belittle, accuse, or attack the other side

designated (given) power power that one party gives to another party or gives to the relationship itself rather than keeping it for themselves

dispute what occurs when the parties in conflict (a) recognize they are opposed to each other, (b) view each other's opposition as an injury, and (c) lay claim to some form of redress

distributive (either/or) power power aimed at controlling and defeating the other party

divergent thinking a type of thinking that starts from a single point or issue and expands outward, encompassing a wide range of solutions

duty of care a legal obligation to act with reasonable prudence when performing acts that may harm others

either/or thinking assuming that only one of two conflicting notions can be correct

emotional intelligence the ability to understand our own emotions and the emotions of others

escalation the growth of a conflict in intensity, complexity, and size

ethnorelativism a mindset in which one accepts that all cultures are valid

evaluative mediation an approach to mediation by which the mediator offers the parties advice and opinion about the appropriate settlement of the conflict

examination-in-chief the questioning of a party's own witness under oath at trial

expanding the pie creating new benefits for both parties in a negotiation

expulsion removing a student from the school due to behavioural or criminal concerns

externalizing conversations the stage in a narrative mediation at which the disputing parties are encouraged to talk about the "conflict story" as if it were external to them, influencing them both

facilitative mediation an approach to mediation that aims to help disputing parties communicate and problem-solve themselves, on the grounds that they are better equipped than the mediator to resolve their conflict satisfactorily

family mediation mediation that deals with matters affecting the family, including divorce, custody and access, and the division of family property

frame of reference a person's subjective reality, shaped by his or her particular experience and culture, and the basis for their perception of the world

framing the issues establishing and clearly defining the parties' specific concerns

frozen words absolute words, such as "always" and "never," that are usually inaccurate and tend to provoke defensiveness in the other party

gamesmanship a light tactic of contention that involves an attempt to destroy or upset the other party's rhythm in some way

gender socially constructed notion of what is male and what is female

gender expectations culturally determined notions of how men and women are supposed to behave

Green Hat thinking creative thinking

ground rules the rules for the conduct of the mediation, covering such topics as the need for respectful behaviour and active listening, caucusing, and the circumstances in which the process might be terminated

hearsay evidence evidence composed of statements made by people who are not testifying before a court; these statements, heard by a party who is testifying before a court, will not be allowed in as evidence because the person testifying can attest to the fact the statement was made, but not to the truth of it; the opposing party will not be able to cross-examine the testifier to determine the veracity of the statements

heavy tactics of contention tactics involving arguments and threats, often leading to the use of violent force

Hero's Journey the narrative pattern according to which an ordinary person undergoes lessons and hardships and, by facing his or her fears, becomes extraordinary—a hero

"I" messages messages that require people to express themselves from their own perspective in language that does not blame the other party

ignoring pretending a conflict does not exist or suppressing conscious awareness of it instead of actively addressing it

impartiality the principled neutrality that prevents the mediator from taking sides or giving preferential treatment in a negotiation

incremental change the gradual change of mind that occurs when a person starts finding numerous exceptions to a rule he or she once thought absolute

individualistic cultures cultures that value the individual over the group and tend to prize such qualities as independence, creativity, freedom of thought and expression, and authority in decision making

inquisitional approach an approach to workplace conflict whereby the manager uses his or her authority to settle a dispute between two co-workers

integrative (both/and) power power used with, rather than against, another party, to the end of mutual gain

intercultural conflict conflict involving cultural differences between the parties—differences related to their frames of reference, values, myths, and stories

interest the legitimate need that underlies the position a person takes in a conflict

interest conflicts conflicts arising from competition over substantive, procedural, or psychological interests

justifying questions questions that are used to resolve inconsistent or contradictory statements and to ensure clarity and understanding

latent content the part of a message, often conveyed non-verbally, that is not expressed explicitly but is there by suggestion

legitimate power power that is based on one party's formal authority over another party in a social structure

light tactics of contention tactics that are designed to win the contest without injuring the other party (for example, persuasion, guilt trips, or simple requests)

loss transfer a mechanism by which, under certain circumstances, automobile insurers who pay no-fault benefits (the first-party insurer) may be reimbursed by another insurer (the second-party insurer) for all or part of a claim

managerial prerogative the manager's right to make decisions

mandatory mediation the formal requirement that parties who have brought an action in court must attempt to settle their dispute by participating in a minimum of three hours of mediation

manifest content what the words of a message actually communicate; the literal meaning

maximalist position an aggressively high opening bid designed to preset the range of negotiation

mediation the process by which a neutral or third party, upon being asked to do so, helps parties negotiate a dispute

mediation brief a short document that the disputing parties create during the pre-mediation stage of a negotiation, setting out the history and context of the dispute

mediators' roster a list of approved professionals who offer mediation services to participants in a particular program, such as the Mandatory Mediation Program

microskills skills that are useful in very particular situations

minutes of settlement the written document containing the final terms the parties have agreed upon in settling their dispute

narrative mediation a kind of mediation that aims to resolve conflict by uncovering and breaking down the disputants' stories so that they can be reconstructed into a larger narrative that integrates both parties' interests

negotiation a process in which two or more parties communicate directly in search of agreement on some action that one or more of them will undertake

new, shared meaning the shared understanding that can develop, through dialogue and an exchange of ideas, between parties in conflict

objective measurable criteria standards of measurement or evaluation that would be acceptable to an unbiased third party

Ontario Mandatory Mediation Program a court-annexed mediation program under which parties involved in certain kinds of civil action are required to attend at least three hours of mediation in a bid to resolve their dispute without the court's involvement

open mediation a mediation process requiring that the mediator report details of the proceedings to a judge; a non-confidential mediation

open-ended question a question that allows the person responding to answer with a variety of answers and to have control of the conversation and room to express feelings and underlying interests

opening bid the initial offer in a negotiation

organizational culture the beliefs, values, and assumptions shared by an organization's members

paradigm shift the change of mind that occurs when a person integrates his or her old views with new perceptions and understands that experience will further refine these views

paraphrasing repeating in your own words what someone else has said

phases of escalation the stages a conflict moves through as it intensifies—from light tactics of contention to heavy ones, from narrow issues to general ones, from moderate to destructive aims, from the involvement of few to the involvement of many, and from rational perspectives to demonizing ones

polarization the process by which parties in conflict become entrenched in disagreement, each assuming that their own view is the only correct one

position the particular result a party wants to gain from a negotiation (as opposed to the *interests* that underlie this want)

positional or distributive bargaining bargaining aimed at getting as much as possible for the negotiating party, with no concern for the other side's needs

power in a dispute situation, the ability to make the other party think, believe, or behave in a way they would not voluntarily

power-based approach an approach to conflict resolution whereby people in positions of authority—managers, officers, religious leaders, boards of directors—use their power to resolve disputes

preferred story a new narrative, composed by the parties in a narrative mediation as they resolve their dispute, that is based on their new understandings of themselves, of each other, and of the conflict itself

preliminary contact the parties' meeting or discussion prior to the start of negotiation

principled negotiation negotiation aimed at preventing parties from getting entrenched in positions; it works by separating people from the problem, focusing on interests rather than positions, and using objective criteria to assess creative solutions

probing questions questions used for exploring a subject when the respondent seems wary of full disclosure

problem solving a method that integrates both parties' interests and seeks mutually beneficial solutions

Red Hat thinking thinking based on emotion and feeling rather than reason and logic

reflecting providing feedback that shows that the speaker's feelings and emotions have been recognized

reflective journal a journal that records how the day went with positive outcomes, challenges, emotional reactions, and insights. The journal can be reviewed to support behavioural and cognitive changes in one's life

reframing looking at a situation from a different perspective, often a more positive one, and restating it

relationship conflicts conflicts caused by stereotyping and misperception, often involving strong emotion

resistance point the lowest point of acceptability in a party's preset bargaining range

restitution compensation the victim receives from the offender for the losses suffered because of the offender's crime

restitution agreement the settlement that emerges from a mediation between a victim and an offender

restorative justice a model of justice that treats crime as a violation of relationships and aims to restore the victim, the offender, and the community, and, ultimately, to prevent a recurrence of the crime

retributive justice system our society's main system of justice, which treats illegal behaviour with punishment alone

retrospective reflection looking back on interpersonal interactions and thinking critically about which behaviours worked well and which did not

rights-based approach an approach to conflict resolution that allows the disputing parties to present their case before an authoritative third party who will decide on a winner according to established criteria

ritual sharing the first stage of a collaborative negotiation and the point where parties develop rapport, discover common ground, and learn about each other's interests

rules of natural justice a system of rules, based on English common law, that defines the elements of a fair hearing

self-determination the parties' right to make decisions for themselves

self-image the individual's subjective perception of himself or herself

sentencing circles a meeting of victims, offenders, their families, and concerned community members, who gather in a circle at the post-conviction phase to discuss the impact of the crime and to work together—along with members of the legal community—to recommend a restorative sentencing

shuttle mediation a mediation process in which there is no face-to-face contact between the disputants; the mediator "shuttles" back and forth between the parties until they reach agreement

stakeholders the people who have a stake in the outcome of a dispute

stereotyping assuming that people from a certain social category all have certain characteristics

structural conflicts conflicts that arise from inequities or constraints in a social structure and that often take the form of destructive behaviour or interactions

summarizing condensing the speaker's message while including all of the relevant points

superordinate goals goals that transcend the conflict situation and appeal to both parties

target point the most desirable outcome for a negotiating party

terms of agreement the conditions on which agreement has been reached and the conflict resolved

totalizing descriptions descriptions that reduce the complexities of a dispute to sweeping generalizations about the conflict and the disputants

transformative theory of mediation an approach to mediation that aims to transform the disputants by teaching them to recognize one another's interests and by helping them to become better communicators and problem solvers

value conflicts conflicts that arise when people have different criteria for valuing ideas or behaviour or have goals based on mutually exclusive value systems

victim–offender reconciliation a form of mediation that works to reconcile victim and offender by having the latter make reparations for the harm done to the victim

WATNA the worst alternative to a negotiated agreement; the worst possibilities if the upcoming negotiations fail

White Hat thinking traditional logical thinking based on information that is known, available, or potentially discoverable

Yellow Hat thinking positive thinking

yielding resolving conflict by giving up one's own aspirations and accepting the other party's as more important

"you" messages messages that use the pronoun "you" and thereby tend toward blame and accusation

zero-sum thinking the belief that the world has finite assets for which its inhabitants must contend on a win–lose basis; the basis of a competitive approach to conflict

Index

Credits

Page 5 (photo, my way/your way): © Stuart Miles/ Shutterstock

Page 9 (photo, Carl Rogers): © Bettman/Getty

Page 15 (Figure 2.1, Four Responses to Conflict): Based on data from Rubin, J.Z., Pruitt, D.G., & Kim, S.H. (2004). *Social conflict, escalation, stalemate and settlement* (2nd ed.). New York: McGraw-Hill.

Page 33 (Figure 3.2, Conflict Onion): Coltri, Laurie S. (2010). *Alternative Dispute Resolution: A Conflict Diagnosis Approach* (2nd ed.) © 2010. Reprinted by permission of Pearson Education, Inc., New York, New York.

Page 41 (photo, hockey game): © Tribune Content Agency LLC/Alamy Stock Photo

Page 94 (photo, Chinese calligraphy): © flySnow/iStock

Page 130 (photo, mediation meeting): © Rawpixel/ Shutterstock

Page 175 (photo, police in community): © Creative Touch Imaging Ltd./NurPhoto via Getty Images

Page 180 (Case Study #4): Favaloro, Geoffrey J. (1998.) "Mediation: A Family Therapy Technique?" *Conflict Resolution Quarterly, 16*(1), 101–108. © Wiley Periodicals Inc., A Wiley Company.